How to Buy a Diamond and its National Diamond HelpLine
are endorsed by the National Bureau of Fraud Prevention
in Washington, D.C.

"Whenever anybody asks me about buying a diamond, I give them this book. It's filled with a lot of common sense, practical advice. Diamond buying can be difficult. This book can help."

Rob Bates, Editor, *National Jeweler* magazine

"This book helps make dreams come true."

Houston Chronicle

"Get a diamond education!"

New Man Promise Keepers

"Educate yourself before you make the big purchase."

Money's Worth

"Inside information on purchasing a diamond."

Library Journal

"If diamond buying figures into your future…*How to Buy a Diamond*… gets you your money's worth."

Tribune Media Services

"Expert advice for diamond buyers."

Tribune Review

"Spending even thirty minutes with *How to Buy a Diamond* can save anyone time, aggravation, and hard-earned money."

Black Elegance

"A cut above."

Dallas Morning News

"Takes the intimidation out of diamond shopping."

Mobile Register

"*How to Buy a Diamond* offers consumers an easy-to-understand crash course in the basics of diamonds and diamond shopping."

Orlando Sentinel

"The book enables a person to walk into a jeweler's store with confidence and to walk out with the right diamond at the right price."

Argus Press

"*How to Buy a Diamond*—give this to him early!"

Complete Woman

"If we didn't believe in the book we wouldn't sell it!"

American Museum of Natural History, New York

"Pure genius!"

Erno Rubik, inventor of the Rubik's Cube

"Simply fantastic!"

Jim Harris, cofounder, Compaq Computers

How to Buy a
DIAMOND

Insider Secrets for Getting
Your Money's Worth

FRED CUELLAR

 sourcebooks

Copyright © 2012 by Fred Cuellar
Cover and internal design © 2012 by Sourcebooks, Inc.
Cover photo © Davies & Starr/Getty Images

Sourcebooks and the colophon are registered trademarks of Sourcebooks, Inc.

This publication is designed to provide accurate and authoritative information in regard to the subject matter covered. It is sold with the understanding that the publisher is not engaged in rendering legal, accounting, or other professional service. If legal advice or other expert assistance is required, the services of a competent professional person should be sought. —*From a Declaration of Principles Jointly Adopted by a Committee of the American Bar Association and a Committee of Publishers and Associations.*

All brand names and product names used in this book are trademarks, registered trademarks, or trade names of their respective holders. Sourcebooks, Inc., is not associated with any product or vendor in this book.

Published by Sourcebooks, Inc.
P.O. Box 4410, Naperville, Illinois 60567-4410
(630) 961-3900
Fax: (630) 961-2168
www.sourcebooks.com

Library of Congress Cataloging-in-Publication Data

Cuellar, Fred.
  How to buy a diamond : insider secrets for getting your money's worth / Fred Cuellar.—7th ed.
  Includes index.
  1. Diamonds—Purchasing. 2. Rings—Purchasing. I. Title.
TS753.C83 2012
736'.23—dc23

                          2011047806

              Printed and bound in the United States of America.
                  VP 10 9 8 7 6 5 4 3 2 1

This book is dedicated first to my mother and father. This book would not have been possible without their love and support.

Second, I dedicate this book to every man in love and doing his best to make the love of his life happy by buying the perfect diamond.

Third and most of all, I dedicate this book to the love of my life, LaTeace. She makes life worth living, and I could not imagine a better companion with whom to spend all the days of my life.

Acknowledgments

LaTeace

Hector & Elvira

Greg J. P. Godek

Alfonso & Delia Cuellar

Alfredo & Jovita Montalvo

George & Betty Woody

Elisa & Knox Wright

Maxine & Clayton Prawl

Sha Shane, Cytinya & Clayton Jr.

Rick & Kerry Antona

Grayland Noah

Jose Garcia

Diep N. Doan

Betiel Ghirmay

Kamilah E. Humphrey

Neil & Rhonda Malhotra

Mr. and Mrs. O. Keith Owen III

O. Keith Owen IV

Julie Seitz

Ricardo Calderon

Barry Berg

Houston Astros

Pauline Palomo

Casablanca Press

Lou Lamoriello

Jim Harris

Arlene Ball

Dallas Cowboys

New Jersey Devils

Houston Rockets Players

Nick Mills

Mr. and Mrs. Ricardo V. Antona Sr.

Pierre Lacroix

Colorado Avalanche

Detroit Redwings

Denver Broncos

Dallas Stars

New York Yankees

Philip Anschutz

Tyra Banks

Oprah Winfrey

Harpo Inc.

Visible Changes

John and Maryanne McCormack

Johnny McCormack

Houston Dynamo

Martin Rapaport

Jeff Smith

Edward Jay Epstein

University of Houston

A special thanks to Diep for her research and editorial assistance.

Table of Contents

Preface

BUYING A DIAMOND MAY be one of the most important purchases of your life. Think of it. If you are a man, you're probably selecting a diamond to present to your bride-to-be as a shining symbol of eternal love. Only a diamond can say it all: your love for her is clear, pure, brilliant, perfect, and indestructible. If you're a woman buying a diamond for the most important man in your life, the symbolism is much the same. The diamond says, "You are the one."

For most people, the engagement ring is the first—and surely the most important—diamond they will ever buy. Selecting the right diamond, therefore, is a big responsibility. Let's make sure you get it right!

Yes, diamonds are romance, the highest expression of love, glamour, elegance, wealth, and refinement. (No one ever sang, "Cubic zirconia is a girl's best friend!") But diamonds can also be viewed as a commodity. There are different grades of diamonds, and each grade has a different value. And—very importantly—dealers are trying to make as much money from you as they can. You know the old expression, "A fool and his money are soon parted." Nowhere is that more true than in the diamond market. Diamond dealers can fool you in a hundred ways. Don't be fooled! In this book, I'll teach you how to judge diamonds so that when you make that all-important purchase, you get your money's worth.

CHARLIE'S GIFT

One day a few years ago I boarded a jetliner in Houston, bound for New York. When I had stowed my carry-on bag and buckled myself in, I looked over to see who I had for a seatmate. I saw a small, elderly lady sitting straight and prim in her seat, clutching her handbag and trying very hard not to appear concerned. I guessed this lady had not flown often in her life. I leaned over and reminder her gently that she would have to stow her handbag before takeoff. "Oh, thank you," she said. "I'm a little nervous, to be quite frank. I've never flown before."

I asked her why she was travelling to New York.

"Well," she said with a sigh, "I'm going to live with my daughter. She's meeting me at the airport. You see, my husband of fifty-five years passed away recently, and my daughter doesn't want me living alone."

I offered condolences, and trying to brighten her up, I said she was lucky to have enjoyed such a long marriage.

"Thank you. Yes, I was fortunate. We had a good marriage, and now it seems like the time went by so fast...seems like just yesterday we were saying our vows." She was quiet for a long moment, replaying some cherished moments of her married life, before she returned to our conversation.

"And what about you?" she asked. "Why are you going to New York?" I told her I was in the diamond business and was going there to close a deal on some diamonds.

"Oooh, diamonds!" Her lined face brightened. "Charlie—that was my husband—always said I'd have a diamond one day. When we got married, all we could afford were the wedding bands. Then came the children, and with one thing or another, we never did have enough money for luxuries. Every anniversary, Charlie would say, 'My dear, next year we'll get you that diamond!' But now there is no next year."

She bowed her head and tried not to let me see the tears, but eventually she had to dab them away with a handkerchief tugged from the pocket of her old coat.

In that moment, this sweet woman's tears revealed to me why I was on that plane, sitting beside her. I asked her name.

"Evelyn," she told me. "Evelyn Benson."

"Well, Evelyn," I said, "my name is Fred Cuellar, and I just realized that fate has brought us together. What is your ring size?"

"I—I don't know, really," she stammered. "Why?"

"Because I am here to give you your diamond ring. Charlie had something to do with sitting us together. I'm sure of it." I guessed her ring size at about a six; I had a grin sized extra large at this point.

"But I can't afford it," she protested. "We never could."

"Evelyn," I told her, "I am not selling you a diamond ring. I'm giving it to you at Charlie's request."

Well, that made her cry even more; however, the tears were happier now, and she gave me a big hug when we parted company at JFK airport.

When I got back to Houston, I put together a modest but very nice diamond engagement ring and mailed it to Evelyn at the address in upstate New York she'd given me. Putting that package in the mail made me feel like a million dollars. No, better than that.

Six months later, I received a small package at my Houston office. When I opened it, I found the diamond ring I'd sent to Evelyn Benson. With the ring was a note from her daughter:

> "Dear Mr. Cuellar, I'm returning the ring which you so graciously allowed my mother to wear for the last six months. Not a day went by that she didn't show it to someone, proud as can be. She told people it was a gift from her late husband Charlie (my dad). I'd never seen her as happy with anything in my life. My mother passed away last week, so I am returning your ring with many thanks for the joy you brought my mother. Sincerely, Jane Adams."

Foreword

By Gregory J. P. Godek

I'M PROUD TO INTRODUCE you to Fred Cuellar. He's not only a jeweler, he's an educator. He not only advises the Saudi royal family on their gemstone investments, he also advises guys buying their first diamond engagement rings. He not only runs a cutting house, he's an outrageous entrepreneur. He's not only the creator of the most expensive toy in the world (the $2 million Fifteenth Anniversary Rubik's Cube), he's also the creator of simple yet elegant diamond engagement rings. He's not a typical, quiet jeweler. He's a frequent guest on radio and TV, including *The Today Show*. He not only creates jewelry for Harley Davidson, many professional sports teams, and lots of celebrities, he also creates jewelry for regular folks like you and me. He's not only a sought-after lecturer, he's also now a bestselling author. He's not only the creator of the 1996 Super Bowl rings for the Dallas Cowboys, he's also the creator of diamond rings that grace the hands of thousands of men and women throughout the world. He's not just any jeweler; he's a maverick who imports his own diamonds. He's not only a creative genius when it comes to jewelry, he's also a sensitive advisor who understands people's feelings as they make a very emotional and meaningful purchase. And he's not only recognized as one of the world's leading diamond experts, he's also a regular guy.

You'll learn all this as you read this awesome book. You'll also learn how to be a wise and discriminating diamond customer, a person who won't be intimidated by jewelers or diamond brokers—or by friends who think they know all about diamonds. You'll learn how to choose the perfect diamond: one that reflects your love (as well as your new-found knowledge of diamonds). And you'll learn how to save money in the process. That's a lot to get out of one little book, isn't it?

Fred's book speaks for itself, but I'd like to add my personal guarantee. I guarantee you that the right diamond for your loved one will have a significant impact on your relationship. Diamonds really are the perfect gift of love.

Congratulations on acquiring this book. You will find that it is not only a great investment, but it is also fun to read, easy to understand, and at the same time wise and witty. Enjoy!

—Gregory J. P. Godek
author, *1001 Ways To Be Romantic*

Introduction

My FIRST EXPERIENCE WITH diamonds, long before I became a gemologist and diamond merchant, happened for the best of all reasons: I was a young man in love, with a burning desire to offer my bride-to-be a diamond ring and ask for her hand in marriage. It seemed simple enough. Between college classes, I would stop by a jewelry store, select a diamond worthy of my beloved, and be on my way. I thought it would be easy—and it was, until I glanced at my first price tag.

After I was resuscitated by the jeweler, I realized this wasn't going to be as easy as I had thought. The only "rock" I could afford then was one I could pick up off the ground.

That experience, however, led to a management trainee position with a major jewelry chain, followed by an opportunity to run a jewelry store. Then I became a wholesaler, and over time my business evolved into what it is today, where I can practice what I preach about buying and selling diamonds.

Keeping in mind my own first experience with diamond buying, I have always tried to teach my customers everything they should know before making their purchase. If you were planning to buy a new car or a washing machine, you'd probably read *Consumer Reports* to educate yourself before the purchase, and you'd at least want to kick the tires and look under the hood before you put your money down. That's what this book is all about. It puts you in charge of the transaction by showing you how to tell one diamond from another, what makes a diamond expensive, and what "investment grade" diamonds are. I'll also show you the tricks of the trade, how to avoid shysters—in short, how to get the most for your money.

When I first published *How to Buy a Diamond*, it created quite a stir. Honest diamond dealers—and there are many—loved the book. They said to me, "Fred, we've needed this for a long time, because it's hard to compete with dealers who cheat." The dishonest diamond dealers— and there are many of them, too, unfortunately—hated the idea of educating consumers, of revealing the "tricks of the trade." They were the ones who made threatening phone calls, who vowed to put me out of business. "You can't do this," they warned. "You can't let the suckers (that's you) see behind the curtain. You'll ruin us!" So of course they threatened to ruin me instead and even went so far as to make attempts on my life! Things got so bad I had to hire a bodyguard to stay at my side for a couple of years. During that time, a lot of people saw me on TV, heard me on the radio, read about me in their newspapers, and bought my book. Becoming well-known made me harder to threaten. Now I'm the jeweler to the Super Bowl Champion Dallas Cowboys and Denver Broncos, and I service the diamond needs of nineteen other pro sports franchises. I supply jewelers with their diamonds and colored stones and supply replacement diamonds for three major insurance companies, and I'm one of just two suppliers of diamonds to the Saudi royal family. But I also provide fine diamonds to private clients, individuals who may be just like you. And what matters most to me is that I've helped thousands of ordinary people get diamonds at fair prices. Helping you get a good deal on a diamond is just as important to me as creating a ring for baseball star Roger Clemens, because it takes me back to when I was a young man in love, shopping for an engagement ring.

Read my book. Call my HelpLine if you have questions. And walk through your jeweler's door with confidence that you'll walk out with the right diamond at the right price.

The Shortcut

◆━━━━━━━━━━━━━━━━━━━━━━━━━━━━━◆

ALTHOUGH THIS BOOK HAS been written and designed for ease of use, I realize that some of you may be in a bit of a hurry. If you just need a crash course on what quality diamond to buy—or want a quick refresher course on the rest of the book before you head out the door to the jeweler—go directly to chapter 2 and read the section, "What Kind of Customer Are You?" Following the recommendations in that chapter you should:

- go to a reputable jewelry store.
- request the quality you have selected.
- get an independent appraisal guaranteeing your selection, and then you are done.

Remember, if at any point in the buying process you feel overwhelmed, intimidated, or underinformed, you can always come home and read the chapters relating to your questions. In fact, you might just want to keep this book in the car!

B.E.S.T.

WHAT ARE THE FOUR things all consumers need to do to get their B.E.S.T. start before they buy the perfect diamond?

Budget—Figure out what you have to spend and stick to it. One month's salary is a good guideline.

Expectations—Listen to her. Try to understand her expectations (her needs and wants) so you will have a feel for what to pick out.

Savvy—Become savvy! Know what any given diamond should cost and what the best qualities are to wear. Knowledge is power. You will never win the race without training.

Timetable—Figure out when you want to give it to her and do not rush. Haste makes waste. Give yourself enough time to study up, shop around, and plan the perfect proposal.

Chapter 1

The 4 Cs

Clarity, Color, Cut & Carat Weight

◆────────────────────────────────────◆

DIAMONDS HAVE BEEN PRIZED through the ages for their beauty and rarity. How beautiful—and how rare—they are is determined by the four Cs. First, let's define them.

The Four Cs

Clarity	Color	Cut	Carat Weight
This indicates how clear the diamond is, how free from blemishes and other imperfections.	Diamonds are found in a variety of colors, but in general, the whiter the better.	This refers to not only the shape of the stone but its proportions, factors which determine the sparkle of the diamond.	This is actually the weight of the stone, not its dimensions or size.

The price you'll pay for a diamond depends on the four Cs. They determine what I call the fifth C: Cost.

WHAT IS A DIAMOND?

Diamonds are pure crystallized carbon, often containing minor traces of impurities. Diamonds are formed at very high pressure and very high temperatures deep in the earth, and diamond is the hardest natural substance on earth.

Before we learn how to grade the quality of a diamond and determine what it should cost, let me share some acquired wisdom about diamond buying. Don't ever lose sight of the fact that you're probably buying a diamond to make the love of your life happy. If you ask a woman what she'd like in a diamond, she's not going to say, "Honey, I want a one-and-a-half carat, VS1, F(1) in a Class II cut." (If she does, better rob a bank—this woman's going to be expensive!) What she will say is something like, "Honey, I want it to be big, clear, white, and sparkly." It's your job to take those general adjectives, translate them into diamond grades, decide on a stone, and get your money's worth.

Remember: Focusing on only one C will rarely satisfy anyone. You can buy a one-carat diamond for a few hundred dollars if you ignore color, cut, and clarity. The idea is to find a balance.

Also Remember: Never buy a diamond that's already in a setting. The setting makes it almost impossible to examine the stone carefully. Buy the diamond first, then decide what setting to put it into.

THE HOPE DIAMOND

One of the most famous diamonds in history, the Hope diamond, came from India and weighted 112 3/16 carats when it was acquired around 1642 by French merchant Jean Baptiste Tavernier, who was struck by its "beautiful violet" color. He sold it to the King of France, Louis XIV, who had it recut to a 67 1/8 carat stone. The blue diamond passed through ownership by French and British royalty, famed jeweler Pierre Cartier, and U.S. socialites before it was purchased by jeweler Harry Winston along with the 94.8-carat Star of the East diamond in 1949. In 1958, Winston donated the Hope diamond to the Smithsonian Institution, where it quickly became a star attraction.

Resettings and recuttings over the centuries reduced the Hope diamond to its present 45.52 carats, 40 percent of its original size. Today, it is set in a spectacular pendant surrounded by sixteen white diamonds and still attracts countless admirers at the Smithsonian.

Carat Weight

When you ask someone what they want in a diamond, usually the first thing they'll say is "big." So let's talk first about carat weight.

What is a "carat"? We already know it's a measure of weight, not size, but it's also a word with a fascinating history. Carat is derived from carob, the bean that's often used as a chocolate substitute.

Carob trees grow in the Mediterranean region, and in ancient times, a diamond of one carat or carob was equal in weight to a single bean or seed of the carob tree. In the Far East, rice was used—four grains equaled one carob bean. Eventually the carat was standardized at 200 milligrams (1/5 of a gram), and the grain was standardized at 50 milligrams. Sometimes you will hear a diamond dealer refer to a one-carat diamond as a "four-grainer."

Diamond Factoid

Seventy-six percent of all new brides in the United States will wear a diamond ring; 4.6 percent of these rings will be inherited.

Diamond weights are also referred to in points. One carat equals 100 points, so a 75-point diamond would weigh 3/4 of one carat. (It's not a diamond with 75 points on it, as some people think!)

FRACTIONAL CRYSTALLIZATION

In a perfect world, carbon atoms destined to be diamond crystals live in just the right amount of pressure at just the right temperature for just the right amount of time to create the strong bonds that produce elegant diamond crystals. But sadly, nothing lives in a perfect environment—not carbon, not us.

If there is too much pressure and heat as the young diamond starts to form, the crystal structure develops stress fractures and many times collapses upon itself and breaks only to try to grow again upon its fractured self. When not enough pressure and heat exists, the diamond isn't able to make the necessary attachments and bonds it will need later in life to fulfill its destiny with light. The vast majority of diamonds are created through a form of fractional crystallization (imperfect environment). These diamonds tend to look smaller than other diamonds of the same weight because of their chaotic, dense atomic structure.

THE "MAGICAL" ONE CARAT

You've no doubt heard or seen the marketing slogans, "A diamond is forever"; "Say you'd marry her all over again with a diamond anniversary ring"; and "A one-carat diamond is one in a million." These all come from old ad campaigns by De Beers. Through their clever marketing, they have established the one-carat diamond as the minimum size to buy.

20 PERCENT RULE

Question: If you're looking at two diamonds of the same shape and quality, how much larger does diamond B have to be than diamond A to look bigger?

Answer: When you have two diamonds of the same shape and quality and want one of them to look noticeably larger than the other one, it must have a minimum of 20 percent more in carat weight. This is known as the 20 percent rule.

That's one reason for the substantial price jump when a diamond reaches one carat. Another reason is that a good one-carat diamond is one in a million. But don't be swayed by advertising. There's no magic in size, and the average diamond purchased in the United States is 38 points—just over 1/3 of a carat.

CLARITY

The clarity of a diamond depends on how clear or "clean" it is—how free it is of blemishes and inclusions when viewed with the naked eye and with a 10X loupe or magnifier. Let's define our terms.

Blemishes: Imperfections on the outside of a diamond.

Chip: A little piece missing caused by wear or the cutting process.

Scratch: A line or abrasion.

Fracture: A crack on the diamond's surface.

Polishing lines: Fine lines on the stone's surface formed during the polishing stage.

Natural: An unpolished part of the diamond.

Extra facets: Additional polished surfaces that shouldn't be there and spoil the symmetry of a diamond.

Bearding: Very small fractures on an edge of the diamond.

BIG DIAMONDS

The biggest diamond ever found in the world is the Cullinan diamond from South Africa: 3,106 carats.

The biggest diamond ever found in the United States is the Uncle Sam from Arkansas: 40 carats.

On November 15, 2010, a 24.78 carat fancy intense pink diamond was sold by Sotheby's in Geneva for $45.6 million, the highest price ever paid at auction for a diamond.

Inclusions: Imperfections inside a diamond.

Carbon: Black spots inside a stone.

Feather: Internal cracking.

Crystal: White spots inside a stone.

Pinpoint: Tiny spots smaller than a crystal.

Cloud: A group of pinpoints that may give the impression of a single large inclusion.

Loupe: (pronounced "loop") A small magnifying glass used to view gemstones. Any good jeweler will let you use one and show you how. They should be 10X or 10-power magnification, and the housing around the lens should be black so as not to distort the color of the stone. The Federal Trade Commission requires diamond grading to be done with a 10X magnifier, and any flaw that can't be seen under 10X magnification is considered nonexistent.

Here are the clarity grades of diamonds, as established by the Gemological Institute of America (GIA), and their corresponding definitions using hard-grading standards (see page 14):

FLAWLESS

Free from inclusions and blemishes when viewed under 10X magnification. *Very rare and very expensive.*

INTERNALLY FLAWLESS

Free from inclusions; may have slight blemishes when viewed under 10X magnification. *Also very rare and very expensive.*

VVS1 AND VVS2 (VERY, VERY SLIGHTLY INCLUDED)

Has minute inclusions or blemishes the size of a pinpoint when viewed under 10X magnification. *Rare and expensive.*

VS1 and VS2 (Very Slightly Included)

Has inclusions or blemishes smaller than a grain of salt when viewed under 10X magnification. No carbon, fractures, or breaks. *High quality.*

SI1 (Slightly Included)

Has inclusions or blemishes larger than a grain of salt when viewed under 10X magnification, and these inclusions can be carbon or fractures. Almost all SI1 diamonds are "eye-clean," which means the flaws can't be seen with the naked eye. *Good quality.*

SI2 (Slightly Included)

Has inclusions or blemishes larger than a grain of salt when viewed under 10X magnification, and some of these flaws may be visible to the naked eye. *Borderline diamond.*

I1 (Imperfect)

Has inclusions and blemishes visible to the naked eye. Commercial grade. *Not my taste!*

I2 (Imperfect)

Has inclusions and blemishes visible to the naked eye that can make as much as one fourth of the diamond appear cloudy and lifeless. *Same as above.*

I3 (Imperfect)

Has many, many inclusions and blemishes visible to the naked eye. Not a pretty diamond. Very little luster or sparkle. *Bottom of the barrel.*

Fred's Advice: Aim for a VS2 diamond. Many people unwittingly buy SI1 and SI2 stones, but if you shop carefully, you can buy an VS2 stone for the same price that most SI2 stones are sold for.

Hard and Soft Grading
(What is the truth?)

Everyday people use clarity and color grades to help them compare one diamond to another, but what if the people who are doing the grading are fudging the truth? What would keep a vendor from calling a diamond of a low clarity or color grade a higher grade? Nothing, because the Federal Trade Commission allows jewelers to be up to two grades off on their clarity and color grades if they give disclaimers that their grading represents ranges or if they use third-party labs. So, the shady jeweler takes the monkey off his back by introducing a third-party lab report and says they are responsible for the accuracy of the quality. But here's the hitch: the lab (who is typically paid by the jeweler) puts a disclaimer on their report saying that they aren't responsible. Here is a direct quote taken from GIA's latest lab report:

> This report is not a guarantee, valuation or appraisal and GIA Laboratory ("GIA") has made no representation or warranty regarding this report, the diamond described herein or any inscription thereon.

The three things you need, a guarantee, valuation, and appraisal, you don't get! So what are you to do? Look for this simple eight word sentence anywhere on their evaluation paperwork or receipt:

> "This document is a guarantee, valuation and appraisal"

Any document that has this statement has been hard-graded. Hard-graded means that no competent accredited gemologist will ever say the diamond is lower than is stated. If they do, you are entitled to a full refund on the diamond. Hard-grading is typically done by a minimum of three gemologists, and the worst-case scenario grade is the one accepted. A soft-graded stone is usually a best-case scenario (from the sellers' view point) and is not guaranteed to be any more accurate than within two full grades. Soft-grading is a range; hard-grading is the brutal truth. It's a funny world we live in; most people would rather believe a beautiful lie than an ugly truth. Don't fall for the beautiful lie of lab reports that don't guarantee anything.

HOW TO SPOT CLARITY GRADES

*Note: All plottings that follow show what inclusions and blemishes look like in the different clarity grades when viewed under 10X magnification. *Actual color photographs of inclusions and blemishes can be found at the photo gallery online at my website www.diamondcuttersintl.com.*

In the plotting of the flawless diamond, you will notice there are no marks, meaning the diamond has no inclusions or blemishes.

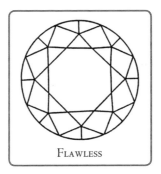

FLAWLESS

In the plottings of the internally flawless diamond, there are no inclusions. But you will notice the slight markings representing slight blemishes.

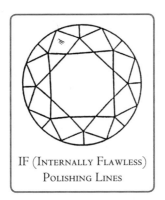

IF (INTERNALLY FLAWLESS)
POLISHING LINES

IF (INTERNALLY FLAWLESS)
SCRATCH

In the VVS plottings, you'll see some very minor inclusions and blemishes.

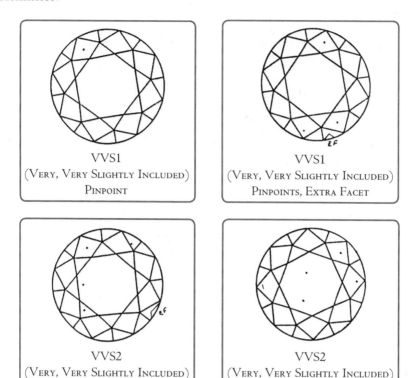

VVS1	VVS1
(Very, Very Slightly Included)	(Very, Very Slightly Included)
Pinpoint	Pinpoints, Extra Facet
VVS2	VVS2
(Very, Very Slightly Included)	(Very, Very Slightly Included)
Pinpoints, Extra Facet	Pinpoints, Scratch, Bearding

Important note: An untrained person will have a very difficult or impossible time trying to find the inclusions or blemishes in a VVS1, or VVS2, internally flawless or flawless diamond. Unless you're a gemologist, don't expect to. These top four grades will appear, to the average person, perfectly clean. You should only be purchasing one of these grades if you're buying the diamond for investment purposes. In my opinion, these grades are too high a quality to be worn. That would be like circulating a proof coin: it would ruin your investment.

Diamonds can get abrasions or even chips through normal wear and tear. Some people find this hard to believe. They say that because a diamond is the hardest substance in the world, that must mean it's very tough and cannot be damaged. The truth is that even though a diamond is hard (hardness being a stone's resistance to being scratched, and the only thing that can scratch a diamond is another diamond), that doesn't mean a diamond is tough (toughness being a stone's resistance to breakage). You see, a diamond can cleave in four directions, meaning it can be damaged.

A diamond is the hardest thing in the world but not the toughest. I don't recommend wearing the highest clarity-grade diamonds, because it is possible for someone to buy a VVS, or flawless diamond and, through normal wear, lower the clarity grade to a VS or even SI grade.

In the VS plottings, the pinpoints become a little easier to see. Also, we start to see some of the other types of inclusions and blemishes.

VS1
(Very Slightly Included)
Pinpoints

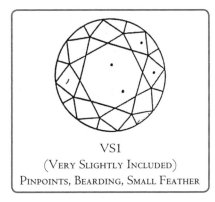

VS1
(Very Slightly Included)
Pinpoints, Bearding, Small Feather

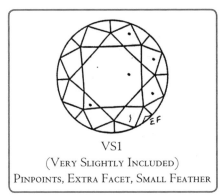

VS1
(Very Slightly Included)
Pinpoints, Extra Facet, Small Feather

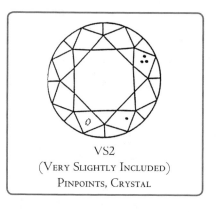

VS2
(VERY SLIGHTLY INCLUDED)
PINPOINTS, CRYSTAL

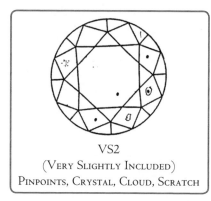

VS2
(VERY SLIGHTLY INCLUDED)
PINPOINTS, CRYSTAL, CLOUD, SCRATCH

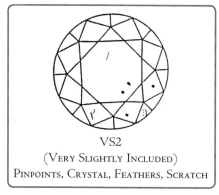

VS2
(VERY SLIGHTLY INCLUDED)
PINPOINTS, CRYSTAL, FEATHERS, SCRATCH

In the SI plottings, we start to see larger crystals, pinpoints, feathers, and the introduction of carbon.

SI1 (SLIGHTLY INCLUDED)
FEATHER, PINPOINTS

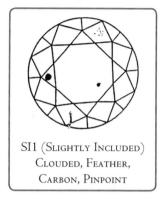

SI1 (SLIGHTLY INCLUDED)
CLOUDED, FEATHER,
CARBON, PINPOINT

SI1 (SLIGHTLY INCLUDED)

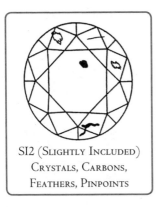

SI2 (Slightly Included)
Crystals, Carbons,
Feathers, Pinpoints

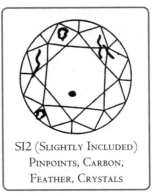

SI2 (Slightly Included)
Pinpoints, Carbon,
Feather, Crystals

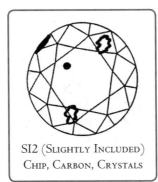

SI2 (Slightly Included)
Chip, Carbon, Crystals

In the imperfect plottings, I get an opportunity to really do some drawing! You will see every type of inclusion and blemish in these grades.

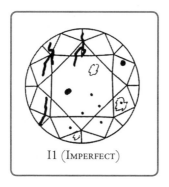

I1 (Imperfect)

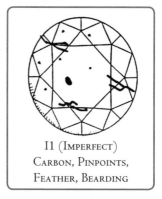

I1 (Imperfect)
Carbon, Pinpoints,
Feather, Bearding

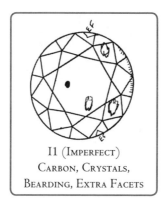

I1 (Imperfect)
Carbon, Crystals,
Bearding, Extra Facets

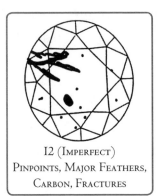

I2 (Imperfect)
Pinpoints, Major Feathers,
Carbon, Fractures

I2 (Imperfect)
Carbon, Major Feathers,
Chips, Clouds

I2 (Imperfect)
Crystals, Chips, Clouds,
Carbon, Fractures

I3 (IMPERFECT)
CHIPS, CARBON, MAJOR
FEATHERS, CRYSTALS,
PINPOINTS

I3 (IMPERFECT)
MAJOR FEATHERS,
BEARDING, CRYSTALS,
CLOUDS, FRACTURE CHIPS

I3 (IMPERFECT)
CLOUDS, CRYSTALS,
PINPOINTS, CARBON,
FRACTURE CHIPS

COLOR

Diamonds come in virtually all colors of the rainbow, from the "beautiful violet" of the Hope diamond to shades of blue, brown, gray, orange, etc. But colored diamonds are very rare and precious. Chances are all the diamonds you'll see in your diamond shopping will be white or yellow, and the whiter the better. The yellow color in diamonds comes from nitrogen, and as a rule, the more yellow the stone, the less value it has. There's a good reason for this. The yellower the stone, the less sharp and sparkly it appears. A whiter stone lets more light pass through it, making it sparkle and shine. The exception to the rule is the canary diamond, which is a beautiful bright yellow and very expensive.

Pink Diamonds—Pink diamonds have been around for hundreds of years, dating back before the fifteenth century. However, their presence seemed imperceptible because of their scarcity. It wasn't until the opening of the Argyle Diamond Mine in Australia in the 1980s that there was a sufficient supply to market them on a worldwide scale. The color of a pink diamond is due to a microscopic imperfection at the atomic level. No trace ingredient here but rather an irregular growth pattern at a sub-molecular level. Fancy pink diamonds typically go for $100,000 per carat, with deep pinks easily running the gamut to over $250,000 per carat.

Blue Diamonds—The secret ingredient behind some of the world's most renowned diamonds, like the Hope Diamond in Washington, D.C.'s Smithsonian Institute, is boron. Just as nitrogen was stirred into the mix of canary, boron gas turns a white diamond blue. Blue diamonds are one of the rarest colors of the rainbow, fetching prices from $100,000 per carat to $664,675 per carat, as was paid for a 13.39 carat fancy deep blue at auction in 2008.

Green Diamonds—As we continue to climb the scale of the world's most valuable colored diamonds, we find green coming in second place. With prices that range from $500,000 per carat to $750,000 per carat, green diamonds owe their beautiful color to high-energy gamma or neutron radiation (not alpha or beta). The Ocean Dream, a 5.51-carat, modified triangular brilliant by Cora Diamonds Corporation, is a classic example of the magnificence of Mother Nature on a good day.

Red Diamonds—Red diamonds are atop the food chain when it comes to the world's most expensive bauble. Ranging upwards to almost $1 million per carat (the Hancock Red set a world record of $926,316 per carat), these rocks aren't for the light of wallet or the impatient. Like the pinks, their atomic structure is imperfect. But if nature hadn't gone amok, we wouldn't have the handful of samples available to study. There are currently clients that have been waiting over fifteen years in line to get the next red when it hits the market.

Some people are more sensitive to the color of diamonds. What may appear slightly yellow to you may look clear to another person, so it will take a higher color grade to satisfy you.

The best way to judge the color of a diamond is to compare it to a master set or a colorimeter. (See the "Color Typing" section for more information on colorimeters.) A master set of diamonds has been graded in a laboratory. A colorimeter is a device that grades the diamond automatically without the need of human eye participation.

Either ask the jeweler for a set and compare the diamonds you're thinking of buying with the diamonds in the master set or have the jeweler place the diamond in the colorimeter to get an accurate grade.

Fred's Advice: Go for grades H or I. Once mounted, they'll look just as good to the average person as the higher grades, without costing a bundle. The average diamond purchased in the United States is color grade M or N, but the customer is usually told it's higher.

Here's the GIA Color Grading Scale and their corresponding definitions using hard-grading standards:

D, E, F:	Colorless
G, H, I:	Nearly colorless
J, K, L:	Slightly yellow
M, N, O:	Light yellow
P, Q, R, S, T,	
U, V, W, X:	Darker yellow
Z:	Fancy colors

Even though there are several grades in each category, there are slight differences between the letter grades. D is the whitest and most valuable, while X is a dingy yellow and least expensive. Z grade and beyond—colored diamonds—are the rarest and most expensive.

UNDER THE RAINBOW

Just as all white diamonds aren't created equal, neither are colored diamonds. Within each of the major colors (hues), there are four main intensity (saturation) levels: fancy light, fancy, fancy intense, and fancy vivid. Within the four saturation levels, there are tone (darkness) modifiers and hue modifiers (secondary or multiple combinations of hues mixed together).

> Example: In a fancy, deep orangey-yellow diamond, the "fancy" is the saturation level (listed always first), followed by "deep" (the tone modifier), then "orangey" (the hue modifier), and then finally yellow (the hue or main color of the stone).

The most expensive saturation level is fancy vivid, followed by fancy intense, fancy, and fancy light. Tone modifiers are either dark or deep. When a tone modifier is present, it complicates things; sometimes for the better, sometimes for the worse.

Try to avoid diamonds with tone modifiers, but this is just a general rule. It is possible for a diamond to be a fancy, deep pink and be as pretty and valuable as a fancy pink. This is a case-by-case basis.

If a diamond has a hue modifier, it means the diamond is not 100 percent one color.

Examples:

Light, fancy orangish-yellow,

Light, fancy orangey-yellow, or

Light, fancy orange-yellow.

Orangish is a hue modifier indicating there is just a hint of orange in the primarily yellow stone (most expensive).

Orangey is a hue modifier indicating there is a splash of orange in the primarily yellow stone (second most expensive).

Orange is a hue modifier that says there are equal amounts of orange and yellow in the stone (the least expensive).

As a general rule, hue modifiers make the diamond less expensive. For example, a fancy, orangish-yellow will always be less expensive than a fancy yellow diamond.

"COGNAC" AND "BLACK" DIAMONDS

"Cognac" (brown) diamonds are a by-product of plastic deformation of the atomic crystal lattice structure. In other words, brown diamonds are brown because they have an irregular or broken atomic structure that grew in an environment of fractional crystallization. This is an environment where too much force was placed upon the carbon atoms and/or the atoms were constantly exposed to drastic changes in temperature (heat).

Brown diamonds, also referred to as "champagne" when the hue is lighter, have been relatively inexpensive for years. A one-carat brown diamond has gone for just a couple hundred dollars a carat. However, consolidators have recently begun gobbling up brown diamonds to heat treat (bake) them in a process called HTHP (high temperature, high pressure), where the atomic structure is rearranged to make the diamond look whiter. There is a difference of opinion on whether HTHP diamonds are structurally sound, but I believe they aren't worth the money. "Cognac" diamonds have little or no secondary market value and should only be bought as a novelty item.

Black diamonds are black because they have been irradiated by man. While it is possible to find a black natural diamond (carbonado), all the black diamonds that are available for purchase have been treated. Prices of black diamonds run very low; approximately $100.00 to $300.00 per carat. Just like the brown, black diamonds serve only the novelty market.

Color Typing

Let's start this piece by asking what might, on the surface, seem like a very simple question: shouldn't two diamonds of the exact same weight, same clarity, same color, exact same proportions, nonfluorescent, same purchase date, same lab-grading report date, and both bonded with the exact same markup cost the same? Well, if you ask the labs or check with any of the major price guides like Rapaport, the answer would be a resounding yes.

But pick up your phone, visit your local jeweler, or surf the Web, and I promise you that you'll find twins that are not the same price. In fact, not only are they not the exact same price, in some cases they're not even close. You'll even find two identical diamonds at the same location with totally different prices. Why? How can this be? It's true that not all SI1s are created equal. Some have centralized inclusions, while others have perimeter inclusions, making those SI1s more desirable and valuable. But what about the VSs? I can honestly tell you I've never met a VS diamond I didn't like. So where's the answer? The answer is in the color. What the industry has been aware of but hasn't shared with the rest of the world is "color typing."

In the spring of 1999, a wonderful gemological color-grading device hit the market: the Gran Fall Spectrum Colorimeter DC2000fs by Gem Instruments. For the first time, we can actually prove that not all Hs, Gs, or Fs are created equal. This new colorimeter is so precise that we can actually break down each color grade into five color types. For example, instead of asking someone what color a diamond is, we should ask what its color and type is. Example: an H can be an H(1), H(2), H(3), H(4), or H(5); H(1) being the best borderline G, while H(5) is a borderline I color. When you combine colors and types with grade bumping (see page 172), two diamonds can have the perception of being the same but be from different parts of the rainbow.

When will the labs start breaking down each color into types?

Who knows! I know the price guides won't be the vanguard until at least one lab steps up to tell us that not all identical diamonds of the same color are created equal. Naturally an F(1) should cost more than an F(5). But if the labs won't tell you, how can you determine a diamond's color and type without their help? It's easy—have the store run a colorimeter tape and attach it to the appraisal so you will know if your G is a strong G or a weak one. Make the sale contingent on an independent appraisal that agrees with the colorimeter tape. I wish the labs did color typing because the technology is now available, but color typing is just not profitable for labs. Jewelers are naturally going to send their stones for evaluation where they get treated the nicest and the labs are the least critical. That's why there are five European Gemological Laboratory (EGL) or International Gemological Institute (IGI) lab-grading reports out there for every one Gemological Institute of America (GIA) lab-grading report. The labs may never recognize color typing, but that doesn't mean jewelers don't have access to colorimeters. Knowledge is power. As the buyer, you have every right to know a diamond's color and type. Just ask.

QUICK AND EASY GRADING TIPS

Clarity

1. If you can see any inclusions or blemishes with your own eyes, the diamond is no better than I1.
2. With a 10X loupe, if you see any black spots, cracks, or anything larger than a grain of salt, the diamond is no better than SI1.
3. With a 10X loupe, if you can see nothing wrong with the diamond, only then could it be a VS1 or VS2 or higher.

MORE ABOUT COLOR: FLUORESCENCE AND PHOSPHORESCENCE

Fluorescence is a diamond's reaction to ultraviolet (UV) light. Some diamonds glow in different colors under UV light, and the general rule is to avoid them. If you put a diamond under UV light and it glows strong blue, the diamond may look dull in sunlight. Diamonds with strong fluorescence may be worth up to 20 percent less than diamonds that do not fluoresce. Faint fluorescence that doesn't fog the diamond is okay.

Phosphorescence is a type of photoluminescence related to fluorescence. A phosphorescent diamond also reacts to ultraviolet (UV) light, but instead of immediately emitting a glow when ultraviolet light is present, the diamond will absorb some of the radiation from the light and emit it even after the exposure to the UV light is over. Translation: phosphorescent diamonds can look poor (foggy and hazy) outdoors and continue to look poor for hours later even though the diamond is no longer being exposed to harmful UV rays. Metaphorically, we could say a phosphorescent diamond is susceptible to sunburn. Not a good thing.

DIAMOND MYTH

"Yellow diamonds are worthless."

Yellow diamonds are worth less than white diamonds, but they still have value. And if a diamond contains so much nitrogen that it's very bright yellow, it can be worth quite a bit. Bright yellow diamonds are known as "canary diamonds," and they're more valuable than light yellow diamonds.

CORRESPONDING GRADING

Corresponding grading means matching clarity grades with color grades. For every clarity grade, there's a color grade that *corresponds* or makes the best match in determining value.

Diamonds that have corresponding grading sell for higher prices originally, and they also appreciate in value more than diamonds that don't and therefore have higher resale value. Buying a diamond with noncorresponding clarity and color grades is like buying a pink Porsche: It's okay as long as you don't try to resell it. The market for pink Porsches just isn't as good as the market for, say, red Porsches.

Here's a list of clarity grades and their corresponding color grades. Notice that for each clarity grade, there's a *perfect* match and a high and low color that also works well.

Clarity Grade	Color Grade	Average Annual Increase in $ Value
Flawless and Internally Flawless	D (Perfect) E (Low)	10.00%
VVS1, VVS2	D (High) E (Perfect) F (Low)	9.25%–9.99%
VS1, VS2	F (High) G (Perfect) H (Low)	8.50%–9.24%
SI1, SI2	H (High) I (Perfect) J (Low)	6.50%–8.49%
Lower	No corresponding color grades	

The value of a stone is always based on the *lowest* clarity or color grade and its highest corresponding grade. For example, let's say you purchased a stone with a clarity grade of SI1 and a color grade of G. You can see above that G is not a corresponding color for an SI1 stone. The SI1-G diamond will cost you more than the SI1-H but will appreciate no more over time than the SI1-H.

When you *don't* correspond the grades—say, you buy high clarity and low color, or high color and low clarity—you'll never get your money back for the higher grade. For example, an SI1-F would resell no higher than the value of an SI1-H, and a VS1-I would resell no higher than the value of an SI1-I. A diamond that is *not* correspondingly graded could be expected to appreciate 2 percent to 4 percent per year.

CUT

Okay, we're three-fourths of the way to becoming diamond experts! We've learned to check the carat weight of a diamond. We know how diamonds are graded for clarity and how to look for a diamond that's "clean." We also know that diamonds range from D to X, "colorless" to "darker yellow" on the color scale. Now we'll learn about the fourth C: Cut.

The first thing to know is that the cut of a diamond indicates more than its shape. The cut also determines how sparkly your diamond will be! It's not enough that a diamond is big and clear and white. No diamond can be truly attractive unless it sparkles, and it won't sparkle unless it's properly cut. You can buy a one-carat diamond, graded SI2 or higher for clarity, and rated J or better on the color scale, and it still won't sparkle unless the cut is good.

The Vivid White Diamond®

When one defines sparkle in a diamond, there are only two things that matter—efficiency and amplified light return.

Efficiency rating (E.R.) is a measure of the refracted light entering a diamond that is returned to your eye.

Amplified light return (A.L.R) is the number of visible internal light reflections that a diamond has per every ray (signal) of light that enters it.

Weighted light return (more commonly known as brightness) = E.R. × W.L.R

A typical run-of-the-mill diamond has an efficiency rating of 35.5 percent and an A.L.R rating of five. Translation: the typical diamond returns 35.5 percent of refracted light back to the viewer's eyes; leaks/wastes 64.5 percent through the pavilion floor of the diamond and only redirects the light internally five times before it leaks out or is returned to be viewed.

A pinball machine is a good analogy here. Think of every ray of light as a pinball. Once the pinball is shot (refracted) into play within the machine (diamond), you score more points (flashes of light) every time the pinball bounces around (internal light reflections) before it is returned back to you in the form of sparkle (sparkle equals efficiency rating multiplied by internal light reflections). So we could say that the typical diamond returns 35.5 percent of absorbed light and amplifies it five times to give you a sparkle return of 177.5 percent. You get 77.5 percent more light than you put in even though there was a lot of waste.

This is why most people who see practically any diamond will, at first glance, be impressed. The truth is even bad diamonds can look pretty good. But what if we're not just looking for pretty good? What if our goal is to have the highest efficiency rating and the highest amplified light return? What would that look like?

If we're looking for the most breathtaking diamond in the world, we're going to have to be patient. Typically, diamonds today are cut from two types of rough (name for what diamonds look like out of the ground): macles and flats.

MACLE

FANCY SHAPES

FLAT

SMALL STONES, TRILLIANTS
AND BAGUETTES

These are also called irregulars or preemies (300 to 400 million years old). Preemies are rough diamonds that Mother Nature did not allow to go to full-term. Full-term crystals, also referred to as sawables, are the most valuable. They are typically found in octahedron, cubic, and dodecahedron shapes.

OCTAHEDRON

CUBE

DODECAHEDRON

The key to having the best-finished product begins by choosing a full-term rough. It takes a minimum of 800 million years, not 400 million years, for Mother Nature to deliver a magnificent, fully crystallized, full-term rough. The irregulars are flat, skipping-stone-looking pieces of rough that have an irregular carbon atomic structure. (Don't forget that shape determines function!) If we don't have a nice shape to work with, we won't be able to cut the diamond properly.

Ninety-eight percent of the diamonds being sold today are being cut from premature rough, and only two percent are being cut from full-term rough. Once we've got the rare full-term rough, we go through a second screening process and throw out any rough that has too much nitrogen or is too heavily included. In order to reach our goal, the diamond must not be any lower than a hard-graded VS2 clarity or H5 color. By hard graded, I mean the vendor guarantees that no accredited gemologist will ever grade the diamond lower than the assigned grade or you get your money back. Other rating agencies—GIA, EGL, IGI, AGS, etc.—all soft-grade their stones, which means they don't guarantee their grades.

Once we have the desired full-term rough with the correct grades, we can move on to a master cutter. It doesn't do any good to have the world's greatest material if we put it in the hands of a poor craftsman. The master cutter will make sure the diamond is cut to class 1 or class 2 specifications (see pages 50–51). But basically, the diamond will have to meet strict proportion guidelines in order to handle the light properly.

So, to sum it up, a hard-graded, full-term rough (most expensive) cut by a master cutter (more expensive) equals a quality finished product. The name given to this most breathtaking diamond is the Vivid White Diamond®. You can view a photograph of one at http://www.diamondcuttersintl.com. The Vivid White Diamond® has an E.R. of 91% and A.L.R of 100. So if we want to calculate the sparkle of this gem we multiply the E.R. by the A.L.R.: 91% × 100 = 9100% light return. 100% goes in; 9100% comes out!

The reason Cartier, Graff, Van Cleef & Arpels, and Harry Winston get $35,000 to $56,000 for a single one-carat diamond is actually rather simple: they are all vivid white diamonds! When buying from online consolidators like Blue Nile, Amazon, or eBay; mall stores like Zale's,

Tiffany's, Kay's, Jared's, Robbins Brothers; and big box stores like Walmart, Costco, or Sam's Club, you're buying diamonds that get 77% more light return in good lighting conditions. But when you buy a Vivid White Diamond®, you are getting 9000% more amplified light.

Some old sayings are still true today, "You get what you pay for." By the way, the number one complaint a woman has about her diamond isn't about its size but its sparkle. So, if you really want to make her happy, buy the Vivid White Diamond®.

DIAMOND MYTH

"Diamonds are indestructible."

False! Diamonds are the hardest natural substance known on earth, but they are not the toughest. There's a difference between the hardness and the toughness of materials. A sharp blow can certainly damage your diamond.

To understand what I mean, first let's look at some shapes. Diamonds can be cut into a wide variety of shapes. Shown on the following pages are some of the most popular.

OFF-MAKES

This is the number one problem with diamonds! An "off-make" is a poorly proportioned diamond, and no matter how white, how clean, or how big a diamond is, it won't achieve maximum sparkle, fire, and brilliance unless it's cut correctly. Always make sure a diamond is well-proportioned by following the Proportion Questionnaire Sheet guidelines.

Modern Diamond Cuts

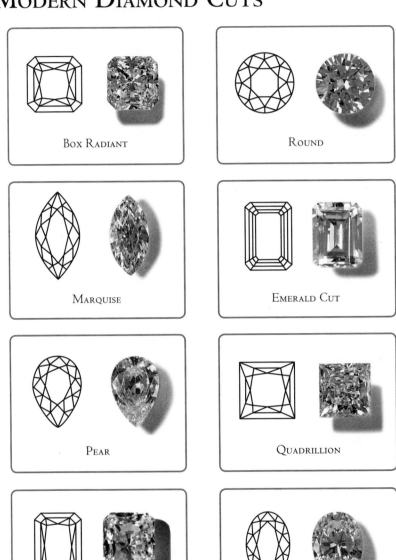

Box Radiant

Round

Marquise

Emerald Cut

Pear

Quadrillion

Standard Radiant

Oval

Old-Era Diamond Cuts

The old-era or nonmodern cuts tend to be off-make or poorly proportioned diamonds.

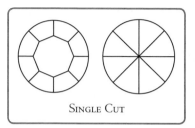

16 or 17 facets

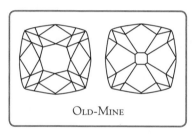

High crown
Deep pavilion
Large culet*

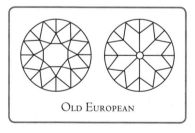

High crown
Deep pavilion
Large culet*

Creates appearance of a hole in the center of the diamond when viewed from above.

Now that you've had a look at some diamond shapes, let's go over the parts of the cut diamond.

There are three basic parts to every cut diamond: the crown (top), the girdle (around the middle), and the pavilion (the bottom).

The crown consists of a large flat area on top called the table and a number of facets. As the diamond catches the light, the job of the crown is to split the light entering the diamond into *white light*, which gives the stone its brilliance and colored light, which gives it fire or dispersion.

THE PARTS OF A DIAMOND

The girdle is the thin band around the widest part of the diamond. The function of the girdle is to protect the edge of the stone from chipping. (Even though diamond is the hardest natural substance on earth, it can be chipped!)

The pavilion has the most important job, which is to reflect the light that passes through the crown back into your eyes. Think of it as a cone lined with mirrors. The light enters the diamond through the crown, splits into white and colored light, and bounces off the facets of the pavilion back up through the crown, where you see it as *sparkle*!

But to achieve the maximum sparkle—that magic combination of brilliance and fire—the diamond must be well-cut and cut in the proper proportions. The size of the table, the symmetry of the facets, the thickness of the girdle, and the angle of the pavilion must all work together to give the diamond the sparkle you want. Let's take these areas one at a time to see how they affect the quality of the diamond.

Table

The size of the table, as a percentage of the crown, is important because it determines the amount of *brilliance*, or white light, the diamond will reflect. For example, if the table is 60 percent of the diameter of the crown, 60 percent of the light you see will be *brilliance* and 40 percent will be *fire* or dispersion. *Avoid a diamond with a table area of 65 percent or higher.* It will give the diamond too much brilliance and not enough fire—and the diamond will look fuzzy or foggy. (The only exception to this rule is square and rectangular cut diamonds that can have a 65 percent table. This includes all princess cuts, asschers, and radiants.)

Here's the formula:
Table area 53–60% = GREAT!
Table area 61–64% = GOOD!
Table area less than 53% or greater than 64% = AVOID!*
*except square and rectangular cuts

So, how do you determine exactly what the table area is? It's obviously a measurement that's pretty difficult to make unless you have the right instruments. You may not be able to measure it, but from the given chart, you know what it should be—*so, ask the dealer!* And tell the dealer you'll have his answer checked by an independent appraiser so he might as well tell you the truth.

Sarin & Megascope

In previous editions of this book, from 1991 to 1998, I never made reference to the tools used to measure the angles and percentages in a diamond. Since as far back as I can remember, hand calipers and proportion comparators were all that were available. Most people refer to this type of measurement as H.E.M. (Human Eye Measurement) because good eyesight and a steady hand were required for accuracy. Well, the days of H.E.M. are over. Technology has brought us two wonderful computers that can measure all the proportions of a diamond in less than fifteen seconds and be thirty-five times more accurate. These two new mechanical marvels are the Sarin machine and the Megascope. Literally, all you have to do is drop a diamond into these devices' chambers, and poof! all the measurements are posted on a monitor.

Presidium Electronic Gemstone Gauge

The old standby gemstone gauge has been thrust into the digital age. Enter the Presidium Electronic Gemstone Gauge. It has a digital display and is accurate to the hundredth of a millimeter.

Facets

The typical diamond is cut with fifty-eight facets, thirty-three on the crown and twenty-five on the pavilion. On a well-proportioned stone, these facets will be uniform and symmetrical. If they are not, the diamond's ability to refract and reflect light will suffer. Furthermore, a poorly cut diamond just won't look right to the eye. The sad fact is that *78 percent of all rounds and 92 percent of all other shapes on the market are poorly proportioned!* Poorly proportioned stones are more profitable for the dealer, because they retain more of the weight of the "rough" or uncut diamond. That allows the dealer to sell it as a bigger diamond than it should be and get more money for it, even though it sparkles less. *Look closely! Choose a diamond that's well-cut, even if you have to search a while to find it.*

Girdle

This is a Goldilocks problem. You don't want a diamond with a girdle that's too thin or one that's too thick—you want one that's just right! The whole purpose of the girdle is to protect the edge of the stone from chipping. A girdle that's too thin doesn't give enough protection. A girdle that's too thick *does* protect against chipping, but it doesn't look good. So you want a diamond with a medium girdle, neither too thin nor too thick. How do you tell? Look at the diamond from the side. If it looks like there's a white chalk line around the middle of the stone, the girdle is too thick. If you don't see any girdle at all with the naked eye, look at the same area of the stone with a 10X loupe. If you can't see a girdle with the loupe, it's too thin.

DIAMONDS IN THE ROUGH

An uncut diamond, as it is found in nature, is called "rough." As a rule of thumb, it takes a three-carat rough to produce a good quality one-carat cut stone. Often, poorly proportioned diamonds are the result of a diamond cutter trying to make a one-carat stone from a two-carat rough.

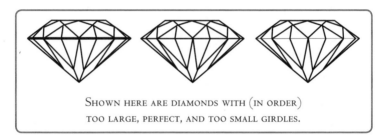

SHOWN HERE ARE DIAMONDS WITH (IN ORDER)
TOO LARGE, PERFECT, AND TOO SMALL GIRDLES.

PAVILION

The job of the pavilion is most important of all: to reflect light into your true love's eyes. I think it's important to understand that when you look at a diamond and see it sparkle, you're not just seeing light reflected off the surface of the diamond. The light enters the diamond through the table and the facets of the crown, passes through the diamond, and is reflected back by the facets of the pavilion.

Here's the important part: The angle of the pavilion for a round diamond must be between 40–41.5 degrees; 40.75 degrees is perfect. For marquise, pear, and ovals, the perfect angle is 40 degrees, but an acceptable range is 39.25–40.75 degrees. For emerald and rectangular cuts, perfect is 45.05 degrees, and an acceptable range is 43.3–46.8 degrees.

If the pavilion angle is not exactly right, it will not reflect the light properly, and the diamond won't have the sparkle it should. In a round diamond, there's a dramatic loss of sparkle if the angle is even a tenth of a degree above 41.5 or below 40 degrees. In a marquise, pear, or oval, maximum sparkle is achieved with a 40 degree pavilion angle, but the angle can be increased or decreased by as much as three-fourths of a degree with only a 10 percent loss of sparkle. Emerald and rectangular cut diamonds have the widest allowable variance of 1.75 degrees. Each extreme will also cause a 10 percent loss of sparkle.

As I mentioned, 92 percent of fancy shapes are poorly cut. A great many people in the diamond industry believe that if that many are cut wrong, it must make it right. It doesn't! Some even argue that the angle can't be accurately measured on a fancy shape. Wrong! You simply measure the pavilion angle at the diamond's widest point. GIA has relaxed its guidelines for fancy shapes, but you and I have not! Insist on the correct angle, and if you don't get it, keep looking.

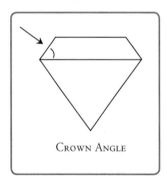

CROWN ANGLE

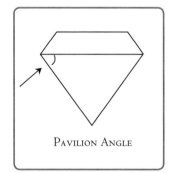

PAVILION ANGLE

BUYING TIP

If a diamond dealer can't (or won't) answer your questions, assume the worst! For example, if the dealer can't tell you the girdle thickness, assume it's too thin or too thick. If the dealer can't tell you the crown angle, assume it's below 32 or greater than 35 degrees and the diamond is an off-make.

CROWN ANGLE

The angle of the crown is also important, but it doesn't have to be quite as precise as the pavilion angle. *The angle of the crown should be 32.0–35.0 degrees.* If it's smaller than 32.0 degrees, the diamond is what we call "spread-cut." This makes the table area too large and the girdle too thin, and we already know what problems that causes.

If the angle of the crown is *above 35.0 degrees*, it makes the diamond "top heavy." This results in a smaller diameter, making the diamond look smaller than it really is. The last thing you want is a one-carat diamond that looks like a three-quarters carat!

WARPING

Is it possible for a diamond to have more than one crown or pavilion angle? You bet! Now here is the million-dollar question: When a lab report or appraisal is done, which crown and pavilion angle are you given? Are you given the best one? Probably. In an ever-competitive race for your dollar, the cutter, jeweler, and even the appraiser can be caught up in "warping."

Warping is the placement of accurate pavilion and crown angles on a diamond but solely in one location. The rest of the crown and pavilion angles are off. Diamonds without universal crown angles and universal pavilion angles can be very profitable for a cutter because most labs and appraisal services check for the best measurement or at least an average, which allows a cutter to push through a Class III or IV (poorly proportioned) diamond as a Class I or II.

In purchasing your diamond, ask to have the worst angles measured—if the worst are acceptable, then surely the rest will be as well. Or ask for minimum and maximum pavilion and crown angles to see the extremes in both directions. This type of information can be easily found on a Sarin or Megascope report.

CULET

Finally, at the very bottom of the diamond—the base of the pavilion—there may be a small facet called the culet. If this facet is too large, when you look straight down through the table, it will look like the diamond has a hole in the middle. *Make sure the stone has no culet or a very small culet.*

TWO OTHER IMPORTANT DIAMOND MEASUREMENTS

Two other measurements to consider are total depth percentage and length-to-width ratio.

Total depth percentage is a simple, straightforward measurement: Take the height of the stone and divide it by the diameter of the stone. For fancy-shaped diamonds, the diameter is measured at its widest part. The answer should be in the 56.0 percent to 61.0 percent range. If it's not, it means there's something wrong with the crown angle and/or the pavilion angle or the girdle thickness. (The only exception to this rule is square- or rectangular-cut diamonds.)

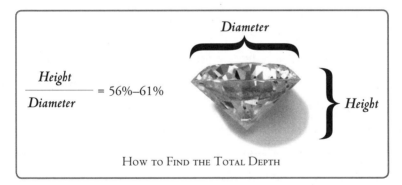

$$\frac{Height}{Diameter} = 56\%–61\%$$

HOW TO FIND THE TOTAL DEPTH

The *length-to-width ratio* is used to determine if a fancy-shaped diamond (anything other than round) is well-proportioned. For example, we don't want to buy a marquise that is so skinny it looks like a banana or one that's so fat it looks like a football.

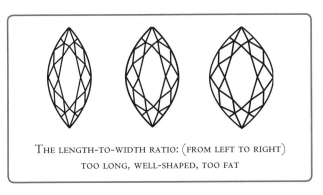

THE LENGTH-TO-WIDTH RATIO: (FROM LEFT TO RIGHT)
TOO LONG, WELL-SHAPED, TOO FAT

Pleasing proportions aside, the length-to-width ratio also affects a phenomenon known as the bow-tie. Let me explain. *Fancy shapes are not symmetrical—only a round one is.* And because fancy stones aren't symmetrical, they all have a bow-tie—two triangular shadows in the middle of the diamond where light leaks out the bottom.

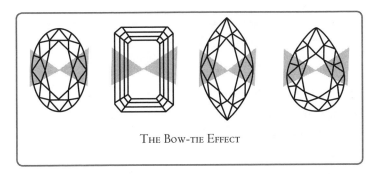

THE BOW-TIE EFFECT

If the length-to-width ratio is off, it will intensify the bow-tie in the stone!

For a marquise diamond, the length should be no less than 1.75 times the width and no more than 2 times the width. For pear shapes, the length should be no less than 1.5 times the width, and no more than 1.75 times the width. For emerald and oval shapes, the length should be no less than approximately 1.3 times the width and no more than 1.75 times the width.

THE 65/68 EXCEPTION FOR STANDARD RADIANTS

My first preference in a standard radiant will always be a beautiful 65/65, 1.22 to 1 length-to-width ratio, 10 percent plus crown height and 45 degree pavilion angle. However, Stan Grossbard of the Original Radiant Diamond Company (his late father was one of my idols) showed me recently that by a slight adjustment of the lower mirror facets on the pavilion, it was possible to use a 68 percent total depth percentage on standard radiants with an attractive outcome. The only drawback is that the higher the depth percentage, the more likely the diamond will appear smaller. I have yet to meet a woman who doesn't appreciate a bigger boat in her ocean regardless of the motion. But let's say you are in a tight squeeze and a 65/65 dream rock isn't available and the choice is a 65/68 or nothing. It has been my experience most women would rather have something over nothing.

Final note: 65/65 standard and box radiants are known as "flagships."

THE 65/65 RULE

The 65/65 rule refers to all square- and rectangular-cut diamonds (princess, emerald, radiant, and asscher). A diamond that is square cut or rectangular is said to be well-proportioned if its table percentage and total depth percentage are each equal or less than 65 percent of the width.

DIAMOND LORE

Diamonds have been treasured throughout history for their special qualities, but for most of that time, they have been very rare and available only to the super-rich. Not until after the discovery of large diamond deposits in South Africa around 1865 did diamonds become plentiful enough to be affordable to people of more modest means. In fact, now diamonds are not rare at all! The market for diamonds is carefully controlled by the big diamond cartels to keep prices artificially high.

Proportions Made Easy

GIA originally made it easier to determine if a diamond is well-proportioned by dividing all cut diamonds into four classes. Here is GIA's original classes of cut system. Although they have abandoned it for their new cut-grade system, I still think it's the best.

Essentially, *Class I* and *Class II* diamonds are well-proportioned; *Class III* and *Class IV* diamonds are not.

Class I diamonds are investment-quality stones, beautifully proportioned and priced to match. For a stone to be rated Class I is like getting an A+ on a test. Class II diamonds get a straight A on the same test, and if your objective is to buy a beautiful diamond to wear, Class II is fine.

Fred's advice: Don't go below Class II. And if the jeweler doesn't know what the GIA classes are—move on!

Proportion and Price

Here's an example of what proportion can mean to price: Let's say you go to two different jewelry stores, Joe's and Mike's. They are both offering a round, one-carat, VS1, G(1) diamond.

Joe's Price: $16,524

Mike's Price: $9,924

Immediately, you notice that Joe's price is $6,600 higher than Mike's. This could be because Joe is just trying to make more money on the same quality diamond. But you look more closely at the diamonds and discover that Joe's diamond is well-proportioned and Mike's is poorly proportioned. In this case, you should buy at Joe's. You're getting your money's worth.

A poorly proportioned diamond is worth as much as 50 percent less than a well-proportioned stone.

One reason for the difference in worth is that it takes a three-carat "rough," which is a diamond as it's found in nature, to produce a well-proportioned one-carat cut stone. But it only takes a two-carat rough to produce a poorly proportioned one-carat stone.

But, you say, one carat is one carat! What's the big deal?

The big deal is that a poorly proportioned diamond will not sparkle nearly as much as a well-proportioned diamond. If a diamond is poorly proportioned, only 30 percent to 40 percent of the light that enters it will reflect back up into your true love's eyes, while a well-proportioned diamond will reflect close to 90 percent of the light. A woman wants a diamond to be "big, clean, white, and sparkly," and it won't sparkle unless it's well-proportioned.

GIA CLASSES OF CUTS

Class I	American/Tolkowsky Cut (15% above cost)*
Table %	53.0–60.0% of diameter of stone for round, marquise, pear, and oval; 58.0–64.0% of diameter of stone for emerald, square, and rectangular
Total depth	59.3–61.0% of diameter of stone for round, marquise, pear, and oval; 58.0–64.0% of diameter of stone for emerald, square, and rectangular
Crown angle	34.0–35.0 degrees for round, marquise, pear, and oval; 33.0–35.0 degrees for emerald, square, and rectangular
Crown height	13.5–16.2% of diameter of stone for round, marquise, pear, and oval; 11.7–16.2% of diameter of stone for emerald, square, and rectangular
Girdle thickness	0.7–2.7% of diameter of stone for all shapes (medium preferred)
Pavilion angle	40.20–41.20 degrees for rounds; 39.25–40.75 degrees for marquise, pear, and oval; 43.8–46.8 degrees for emerald, square, and rectangular
Pavilion depth	42.52–43.57% of diameter of stone for round, marquise, pear, and oval; 47.6–53.1% of diameter of stone for emerald, square, and rectangular
Polish & symmetry	Excellent to Good

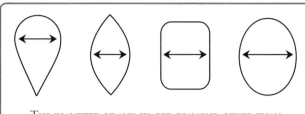

THE DIAMETER OF ANY SHAPED DIAMOND OTHER THAN
ROUND IS THE DIAMOND'S MAXIMUM WIDTH.

Class II	(cost)*
Table %	53.0–64.0% for round, pear, marquise, and oval; 53.0–65.0% for emerald, square, and rectangular
Total depth	56.0–61.0% for round, marquise, pear, and oval; 56.0–65.0% for emerald, square, and rectangular
Crown angle	32.0–35.0 degrees for all shapes
Crown height	11.2–16.2% for all shapes
Girdle thickness	0.7–2.7% of diameter of stone for all shapes (medium preferred)
Pavilion angle	40.0–41.5 degrees for rounds; 39.25–40.75 degrees for pear, marquise, and oval; 43.3–46.8 degrees for emerald, square, and rectangular
Pavilion depth	42.31–43.89% for rounds; 41.51–43.1% for pear, marquise, and oval; 47.1–53.1% for emerald, square, and rectangular
Polish & symmetry	Excellent to Good

Class III	(15-25% below cost)*
Table %	65–70% for round, marquise, pear, and oval; 66–70% for emerald, square, and rectangular
Crown angle	30–32 degrees for all shapes
Girdle thickness	Very thin or very thick for all shapes

Pavilion angle	Any measurement other than 40–41.5 degrees for round or 39.25–40.75 degrees for marquise, pear, and oval; any measurement other than 43.3–46.8 degrees
Polish & symmetry	Fair to Good

Class IV	(50-60% below cost)*
Table %	70% and above for all shapes
Crown angle	30 degrees and below for all shapes
Girdle thickness	Extremely thin to very thin, or very thick to extremely thick for all shapes
Pavilion angle	Any measurement other than 40–41.5 degrees for round or 39.25–40.75 degrees for marquise, pear, and oval; any measurement other than 43.3–46.8 degrees
Polish & symmetry	Fair to Good

*Cost refers to the price guide in this book.

THE BOX RADIANT AND STANDARD RADIANT EXCEPTION

With the recent advancements made by Radiant Diamond Company in lower mirror facet arrangements, it is now acceptable for box radiants to have crown heights range from 9.0 percent to 16.2 percent and standard radiants to range from 10.0 percent to 16.2 percent.

"THE 61 PERCENT FACTOR"

(In honor of Mark Osborne)

Question: Can a diamond whose crown angle is within tolerance of being a Class I or II, whose girdle thickness is neither very thin nor very thick, and whose pavilion angle is also within tolerance of being a Class II actually be a Class III?

Answer: Yes, it is possible for the parts of a diamond to meet Class II tolerances but whose total exceeds the "61 percent factor." The 61 percent factor is when the crown height, girdle thickness, and pavilion depth exceed 61 percent. Mathematically, 61 percent is the magical total depth percentage that a round, pear, marquise, or oval must not exceed in order to remain a Class II (Class I and Class II diamonds are well-proportioned diamonds, and Class III and Class IV are not). Once the total depth percentage exceeds 61 percent, it can be proven very easily by taking the tangent of the crown and pavilion angles and their corresponding crown heights and pavilion depths to show how light enters critical angles in the pavilion of the diamond and leaks out to create a fish eye in round and deep bow-tie shadows in pears, marquise, and ovals.

An avid reader of this book pointed out that I did not send this point home well enough to my readers and to visitors of my website. It is with his encouragement that I correct any omissions or explanations on this very point. With so many laboratories stating that total depths can exceed 61 percent, my lack of emphasis on the importance of the "61 percent factor" might have left too many question marks in the minds of some of the readers of my book, website, and columns. The importance of the "61 percent factor" can now be placed in the limelight that it rightfully deserves.

In closing, someone once asked me how important not going over the 61 percent really was in terms of total depth percentage. My response was short and to the point. Imagine that you are 61 steps from the edge of a cliff; how big a deal is that 62nd step?

Note: Class I has an average of 91 percent light return.

Class II, 88 percent light return.

Class III, 38-39 percent light return.

Class IV, approximately 32 percent.

Artificial Lighting

In 1955, Gemological Institute of America's (GIA) Gem Trade Lab (GTL) began issuing lab-grading reports for diamonds. Concept: In order to assign a value to a diamond, you need to know its quality. GIA hit a homerun by creating a standardized system for grading diamonds (the four Cs; carat weight, clarity, color, and cut). Also, with GIA as an industry watchdog, misgrading or misrepresentation by unscrupulous jewelers might be avoided.

At first, it worked. Jewelers knew that if they had a good diamond, the ideal thing was to send it in for a lab-grading report. Then a funny thing happened; others realized there was money to be made in having the power to bless or condemn a diamond's quality, so they started their own labs (EGL, IGI, HRD, AGS, etc.).

The word certificate (see page 170) started being thrown around, and it was implied that a diamond didn't have any value without its "papers." What the public wasn't aware of was that the labs did not discriminate as to which diamonds they issued reports on. Any diamond sent in, regardless of quality, got "papers" (a lab-grading report) so the jeweler could reference it during the sale.

While you'll read at great length about the current validity of lab-grading reports in Chapter 4, I'd like to focus on a new aspect of lab-grading reports that was incorporated into the reports in January of 2006 by GIA—a cut-grading system.

According to Tom Moses, GTL's vice president, computer-generated models were used to determine the most appropriate set of proportions (for round stones) to increase the amount of sparkle (brilliance plus dispersion) and scintillation of a diamond to the viewer's eyes. After the computer model calculations were done, Human Eye Measurement was needed to solidify the predictions. It has been reported by GTL that over sixty-five thousand observations were made to quantify if human preferences matched what the computer light-tracing experiments predicted would be the most optimal way to cut a diamond. *Note: While sixty-five thousand observations sounds like sixty-five thousand people were used in the trial, in fact only three hundred fifty people were used. Every time they looked at a diamond, even if it was more than once, it was counted as an observation. (One million hits on a website doesn't mean one million unique visitors found the site.)* A reported two thousand diamonds were used for the calculations.

Diamond Myth

"A fancy-shaped diamond is more difficult to cut and more valuable than a round diamond."

Actually, a fancy shape is no more difficult to cut than a round diamond, and a round diamond is generally the most expensive shape simply because of demand. Sixty-five percent of all diamonds sold are round. The emerald cut can be the least expensive because its shape is most like the natural shape of the rough—the uncut diamond.

Regardless, after GTL's models suggested that the current cutting standards for "ideal" or "Class 1" were too strict, the three hundred and fifty participants couldn't agree with GTL's conclusions on which diamonds were more sparkly. Instead of going back to the drawing board, GTL blamed the disagreement on poor lighting. They then cranked up the lighting until the observations matched the predictions.

This leads me to an important point; the models appear to ignore mathematicians Tolkowsky and Ditchburn's work on proportions and light return in respect to their guidelines for maximum and minimum tolerances. If larger table percentages and larger depth percentages are acceptable, it will allow jewelers to sell what was previously considered a poorly proportioned diamond as a well-proportioned one, as was first reported in the May 16, 2004, article in *National Jeweler* by Victoria Gomelsky:

"When the system is introduced, it will profoundly change the way that manufacturers cut diamonds and retailers sell them. The latter are among those who are concerned about the trade's lack of preparedness for such a development. They fear that consumers accustomed to the ideal cut will lose confidence in the industry's ability to agree on the issue of diamonds' appearance. But supporters say a third-party evaluation of cut will help people at all points of the supply chain sell diamonds previously considered unsalable."

In the article "Grading the Make" by Rob Bates, former senior editor of *Jewelers Circular Keystone*, he writes that the only way GIA could get their numbers to jive was to choose a "standardized lighting environment!"

As you well know, you don't live in a standardized lighting environment! We live in cloudy days and fluorescent-lit offices; sunny days and candlelit restaurants. Any test to determine a diamond's beauty must consist of multiple lighting environments. The diamond that averages the best under lighting conditions that range from the best to the worst should be declared the winner. That's how a decathlete is declared the world's greatest athlete, not because he's best in one event but because his cumulative score in ten events ranks him the best.

Well, GIA is undeterred. The exact parameters of GIA's new cut-grading system are laid out in a twenty-six-page article (fall 2004) by Thomas M. Moses and colleagues, "A Foundation for Grading the Overall Cut Quality of Round Brilliant-Cut Diamonds."

One aspect of the new system changes "class" to "category" and adds a fifth category (category five, aka bottom of the barrel) by subdividing Class IV into two new categories.

I just can't sign up for the new far-reaching criteria. The laws of physics haven't been repealed. Reflection and refraction of light from a diamond does not differ today from over fifty years ago when R. W.

Ditchburn, mathematician and author of *Light*, did his initial work on diffraction and resolution with noncoherent illumination.

To imply that a diamond can now be cut with crown angles between 27.0 degrees and 38.0 degrees and pavilion angles from 39.8 degrees and 42.4 degrees and still be a category (or class) two is misguided. It's true that with enough light and enough movement of the diamond, any rock will have some pop, but GIA's methods—standardized lighting, non-use of metrics for scintillation, equalization of polish and symmetry in classifying with fire and brilliance, over-reliance on subjective human observation, addition of star-facet length and lower-girdle-facet length measurements, and durability criteria—are not credible. While I understand that the jewelry industry will benefit from allowing more diamonds into a new category two, it gives the consumer a false sense of value. Even the new category one extends the acceptable crown angles to 36 degrees and increases the pavilion angle to a maximum 41.8 degrees! Of course, the old Class Is and Class IIs will still get the highest marks on this new scale, yet it allows inferior grades to tout the same rankings.

If you accept this new cut-grading system, buying a well-proportioned diamond is going to get tougher, if not impossible.

SUPER CUTS
EIGHTSTAR

Founded by Richard Von Sternberg in 1990, EightStar's mission statement has always been to cut a diamond for maximum light return. This is the only one that probably deserves to be called a true super cut. Practically every single diamond faceted and proportioned from EightStar Diamond Company meets the standards for a Class I. It is important to note, however, that after June 10, 2004, some lesser-quality diamonds made it through the pipeline, so each stone must still be double-checked for accuracy.

A.G.S. 000

A.G.S. stands for American Gem Society. This society or club of jewelers got together decades ago to set higher standards for which jewelers should live by. Yada, yada, yada. Anyway, one of these standards is promoting "ideal" diamonds. But they have coined their own terminology. Instead of four classes of cut, they have a number scale ranging from 0 to 10. An A.G.S. 000 or 1 is sometimes equal to a Class I; an A.G.S. 2 or 3 is sometimes equal to a Class II. An A.G.S. 4, 5, 6, or 7 is sometimes equal to a Class III, and an A.G.S. 8, 9, or 10 is bottom of the barrel, equal to a Class IV.

HEARTS ON FIRE

Hearts on Fire is a brand name for a type of cut diamond marketed by the company Di-Star Ltd. out of Boston. Their contention is if you cut a diamond to "ideal" proportions, turn it upside down, and shoot a blue light through it, heart-shaped patterns will be visible through the pavilion, proving it is a well-cut diamond. Big deal! This is just a marketing ploy.

No matter what language you use, A.G.S. 000, Class I, "Ideal" make, Hearts on Fire, it just comes down to one thing: Is it well-proportioned or not? I call all these cuts "super cuts" because they are perfection personified in cutting a diamond. But with their average 15 percent to 20 percent price premium for an increase in brilliance and dispersion of less than 4 percent, I would stick with a Class II and save the money.

HIGH-DEFINITION DIAMONDS

Fact or Fiction?

Scene: (Also known as "The Setup") A young man walks into a jewelry store to buy a diamond. We'll call the young man Ralph and the store salesperson Buddy.

Ralph: Hi there, I'm Ralph, and I'm looking for a round diamond.

Buddy: Hi, I'm Buddy. What kind of round are you looking for?

Ralph: A shy 1ct, VS1, G, Class II, no fluorescence, natural, and bonded.

Buddy: No problem, what faceting arrangement would you like?

Ralph: Faceting arrangement?

Buddy: Well, are you looking for a Modern Era Cut? And if so, which one?

Ralph: Huh?

Buddy: A Modern Era Cut is not only well-proportioned but comes in 58–144-facet combinations. A Non-Modern Era Cut would be a single cut with 16–17 facets or a full cut with 57–58 facets with Old Miners (squared round) or Old European (high crown, sawed off culet) for weight retention.

Ralph: I definitely want a Modern Era Cut, but I didn't know I could get a multifacet arrangement to my liking. What's the theory behind adding more than fifty-eight facets?

Buddy: Oh, sir, it's not a theory but a proven fact! The more facets, the more brilliance.

Ralph: So a 144-faceted diamond has more brilliance than a 58-faceted diamond?

Buddy: You betcha!

Ralph: Well, if that's true, why would anyone buy less than 144 facets?

Buddy: Personal taste. Some people just can't handle too much brilliance, so they pick the facet number that suits them best. Like picking out what wattage you want your bulb for a lamp.

Ralph: Do these multifaceted diamonds cost more?

Buddy: Oh, yes sir! They are very labor intensive, and only the finest rough (what diamonds look like before they are cut) is chosen.

Ralph: So how do I refer to these diamonds?

Buddy: Well, Ralph, they all have their own names. For example, The Zoe Diamond has one hundred facets and was invented by Gabi

Tolkowsky, the grandson to Marcel Tolkowsky, who invented the American Ideal. There's also the Leo Cut from Leo Schachter that has sixty-six facets for just a little extra zing! Try to think of these multi-faceted rounds as "high-definition diamonds." You'll get a clearer, sharper, more brilliant picture.

Ralph: How many types of these "high-definition diamonds" are out there?

Buddy: Tons. A new one hits the market practically every day! Let me tell you about—

Ralph: No, that's okay. I'll get back with you; I've got a headache.

Fade to black.

THE FACTS

1. The job of a facet with the exception of the table facet is like that of a prism, to break light into the color spectrum, not to increase its magnitude or intensity. Extra-faceted diamonds cannot, I repeat cannot, increase the brilliance or white light return to your eye.

2. All of these "high-definition diamonds" are trademarked or branded, leaving only a few distributors able to sell them through a contract with the cutting company. (Translation: big cost, no secondary market value because of poor distribution.)

High-definition diamonds are not bondable as of 2005, leaving you with no guarantees.

The existence of high-definition diamonds is a fact, but they are just slick marketing campaigns designed to get a bigger piece of an already shrinking diamond pie.

So what's the final word on these "high-definition diamonds"? Leave them alone. The only thing high on these diamonds is the price, and their definition is incomplete.

WHAT'S IN A NAME?

The Branding of Diamonds

Which sounds better: Chilean Sea Bass or Patagonian Toothfish? Consumers overwhelmingly prefer the sound of Chilean Sea Bass. Still, Chilean Sea Bass and Patagonian Toothfish are actually the same thing, but the fish is largely referred to under the preferred name in the United States to attract more sales.

Similarly, there has been a rush to rename diamonds to make them sound more appealing. The following is a list of round and fancy-shaped diamonds that have gone through the marketing mill to acquire your hard-earned dollars. Don't be fooled by just a name! Any diamond you are considering must meet the stringent criteria addressed in this book, or you shouldn't buy it.

Alito	Context Cut	Eternal Cut
Arctic Empress	Corona	Euphora
Arges	Crisscut	Flame
Ashoka	Crossfor	Flanders Ideal Square
Asprey cut	Cupio	
Barocut	Divine	Flower Cuts
Briolette	Dream	Forever 10
Buddha	Eighternity	Fourever Concept
Cadi Calla	88facets	Gabrielle
CaressaCutt	Echno	Genesis
Cento	Eighty-Eight	Half Moon
Chaim Cut	Elara	Hope Original Square
Christmas Tree	Elinor	IdealCut
Cleopatra Diamonds	Escada Cut	Jubilant Crown

Jubilee	Princette	Tabiz
Kotlar Cushion	Quadrillion	Ten Commandments
Lady Heart	Qui Shape	Tiana
Leafz	Qui Vive	T.M. Star Diamonds
Leo	Q'uortia	
Lily cut	Regent Cut	Tollkowsky
Lucere	Rising Star	Trapezoid
Lucida	Rose	Triangular Brilliant
Maharaja Cut	Royal Asscher	
Millennial Sunrise	Royal Brilliant	Trielle
My Girl	Royalcrest	Tycoon
NissenCut	Royal Cuts	Victorian Cut
Noble Cut	Savannah Cut	Vinci Diamond
Phoenix	Signature	Virtue Cut
Prince Cut	Spirit Cut	Web Cut
Princess Plus	Super Ideal Cut	Wild Orchid

Proportion Questionnaire Sheet (P.Q.S): A Worksheet

Now that you know what you're looking for, here's a quick questionnaire that will tell you if a stone measures up.

_____ 1. What is the table?

53–60% (1 pt)

61–64% (0 pt)

Less than 53% or greater than 64% (–1 pt)*

For square and rectangular cuts, deduct 1 point only if 66% or over.

_____ 2. What is the crown angle?

32–35 degrees (1 pt)

Above 35 degrees (–1 pt)

Below 32 degrees (–1 pt)

_____ 3. What is the height of the crown?

11.2% to 16.2% of diameter (1 pt)

Above 16.2% (–1 pt)

Below 11.2% (–1 pt)*

_____ 4. What is the pavilion angle?

40–41.5 degrees (round diamond) (1 pt)

39.25–40.75 degrees (oval, marquise, pear) (1 pt)

43.3–46.8 degrees (square and rectangular) (1 pt)

Anything else (disqualify)

_____ 5. What is the pavilion depth?

42.31–43.89% of diameter (round diamond) (1 pt)

41.51–43.1% of width (oval, marquise, pear) (1 pt)

47.1–53.1% of width (square and rectangular) (1 pt)

Anything else (disqualify)

_____ 6. What is the total depth percentage?

56–61% (round, oval, marquise, pear) (1 pt)

56–65% (square and rectangular cuts) (1 pt)

Above 61% (round, oval, marquise, pear) (disqualify)

Above 65% (square and rectangular cuts) (disqualify)

Below 56% (round, oval, marquise, pear) (disqualify)

Below 56% (square and rectangular cuts) (disqualify)

*Please see Box Radiant and Standard Radiant Exception on page 52.

_____ 7. What is the girdle thickness?

Medium (1 pt)

Thick (0 pt)

Thin (0 pt)

Very thin to extremely thin (–1 pt)

Very thick or extremely thick (–1 pt)

_____ 8. What is the culet size?

None to small (1 pt)

Medium to large (–1 pt)

_____ 9. Is the cutting of the stone symmetrical?

Excellent to good (1 pt)

Fair to poor (–1 pt)

_____ 10. What GIA class of cut is the diamond?

I or II (1 pt)

III or IV (disqualify)

_____ 11. How is the polish?

Excellent to good (1 pt)

Fair to poor (–1 pt)

_____ 12. Are the crown angles and pavilion angles universal?

Yes (1 pt)

No (disqualify)

For the diamond to pass proportionality, it must not disqualify and must have a score of 7+ points.

Chapter 2

Cost

The Fifth "C"

◆──◆

Ok, time to talk real money. The prices listed here are the latest *wholesale* diamond prices at the time this book went to press. These are approximate prices, but because the supply of diamonds is so carefully controlled by the international diamond cartels, prices don't fluctuate very much. You can expect prices to rise no more than 5 percent a year under normal market conditions. Even if you do use the two months' salary guideline, if you follow my advice and buy wisely, you'll only have to spend one month's salary to get what an uneducated buyer would pay double for.

How Much to Spend

I'm sure you have heard the rule of thumb that says you should spend two months' salary on a diamond engagement ring. Well, let's not forget whose thumb we're talking about here: the diamond cartel's. There is no magic in that guideline—it wasn't given to Moses on a tablet; it's not in the Bible or the Dead Sea Scrolls. It's a marketing gimmick aimed at getting you to spend as much money as possible for your diamond. Don't be bullied by the diamond industry into buying something you can't afford! You should examine your own budget carefully and decide what you can afford.

Keep in mind as you look through the price chart that the *price per carat* increases with the size of the diamond. For example, a half-carat VS1-G(1) costs $4,368 or $8,736 per carat, while an actual one-carat VS1-G(1) costs $16,524. That's because the larger stones are rarer.

If you do your homework and shop around, you should be able to buy a diamond at these prices. If you have problems, call my HelpLine: 800-275-4047 or 713-222-2728. The HelpLine operates 24 hours a day, 7 days a week.

DIAMOND PRICE TABLES

1/3 carat (33 points)									
Clarity									
Color	IF	VVS1	VVS2	VS1	VS2	SI1	SI2	I1	I2	I3
D 1	3387	2883	2523	2234	2018	1514	1297	1009	793	505
2	3261	2829	2468	2180	1982	1495	1279	1009	775	486
3	3135	2775	2414	2126	1946	1477	1261	1009	757	468
4	3009	2721	2360	2072	1910	1459	1243	1009	739	450
5	2883	2667	2306	2018	1874	1441	1225	1009	721	432
E1	2883	2667	2306	2018	1874	1441	1225	1009	721	432
2	2829	2613	2252	1982	1838	1423	1207	991	703	432
3	2775	2559	2198	1946	1802	1405	1189	973	685	432
4	2721	2505	2144	1910	1766	1387	1171	955	667	432
5	2667	2450	2090	1874	1730	1369	1153	937	649	432
F1	2667	2450	2090	1874	1730	1369	1153	937	649	432
2	2613	2378	2054	1838	1676	1333	1135	919	631	414
3	2559	2306	2018	1802	1622	1297	1117	901	613	396
4	2505	2234	1982	1766	1568	1261	1099	883	595	378
5	2450	2162	1946	1730	1514	1225	1081	865	577	360
G1	2450	2162	1946	1730	1514	1225	1081	865	577	360
2	2396	2108	1892	1676	1477	1207	1063	847	577	360
3	2342	2054	1838	1622	1441	1189	1045	829	577	360
4	2288	2000	1784	1568	1405	1171	1027	811	577	360
5	2234	1946	1730	1514	1369	1153	1009	793	577	360

Color	IF	VVS1	VVS2	VS1	VS2	SI1	SI2	I1	I2	I3
H1	2234	1946	1730	1514	1369	1153	1009	793	577	360
2	2144	1874	1676	1514	1315	1135	991	793	559	360
3	2054	1802	1622	1514	1261	1117	973	793	541	360
4	1964	1730	1568	1514	1207	1099	955	793	523	360
5	1874	1658	1514	1514	1153	1081	937	793	505	360
I1	1874	1658	1514	1514	1153	1081	937	793	505	360
2	1766	1586	1441	1405	1117	1045	919	757	505	342
3	1658	1514	1369	1297	1081	1009	901	721	505	324
4	1550	1441	1297	1189	1045	973	883	685	505	306
5	1441	1369	1225	1081	1009	937	865	649	505	288
J1	1441	1369	1225	1081	1009	937	865	649	505	288
2	1405	1333	1189	1063	991	919	847	631	486	288
3	1369	1297	1153	1045	973	901	829	613	468	288
4	1333	1261	1117	1027	955	883	811	595	450	288
5	1297	1225	1081	1009	937	865	793	577	432	288
K1	1297	1225	1081	1009	937	865	793	577	432	288
2	1243	1171	1063	991	919	847	757	541	414	270
3	1189	1117	1045	973	901	829	721	505	396	252
4	1135	1063	1027	955	883	811	685	468	378	234
5	1081	1009	1009	937	865	793	649	432	360	216
L1	1081	1009	1009	937	865	793	649	432	360	216
2	1045	991	973	901	847	775	631	414	342	216
3	1009	973	937	865	829	757	613	396	324	216
4	973	955	901	829	811	739	595	378	306	216
5	937	937	865	793	793	721	577	360	288	216
M1	937	937	865	793	793	721	577	360	288	216
2	883	865	793	721	703	631	505	324	252	180
3	829	793	721	649	613	541	432	288	216	144
4	775	721	649	577	523	450	360	252	180	108
5	721	649	577	505	432	360	288	216	144	72

E.G. 1/3 carat SI-1 (clarity) H-3 (color) = $1117

Color	IF	VVS1	VVS2	VS1	VS2	SI1	SI2	I1	I2	I3
D 1	9828	7644	6552	5460	4914	4040	3167	2402	2075	1310
2	9282	7371	6416	5378	4805	3959	3112	2375	2048	1283
3	8736	7098	6279	5296	4696	3877	3058	2348	2020	1256
4	8190	6825	6143	5214	4586	3795	3003	2321	1993	1229
5	7644	6552	6006	5132	4477	3713	2948	2293	1966	1201
E 1	7644	6552	6006	5132	4477	3713	2948	2293	1966	1201
2	7371	6416	5870	5078	4423	3604	2894	2266	1938	1201
3	7098	6279	5733	5023	4368	3494	2839	2239	1911	1201
4	6825	6143	5597	4969	4313	3385	2785	2211	1884	1201
5	6552	6006	5460	4914	4259	3276	2730	2184	1856	1201
F 1	6552	6006	5460	4914	4259	3276	2730	2184	1856	1201
2	6416	5870	5324	4778	4122	3194	2648	2157	1829	1174
3	6279	5733	5187	4641	3986	3112	2566	2129	1802	1147
4	6143	5597	5051	4505	3849	3030	2484	2102	1775	1119
5	6006	5460	4914	4368	3713	2948	2402	2075	1747	1092
G 1	6006	5460	4914	4368	3713	2948	2402	2075	1747	1092
2	5842	5324	4778	4204	3604	2894	2375	2048	1720	1065
3	5678	5187	4641	4040	3494	2839	2348	2020	1693	1037
4	5515	5051	4505	3877	3385	2785	2321	1993	1665	1010
5	5351	4914	4368	3713	3276	2730	2293	1966	1638	983
H 1	5351	4914	4368	3713	3276	2730	2293	1966	1638	983
2	5132	4723	4204	3576	3167	2648	2266	1938	1611	983
3	4914	4532	4040	3440	3058	2566	2239	1911	1583	983
4	4696	4341	3877	3303	2948	2484	2211	1884	1556	983
5	4477	4150	3713	3167	2839	2402	2184	1856	1529	983
I 1	4477	4150	3713	3167	2839	2402	2184	1856	1529	983
2	4232	3931	3549	3058	2730	2348	2157	1856	1502	956
3	3986	3713	3385	2948	2621	2293	2129	1856	1474	928
4	3740	3494	3221	2839	2512	2239	2102	1856	1447	901
5	3494	3276	3058	2730	2402	2184	2075	1856	1420	874
J 1	3494	3276	3058	2730	2402	2184	2075	1856	1420	874
2	3358	3167	2976	2621	2348	2157	2048	1802	1420	874
3	3221	3058	2894	2512	2293	2129	2020	1747	1420	874
4	3085	2948	2812	2402	2239	2102	1993	1693	1420	874

1/2 carat (50 points)
Clarity

Color	IF	VVS1	VVS2	VS1	VS2	SI1	SI2	I1	I2	I3
5	2948	2839	2730	2293	2184	2075	1966	1638	1420	874
K1	2948	2839	2730	2293	2184	2075	1966	1638	1420	874
2	2894	2730	2621	2266	2157	2020	1911	1583	1365	846
3	2839	2621	2512	2239	2129	1966	1856	1529	1310	819
4	2785	2512	2402	2211	2102	1911	1802	1474	1256	792
5	2730	2402	2293	2184	2075	1856	1747	1420	1201	764
L1	2730	2402	2293	2184	2075	1856	1747	1420	1201	764
2	2621	2321	2211	2102	1993	1829	1720	1392	1147	737
3	2512	2239	2129	2020	1911	1802	1693	1365	1092	710
4	2402	2157	2048	1938	1829	1775	1665	1338	1037	683
5	2293	2075	1966	1856	1747	1747	1638	1310	983	655
M1	2293	2075	1966	1856	1747	1747	1638	1310	983	655
2	2157	1966	1856	1747	1638	1583	1474	1201	928	628
3	2020	1856	1747	1638	1529	1420	1310	1092	874	601
4	1884	1747	1638	1529	1420	1256	1147	983	819	573
5	1747	1638	1529	1420	1310	1092	983	874	764	546

E.G. 1/2 carat SI-2 (clarity) G-1 (color) = $2,402

3/4 carat (75 points)

Clarity

Color	IF	VVS1	VVS2	VS1	VS2	SI1	SI2	I1	I2	I3
D 1	15836	11705	10328	8951	8262	6885	6197	4131	2892	1790
2	14803	11360	10087	8847	8090	6816	6128	4097	2857	1756
3	13770	11016	9846	8744	7918	6747	6059	4062	2823	1721
4	12737	10672	9605	8641	7746	6678	5990	4028	2788	1687
5	11705	10328	9364	8537	7574	6610	5921	3993	2754	1652
E1	11705	10328	9364	8537	7574	6610	5921	3993	2754	1652
2	11360	10087	9157	8365	7401	6506	5818	3959	2720	1652
3	11016	9846	8951	8193	7229	6403	5715	3924	2685	1652
4	10672	9605	8744	8021	7057	6300	5611	3890	2651	1652
5	10328	9364	8537	7849	6885	6197	5508	3856	2616	1652
F1	10328	9364	8537	7849	6885	6197	5508	3856	2616	1652
2	10087	9157	8365	7608	6713	6059	5405	3821	2582	1618
3	9846	8951	8193	7367	6541	5921	5301	3787	2547	1584
4	9605	8744	8021	7126	6369	5783	5198	3752	2513	1549
5	9364	8537	7849	6885	6197	5646	5095	3718	2479	1515

Color	IF	VVS1	VVS2	VS1	VS2	SI1	SI2	I1	I2	I3
G1	9364	8537	7849	6885	6197	5646	5095	3718	2479	1515
2	9157	8365	7608	6713	6059	5542	4992	3649	2444	1515
3	8951	8193	7367	6541	5921	5439	4888	3580	2410	1515
4	8744	8021	7126	6369	5783	5336	4785	3511	2375	1515
5	8537	7849	6885	6197	5646	5233	4682	3443	2341	1515
H1	8537	7849	6885	6197	5646	5233	4682	3443	2341	1515
2	8124	7505	6713	6059	5542	5095	4510	3408	2306	1515
3	7711	7160	6541	5921	5439	4957	4338	3374	2272	1515
4	7298	6816	6369	5783	5336	4820	4165	3339	2238	1515
5	6885	6472	6197	5646	5233	4682	3993	3305	2203	1515
I1	6885	6472	6197	5646	5233	4682	3993	3305	2203	1515
2	6437	6093	5852	5336	4957	4510	3924	3236	2169	1480
3	5990	5715	5508	5026	4682	4338	3856	3167	2134	1446
4	5542	5336	5164	4716	4406	4165	3787	3098	2100	1411
5	5095	4957	4820	4406	4131	3993	3718	3029	2066	1377
J1	5095	4957	4820	4406	4131	3993	3718	3029	2066	1377
2	4957	4820	4682	4234	3993	3821	3546	2892	2031	1377
3	4820	4682	4544	4062	3856	3649	3374	2754	1997	1377
4	4682	4544	4406	3890	3718	3477	3202	2616	1962	1377
5	4544	4406	4269	3718	3580	3305	3029	2479	1928	1377
K1	4544	4406	4269	3718	3580	3305	3029	2479	1928	1377
2	4406	4234	4097	3615	3477	3236	2961	2410	1859	1343
3	4269	4062	3924	3511	3374	3167	2892	2341	1790	1308
4	4131	3890	3752	3408	3270	3098	2823	2272	1721	1274
5	3993	3718	3580	3305	3167	3029	2754	2203	1652	1239
L1	3993	3718	3580	3305	3167	3029	2754	2203	1652	1239
2	3924	3649	3511	3236	3098	2961	2720	2134	1618	1170
3	3856	3580	3443	3167	3029	2892	2685	2066	1584	1102
4	3787	3511	3374	3098	2961	2823	2651	1997	1549	1033
5	3718	3443	3305	3029	2892	2754	2616	1928	1515	964
M1	3718	3443	3305	3029	2892	2754	2616	1928	1515	964
2	3546	3305	3167	2926	2788	2651	2513	1790	1411	895
3	3374	3167	3029	2823	2685	2547	2410	1652	1308	826
4	3202	3029	2892	2720	2582	2444	2306	1515	1205	757
5	3029	2892	2754	2616	2479	2341	2203	1377	1102	689

E.G. 3/4 carat VS-2 (clarity) L-1 (color) = $3,167

1 carat (100 points)

Clarity

Color	IF	VVS1	VVS2	VS1	VS2	SI1	SI2	I1	I2	I3
D 1	46818	36720	32130	24786	20563	14872	12485	8446	5508	3121
2	44064	35573	30524	24098	20012	14642	12347	8354	5462	3075
3	41310	34425	28917	23409	19462	14413	12209	8262	5416	3029
4	38556	33278	27311	22721	18911	14183	12072	8170	5370	2984
5	35802	32130	25704	22032	18360	13954	11934	8078	5324	2938
E1	35802	32130	25704	22032	18360	13954	11934	8078	5324	2938
2	34655	30524	24786	21573	17901	13770	11796	8033	5279	2892
3	33507	28917	23868	21114	17442	13586	11659	7987	5233	2846
4	32360	27311	22950	20655	16983	13403	11521	7941	5187	2800
5	31212	25704	22032	20196	16524	13219	11383	7895	5141	2754
F1	31212	25704	22032	20196	16524	13219	11383	7895	5141	2754
2	29376	24786	21573	19278	16249	13082	11291	7849	5095	2708
3	27540	23868	21114	18360	15973	12944	11200	7803	5049	2662
4	25704	22950	20655	17442	15698	12806	11108	7757	5003	2616
5	23868	22032	20196	16524	15422	12668	11016	7711	4957	2570
G1	23868	22032	20196	16524	15422	12668	11016	7711	4957	2570
2	22950	21114	19278	16157	14963	12531	10878	7619	4911	2570
3	22032	20196	18360	15790	14504	12393	10741	7528	4865	2570
4	21114	19278	17442	15422	14045	12255	10603	7436	4820	2570
5	20196	18360	16524	15055	13586	12118	10465	7344	4774	2570
H1	20196	18360	16524	15055	13586	12118	10465	7344	4774	2570
2	19278	17672	15881	14459	13219	11842	10282	7160	4682	2525
3	18360	16983	15239	13862	12852	11567	10098	6977	4590	2479
4	17442	16295	14596	13265	12485	11291	9914	6793	4498	2433
5	16524	15606	13954	12668	12118	11016	9731	6610	4406	2387
I1	16524	15606	13954	12668	12118	11016	9731	6610	4406	2387
2	15836	14872	13495	12393	11842	10695	9547	6426	4315	2387
3	15147	14137	13036	12118	11567	10373	9364	6242	4223	2387
4	14459	13403	12577	11842	11291	10052	9180	6059	4131	2387
5	13770	12668	12118	11567	11016	9731	8996	5875	4039	2387
J1	13770	12668	12118	11567	11016	9731	8996	5875	4039	2387
2	13311	12393	11796	11246	10695	9410	8675	5738	3947	2341
3	12852	12118	11475	10924	10373	9088	8354	5600	3856	2295
4	12393	11842	11154	10603	10052	8767	8033	5462	3764	2249

Color	IF	VVS1	VVS2	VS1	VS2	SI1	SI2	I1	I2	I3
5	11934	11567	10832	10282	9731	8446	7711	5324	3672	2203
K1	11934	11567	10832	10282	9731	8446	7711	5324	3672	2203
2	11475	11154	10419	9914	9364	8262	7528	5233	3580	2157
3	11016	10741	10006	9547	8996	8078	7344	5141	3488	2111
4	10557	10328	9593	9180	8629	7895	7160	5049	3397	2066
5	10098	9914	9180	8813	8262	7711	6977	4957	3305	2020
L1	10098	9914	9180	8813	8262	7711	6977	4957	3305	2020
2	9777	9501	8813	8400	7849	7344	6610	4820	3259	2020
3	9455	9088	8446	7987	7436	6977	6242	4682	3213	2020
4	9134	8675	8078	7573	7023	6610	5875	4544	3167	2020
5	8813	8262	7711	7160	6610	6242	5508	4406	3121	2020
M1	8813	8262	7711	7160	6610	6242	5508	4406	3121	2020
2	8170	7711	7252	6747	6242	5829	5141	4131	2938	1928
3	7528	7160	6793	6334	5875	5416	4774	3856	2754	1836
4	6885	6610	6334	5921	5508	5003	4406	3580	2570	1744
5	6242	6059	5875	5508	5141	4590	4039	3305	2387	1652

E.G. 1 carat VS-1 (clarity) F-3 (color) = $18,360

1.5 carat (150 points)
Clarity

Color	IF	VVS1	VVS2	VS1	VS2	SI1	SI2	I1	I2	I3
D 1	90882	70227	60588	49572	41310	30294	24235	15147	9088	5233
2	85030	67817	58178	48539	40622	29950	23960	14940	9019	5164
3	79178	65408	55769	47507	39933	29606	23684	14734	8951	5095
4	73325	62998	53359	46474	39245	29261	23409	14527	8882	5026
5	67473	60588	50949	45441	38556	28917	23134	14321	8813	4957
E1	67473	60588	50949	45441	38556	28917	23134	14321	8813	4957
2	65063	58178	49572	44064	37523	28573	22789	14183	8744	4888
3	62654	55769	48195	42687	36491	28229	22445	14045	8675	4820
4	60244	53359	46818	41310	35458	27884	22101	13908	8606	4751
5	57834	50949	45441	39933	34425	27540	21757	13770	8537	4682
F1	57834	50949	45441	39933	34425	27540	21757	13770	8537	4682
2	54736	48539	43376	38556	33392	27058	21412	13632	8469	4613
3	51638	46130	41310	37179	32360	26576	21068	13495	8400	4544
4	48539	43720	39245	35802	31327	26094	20724	13357	8331	4475
5	45441	41310	37179	34425	30294	25612	20380	13219	8262	4406

Color	IF	VVS1	VVS2	VS1	VS2	SI1	SI2	I1	I2	I3
G1	45441	41310	37179	34425	30294	25612	20380	13219	8262	4406
2	43376	39589	35802	33048	29261	25061	20104	13082	8193	4406
3	41310	37868	34425	31671	28229	24511	19829	12944	8124	4406
4	39245	36146	33048	30294	27196	23960	19553	12806	8055	4406
5	37179	34425	31671	28917	26163	23409	19278	12668	7987	4406
H1	37179	34425	31671	28917	26163	23409	19278	12668	7987	4406
2	35458	33048	30638	27884	25268	22789	18796	12462	7849	4338
3	33737	31671	29606	26852	24373	22170	18314	12255	7711	4269
4	32015	30294	28573	25819	23478	21550	17832	12049	7574	4200
5	30294	28917	27540	24786	22583	20930	17350	11842	7436	4131
I1	30294	28917	27540	24786	22583	20930	17350	11842	7436	4131
2	29261	27747	26370	23891	21757	20173	16868	11429	7298	4131
3	28229	26576	25199	22996	20930	19416	16386	11016	7160	4131
4	27196	25406	24029	22101	20104	18658	15904	10603	7023	4131
5	26163	24235	22858	21206	19278	17901	15422	10190	6885	4131
J1	26163	24235	22858	21206	19278	17901	15422	10190	6885	4131
2	24717	23065	21825	20380	18658	17213	14872	9983	6678	4062
3	23271	21894	20793	19553	18039	16524	14321	9777	6472	3993
4	21825	20724	19760	18727	17419	15836	13770	9570	6265	3924
5	20380	19553	18727	17901	16799	15147	13219	9364	6059	3856
K1	20380	19553	18727	17901	16799	15147	13219	9364	6059	3856
2	19691	18865	18039	17213	16111	14665	12875	9157	5990	3787
3	19003	18176	17350	16524	15422	14183	12531	8951	5921	3718
4	18314	17488	16662	15836	14734	13701	12186	8744	5852	3649
5	17626	16799	15973	15147	14045	13219	11842	8537	5783	3580
L1	17626	16799	15973	15147	14045	13219	11842	8537	5783	3580
2	17006	16180	15354	14527	13357	12600	11360	8331	5646	3580
3	16386	15560	14734	13908	12668	11980	10878	8124	5508	3580
4	15767	14940	14114	13288	11980	11360	10396	7918	5370	3580
5	15147	14321	13495	12668	11291	10741	9914	7711	5233	3580
M1	15147	14321	13495	12668	11291	10741	9914	7711	5233	3580
2	13701	13013	12324	11567	10396	9777	8951	7023	4820	3305
3	12255	11705	11154	10465	9501	8813	7987	6334	4406	3029
4	10809	10396	9983	9364	8606	7849	7023	5646	3993	2754
5	9364	9088	8813	8262	7711	6885	6059	4957	3580	2479

E.G. 1 1/2 carat VVS-1 (clarity) J-1 (color) = $24,235

2 carat (200 points)

Clarity

Color	IF	VVS1	VVS2	VS1	VS2	SI1	SI2	I1	I2	I3
D1	218400	165984	148512	122304	90418	65520	52416	27955	15725	8736
2	205296	161616	142506	118482	88124	64646	51870	27737	15616	8627
3	192192	157248	136500	114660	85831	63773	51324	27518	15506	8518
4	179088	152880	130494	110838	83538	62899	50778	27300	15397	8408
5	165984	148512	124488	107016	81245	62026	50232	27082	15288	8299
E1	165984	148512	124488	107016	81245	62026	50232	27082	15288	8299
2	160524	142506	120666	103194	80044	61261	49686	26863	15179	8190
3	155064	136500	116844	99372	78842	60497	49140	26645	15070	8081
4	149604	130494	113022	95550	77641	59732	48594	26426	14960	7972
5	144144	124488	109200	91728	76440	58968	48048	26208	14851	7862
F1	144144	124488	109200	91728	76440	58968	48048	26208	14851	7862
2	136500	117390	103740	87360	73710	57876	47502	25990	14742	7753
3	128856	110292	98280	82992	70980	56784	46956	25771	14633	7644
4	121212	103194	92820	78624	68250	55692	46410	25553	14524	7535
5	113568	96096	87360	74256	65520	54600	45864	25334	14414	7426
G1	113568	96096	87360	74256	65520	54600	45864	25334	14414	7426
2	106470	92274	84084	72072	63336	53508	45318	25007	14305	7426
3	99372	88452	80808	69888	61152	52416	44772	24679	14196	7426
4	92274	84630	77532	67704	58968	51324	44226	24352	14087	7426
5	85176	80808	74256	65520	56784	50232	43680	24024	13978	7426
H1	85176	80808	74256	65520	56784	50232	43680	24024	13978	7426
2	80262	76440	70980	62244	54600	48594	42588	23587	13759	7316
3	75348	72072	67704	58968	52416	46956	41496	23150	13541	7207
4	70434	67704	64428	55692	50232	45318	40404	22714	13322	7098
5	65520	63336	61152	52416	48048	43680	39312	22277	13104	6989
I1	65520	63336	61152	52416	48048	43680	39312	22277	13104	6989
2	62244	59842	57658	50232	45755	41824	37892	21949	12776	6989
3	58968	56347	54163	48048	43462	39967	36473	21622	12449	6989
4	55692	52853	50669	45864	41168	38111	35053	21294	12121	6989
5	52416	49358	47174	43680	38875	36254	33634	20966	11794	6989
J1	52416	49358	47174	43680	38875	36254	33634	20966	11794	6989
2	51324	48266	46082	42370	38111	35381	32542	20311	11684	6880
3	50232	47174	44990	41059	37346	34507	31450	19656	11575	6770
4	49140	46082	43898	39749	36582	33634	30358	19001	11466	6661

Color	IF	VVS1	VVS2	VS1	VS2	SI1	SI2	I1	I2	I3
5	48048	44990	42806	38438	35818	32760	29266	18346	11357	6552
K1	48048	44990	42806	38438	35818	32760	29266	18346	11357	6552
2	45536	42479	40404	36582	33961	31013	28064	17800	11248	6443
3	43025	39967	38002	34726	32105	29266	26863	17254	11138	6334
4	40513	37456	35599	32869	30248	27518	25662	16708	11029	6224
5	38002	34944	33197	31013	28392	25771	24461	16162	10920	6115
L1	38002	34944	33197	31013	28392	25771	24461	16162	10920	6115
2	36473	33961	32432	30358	27518	24788	23260	15397	10811	6115
3	34944	32978	31668	29702	26645	23806	22058	14633	10702	6115
4	33415	31996	30904	29047	25771	22823	20857	13868	10592	6115
5	31886	31013	30139	28392	24898	21840	19656	13104	10483	6115
M1	31886	31013	30139	28392	24898	21840	19656	13104	10483	6115
2	29375	28610	27846	26317	23369	20639	18673	12012	9500	5788
3	26863	26208	25553	24242	21840	19438	17690	10920	8518	5460
4	24352	23806	23260	22168	20311	18236	16708	9828	7535	5132
5	21840	21403	20966	20093	18782	17035	15725	8736	6552	4805

E.G. 2 carat SI-1 (clarity) I-2 (color) = $41,824

BUYING SHY

"Buying shy" is a term I coined. It's one of my shrewdest and most valuable suggestions for buying diamonds. Buying shy can save you a lot of money!

Here's what I mean by buying shy: *shopping for diamonds that weigh just under half-carat and full-carat weights*.

For example, instead of a one-carat (100-point) diamond, you'd buy a .90-carat diamond. Instead of a half-carat, you'd buy a .45-carat stone. It's as simple as that.

But Fred, you're saying—why should I buy a smaller diamond than I want?

The simple answer: to save a lot of money. Because the price of a diamond jumps dramatically when it reaches a true half-carat or full-carat, the advantage of buying shy is also pretty dramatic!

And let's see how much "smaller" we're talking about. The diameter of a one-carat diamond is 6.5 millimeters. The diameter of a "shy" .90-carat stone is 6.3 millimeters. The difference is the thickness of a piece of ordinary paper! Looking at the stones side by side, you'd be hard-pressed to tell the difference.

Look at the savings:
.50ct SI1-I: $2,402
.45ct SI1-I: $1,769 **You save $633!**
.75ct SI1-I: $4,682
.62ct SI1-I: $2,979 **You save $1,703!**
1.00ct SI1-I: $11,016
.90ct SI1-I: $7679 **You save $3,337!**

You'll notice that buying shy sometimes means a difference of one point and sometimes a difference of ten points. And you're thinking, "Why don't I buy the .99-carat stone instead of the .90-carat stone? Won't I still get the same price break and a slightly bigger stone?" Yes, but the problem is finding that 99-pointer. Diamond cutters, who are well aware that the full one-carat stone is worth quite a bit more than the 99-pointer, will cheat on the proportions a bit to get the stone up to the full carat. So don't be obsessed with trying to get closer than ten points on full-carat stones, but you will find .90s and 1.90s, etc.

The one potential problem with buying shy is a psychological one. What sort of person is your true love? If she's going to be upset that you didn't get the full carat and will forever think of you as a cheapskate, then it may be worth the extra money.

Your fiancée may never ask how big her 90-point diamond is, but if she does, you might say, "About a carat," and leave it at that. I believe that happiness is a dream that becomes a reality—and if she sees a diamond that is just what she dreamed of, she'll be happy!

Of course, if you're a practical couple and you decide to shop for the diamond together, you should both read this book first and then decide what you're going to shop for.

Fred's advice: When possible, always buy shy! You'll pay a lot less for a diamond that looks just as good.

THE DAY MY WORLD CHANGED (SEPTEMBER 6, 2005)

The Day Before

My father and I were going to New York to have a meeting with the manager of DCINY to see why clients were experiencing unusual delays on the processing of their orders. The meeting should have lasted only thirty minutes…it lasted nine hours.

September 6, 2005

The meeting was at our offices at 579 Fifth Avenue and scheduled for 9:00 a.m. We had the whole day for the meeting and whatever (shopping and eating) because we weren't flying back until Wednesday, September 7. I had no idea when I walked into the office my life was going to forever change!

The Meeting

We exchange pleasantries for a while, and then I got to the point of the meeting.

Me: Neil, as you know, DCINY is falling a little behind in filling all the orders, and we just want to see what's up. (I wanted to say "What's up?" like the Budweiser commercials but realized it was a little lame to use a seven-year-old bit regardless of how much I personally loved to say "Wazzzzzup?")

Long dramatic pause…

Neil: Fred, do you know how for twenty years you've been telling people to buy shy?

Me: Uh-huh.

Neil: Well, they did. And now they're all gone—the good quality ones.

Me: What do you mean they're all gone?

Neil: They are all gone! All the shy stones (.45–.49 ct, .65–.69 ct, 1.45–1.49 ct, 1.85–1.95 ct, 2.85 ct–2.95 ct) are gone, and it's not only those. All the full sizes over three carats are gone. The rough-to-cut 1.25 ct and 1.75 ct box radiants are gone. The rough-to-cut 65/65 princesses in any size are gone. The 65/65 asschers are gone! Fred, they're all gone!

The conversation proceeded from there. For nine hours, we tackled many questions. What rough was still available to fill current and future orders? What type of rationing was needed to stretch the current supply of "fulls"? A full is a hard-weight diamond .50 ct, .75 ct, 1.0 ct, 1.50 ct, 2.0 ct, and rough-to-cut full sizes were still available. Important note: When I tell you, the reader, that the world is running out of diamonds, again, I am only referring to the good diamonds, not the commercial-grade stuff that consolidators like Costco, Sam's Club, Blue Nile, Zales, Jared, Kay, Robbins Brothers, Tiffany, or Bailey Banks & Biddle sell. There is no shortage, nor will there ever be a shortage of commercial grade diamonds.

Everyone defines a "good" diamond as a diamond that holds or appreciates in value over time when you try to sell it. Commercial-grade diamonds on the secondary market sell for only a small fraction of what you paid. That is also the case now for many of the fancy shapes (pear, marquise, emerald cut, asscher, oval, heart, trilliant, baguette) and melee. They have little or no secondary market value. The top price you'll see for any commercial-grade, fancy-shaped, or melee diamonds will rarely be a penny more than 19.7 percent of the original dollar spent. While a good diamond (white, eye clean, Class

1 or 2, non-fluorescent, natural, fully bonded) will always bring you even money (100 percent of what you paid) as long as the vendor you bought it from stays in business. Even if they don't, you'll at least get 40 to 45 percent of what you paid as dump value (the average is 60 percent) or 80 to 85 percent on the secondary market to an end consumer who is not looking to flip the rock. There is no question: If you are going to buy a diamond, it makes no sense purchasing a crummy one with bogus "certificates" that don't guarantee you anything. It leaves you holding a piece of gravel if you ever want to part with your rock.

Anyway, this is what the market (world) is dealing with. Good diamonds in entire categories are extinct except the onesies and twosies. The following Buying Shy Price Lists are like an endangered species, they can become extinct overnight.

Buying Shy Endangered Price List

0.45 carat (45 points)									
Clarity									
Color	IF	VVS1	VVS2	VS1	VS2	SI1	SI2	I1	I2	I3
D 1	5405	4619	4128	3735	2948	2260	2064	1474	1179	786
2	5209	4521	4054	3661	2899	2236	2015	1474	1155	762
3	5012	4423	3980	3587	2850	2211	1966	1474	1130	737
4	4816	4324	3907	3514	2801	2187	1916	1474	1106	713
5	4619	4226	3833	3440	2752	2162	1867	1474	1081	688
E1	4619	4226	3833	3440	2752	2162	1867	1474	1081	688
2	4521	4152	3735	3342	2703	2138	1843	1450	1081	688
3	4423	4079	3636	3243	2654	2113	1818	1425	1081	688
4	4324	4005	3538	3145	2604	2088	1794	1400	1081	688
5	4226	3931	3440	3047	2555	2064	1769	1376	1081	688
F1	4226	3931	3440	3047	2555	2064	1769	1376	1081	688
2	4152	3808	3342	2973	2506	2039	1744	1351	1057	663
3	4079	3686	3243	2899	2457	2015	1720	1327	1032	639
4	4005	3563	3145	2826	2408	1990	1695	1302	1007	614

Color	IF	VVS1	VVS2	VS1	VS2	SI1	SI2	I1	I2	I3
5	3931	3440	3047	2752	2359	1966	1671	1278	983	590
G1	3931	3440	3047	2752	2359	1966	1671	1278	983	590
2	3808	3366	2973	2678	2310	1941	1646	1253	958	590
3	3686	3292	2899	2604	2260	1916	1622	1229	934	590
4	3563	3219	2826	2531	2211	1892	1597	1204	909	590
5	3440	3145	2752	2457	2162	1867	1572	1179	885	590
H1	3440	3145	2752	2457	2162	1867	1572	1179	885	590
2	3317	3022	2678	2383	2113	1843	1548	1179	860	590
3	3194	2899	2604	2310	2064	1818	1523	1179	835	590
4	3071	2776	2531	2236	2015	1794	1499	1179	811	590
5	2948	2654	2457	2162	1966	1769	1474	1179	786	590
I1	2948	2654	2457	2162	1966	1769	1474	1179	786	590
2	2826	2555	2359	2088	1892	1695	1450	1155	786	565
3	2703	2457	2260	2015	1818	1622	1425	1130	786	541
4	2580	2359	2162	1941	1744	1548	1400	1106	786	516
5	2457	2260	2064	1867	1671	1474	1376	1081	786	491
J1	2457	2260	2064	1867	1671	1474	1376	1081	786	491
2	2408	2211	2015	1818	1646	1450	1327	1032	762	491
3	2359	2162	1966	1769	1622	1425	1278	983	737	491
4	2310	2113	1916	1720	1597	1400	1229	934	713	491
5	2260	2064	1867	1671	1572	1376	1179	885	688	491
K1	2260	2064	1867	1671	1572	1376	1179	885	688	491
2	2187	2015	1843	1646	1548	1351	1155	835	663	467
3	2113	1966	1818	1622	1523	1327	1130	786	639	442
4	2039	1916	1794	1597	1499	1302	1106	737	614	418
5	1966	1867	1769	1572	1474	1278	1081	688	590	393
L1	1966	1867	1769	1572	1474	1278	1081	688	590	393
2	1892	1794	1695	1523	1425	1253	1032	663	565	393
3	1818	1720	1622	1474	1376	1229	983	639	541	393
4	1744	1646	1548	1425	1327	1204	934	614	516	393
5	1671	1572	1474	1376	1278	1179	885	590	491	393
M1	1671	1572	1474	1376	1278	1179	885	590	491	393
2	1548	1450	1351	1253	1179	1057	811	565	467	344
3	1425	1327	1229	1130	1081	934	737	541	442	295
4	1302	1204	1106	1007	983	811	663	516	418	246
5	1179	1081	983	885	885	688	590	491	393	197

E.G. 0.45 carat I-2 (clarity) G-1 (color) = $983

0.62 carat (62 points)

Clarity

Color	IF	VVS1	VVS2	VS1	VS2	SI1	SI2	I1	I2	I3
D 1	12187	9479	8124	6770	6093	5010	3927	2979	2573	1625
2	11510	9140	7955	6669	5958	4909	3859	2945	2539	1591
3	10833	8802	7786	6567	5823	4807	3791	2911	2505	1557
4	10156	8463	7617	6466	5687	4705	3724	2877	2471	1523
5	9479	8124	7447	6364	5552	4604	3656	2844	2437	1489
E1	9479	8124	7447	6364	5552	4604	3656	2844	2437	1489
2	9140	7955	7278	6296	5484	4468	3588	2810	2403	1489
3	8802	7786	7109	6229	5416	4333	3521	2776	2370	1489
4	8463	7617	6940	6161	5349	4198	3453	2742	2336	1489
5	8124	7447	6770	6093	5281	4062	3385	2708	2302	1489
F1	8124	7447	6770	6093	5281	4062	3385	2708	2302	1489
2	7955	7278	6601	5924	5112	3961	3284	2674	2268	1456
3	7786	7109	6432	5755	4942	3859	3182	2640	2234	1422
4	7617	6940	6263	5586	4773	3758	3081	2607	2200	1388
5	7447	6770	6093	5416	4604	3656	2979	2573	2167	1354
G1	7447	6770	6093	5416	4604	3656	2979	2573	2167	1354
2	7244	6601	5924	5213	4468	3588	2945	2539	2133	1320
3	7041	6432	5755	5010	4333	3521	2911	2505	2099	1286
4	6838	6263	5586	4807	4198	3453	2877	2471	2065	1253
5	6635	6093	5416	4604	4062	3385	2844	2437	2031	1219
H1	6635	6093	5416	4604	4062	3385	2844	2437	2031	1219
2	6364	5856	5213	4435	3927	3284	2810	2403	1997	1219
3	6093	5619	5010	4265	3791	3182	2776	2370	1963	1219
4	5823	5382	4807	4096	3656	3081	2742	2336	1930	1219
5	5552	5146	4604	3927	3521	2979	2708	2302	1896	1219
I1	5552	5146	4604	3927	3521	2979	2708	2302	1896	1219
2	5247	4875	4401	3791	3385	2911	2674	2302	1862	1185
3	4942	4604	4198	3656	3250	2844	2640	2302	1828	1151
4	4638	4333	3995	3521	3114	2776	2607	2302	1794	1117
5	4333	4062	3791	3385	2979	2708	2573	2302	1760	1083
J1	4333	4062	3791	3385	2979	2708	2573	2302	1760	1083
2	4164	3927	3690	3250	2911	2674	2539	2234	1760	1083
3	3995	3791	3588	3114	2844	2640	2505	2167	1760	1083
4	3825	3656	3487	2979	2776	2607	2471	2099	1760	1083

Color	IF	VVS1	VVS2	VS1	VS2	SI1	SI2	I1	I2	I3
5	3656	3521	3385	2844	2708	2573	2437	2031	1760	1083
K1	3656	3521	3385	2844	2708	2573	2437	2031	1760	1083
2	3588	3385	3250	2810	2674	2505	2370	1963	1693	1049
3	3521	3250	3114	2776	2640	2437	2302	1896	1625	1016
4	3453	3114	2979	2742	2607	2370	2234	1828	1557	982
5	3385	2979	2844	2708	2573	2302	2167	1760	1489	948
L1	3385	2979	2844	2708	2573	2302	2167	1760	1489	948
2	3250	2877	2742	2607	2471	2268	2133	1726	1422	914
3	3114	2776	2640	2505	2370	2234	2099	1693	1354	880
4	2979	2674	2539	2403	2268	2200	2065	1659	1286	846
5	2844	2573	2437	2302	2167	2167	2031	1625	1219	812
M1	2844	2573	2437	2302	2167	2167	2031	1625	1219	812
2	2674	2437	2302	2167	2031	1963	1828	1489	1151	779
3	2505	2302	2167	2031	1896	1760	1625	1354	1083	745
4	2336	2167	2031	1896	1760	1557	1422	1219	1016	711
5	2167	2031	1896	1760	1625	1354	1219	1083	948	677

E.G. 5/8 carat VS-2 (clarity) M-3 (color) = $1,896

0.80 carat (80 points)
Clarity

Color	IF	VVS1	VVS2	VS1	VS2	SI1	SI2	I1	I2	I3
D1	20093	14851	13104	11357	10483	8736	7862	5242	3669	2271
2	18782	14414	12798	11226	10265	8649	7775	5198	3625	2228
3	17472	13978	12492	11095	10046	8561	7688	5154	3582	2184
4	16162	13541	12187	10964	9828	8474	7600	5111	3538	2140
5	14851	13104	11881	10833	9610	8387	7513	5067	3494	2097
E1	14851	13104	11881	10833	9610	8387	7513	5067	3494	2097
2	14414	12798	11619	10614	9391	8256	7382	5023	3451	2053
3	13978	12492	11357	10396	9173	8124	7251	4980	3407	2009
4	13541	12187	11095	10177	8954	7993	7120	4936	3363	1966
5	13104	11881	10833	9959	8736	7862	6989	4892	3320	1922
F1	13104	11881	10833	9959	8736	7862	6989	4892	3320	1922
2	12798	11619	10614	9653	8518	7688	6858	4848	3276	1922
3	12492	11357	10396	9348	8299	7513	6727	4805	3232	1922
4	12187	11095	10177	9042	8081	7338	6596	4761	3189	1922
5	11881	10833	9959	8736	7862	7164	6465	4717	3145	1922

Color	IF	VVS1	VVS2	VS1	VS2	SI1	SI2	I1	I2	I3
G1	11881	10833	9959	8736	7862	7164	6465	4717	3145	1922
2	11619	10614	9653	8518	7688	7032	6334	4630	3101	1922
3	11357	10396	9348	8299	7513	6901	6203	4543	3058	1922
4	11095	10177	9042	8081	7338	6770	6072	4455	3014	1922
5	10833	9959	8736	7862	7164	6639	5940	4368	2970	1922
H1	10833	9959	8736	7862	7164	6639	5940	4368	2970	1922
2	10308	9522	8518	7688	7164	6465	5722	4324	2927	1922
3	9784	9085	8299	7513	7164	6290	5504	4281	2883	1922
4	9260	8649	8081	7338	7164	6115	5285	4237	2839	1922
5	8736	8212	7862	7164	7164	5940	5067	4193	2796	1922
I1	8736	8212	7862	7164	7164	5940	5067	4193	2796	1922
2	8168	7731	7426	6770	6683	5722	4980	4106	2752	1878
3	7600	7251	6989	6377	6203	5504	4892	4019	2708	1835
4	7032	6770	6552	5984	5722	5285	4805	3931	2664	1791
5	6465	6290	6115	5591	5242	5067	4717	3844	2621	1747
J1	6465	6290	6115	5591	5242	5067	4717	3844	2621	1747
2	6290	6115	5940	5373	5067	4848	4499	3669	2577	1747
3	6115	5940	5766	5154	4892	4630	4281	3494	2533	1747
4	5940	5766	5591	4936	4717	4412	4062	3320	2490	1747
5	5766	5591	5416	4717	4543	4193	3844	3145	2446	1747
K1	5766	5591	5416	4717	4543	4193	3844	3145	2446	1747
2	5591	5373	5198	4586	4412	4106	3756	3058	2359	1704
3	5416	5154	4980	4455	4281	4019	3669	2970	2271	1660
4	5242	4936	4761	4324	4150	3931	3582	2883	2184	1616
5	5067	4717	4543	4193	4019	3844	3494	2796	2097	1572
L1	5067	4717	4543	4193	4019	3844	3494	2796	2097	1572
2	4980	4630	4455	4106	3931	3756	3451	2708	2053	1485
3	4892	4543	4368	4019	3844	3669	3407	2621	2009	1398
4	4805	4455	4281	3931	3756	3582	3363	2533	1966	1310
5	4717	4368	4193	3844	3669	3494	3320	2446	1922	1223
M1	4717	4368	4193	3844	3669	3494	3320	2446	1922	1223
2	4499	4193	4019	3713	3538	3363	3189	2271	1791	1136
3	4281	4019	3844	3582	3407	3232	3058	2097	1660	1048
4	4062	3844	3669	3451	3276	3101	2927	1922	1529	961
5	3844	3669	3494	3320	3145	2970	2796	1747	1398	874

E.G. 0.80ct carat SI-1 (clarity) I-1 (color) = $5,940

0.90 carat (90 points)

Clarity

Color	IF	VVS1	VVS2	VS1	VS2	SI1	SI2	I1	I2	I3
D1	29521	23355	20552	15881	12286	11262	10068	6484	4095	2560
2	27979	22654	19852	15554	12115	11092	9982	6442	4053	2517
3	26438	21954	19151	15227	11945	10921	9897	6399	4010	2474
4	24896	21253	18450	14900	11774	10750	9812	6356	3967	2432
5	23355	20552	17750	14574	11604	10580	9726	6314	3925	2389
E1	23355	20552	17750	14574	11604	10580	9726	6314	3925	2389
2	22654	19852	17236	14293	11476	10452	9599	6271	3882	2389
3	21954	19151	16722	14013	11348	10324	9471	6228	3839	2389
4	21253	18450	16208	13733	11220	10196	9343	6186	3797	2389
5	20552	17750	15695	13452	11092	10068	9215	6143	3754	2389
F1	20552	17750	15695	13452	11092	10068	9215	6143	3754	2389
2	19852	17236	15134	13126	10878	9854	9001	6100	3711	2346
3	19151	16722	14574	12799	10665	9641	8788	6058	3669	2304
4	18450	16208	14013	12472	10452	9428	8575	6015	3626	2261
5	17750	15695	13452	12145	10238	9215	8361	5972	3583	2218
G1	17750	15695	13452	12145	10238	9215	8361	5972	3583	2218
2	16725	14842	12862	11668	10025	9044	8233	5887	3541	2218
3	15701	13990	12272	11192	9812	8873	8105	5802	3498	2218
4	14676	13138	11682	10715	9599	8703	7977	5716	3455	2218
5	13651	12286	11092	10238	9385	8532	7849	5631	3413	2218
H1	13651	12286	11092	10238	9385	8532	7849	5631	3413	2218
2	13139	11859	10622	9812	9172	8319	7636	5503	3370	2176
3	12627	11433	10153	9385	8959	8105	7423	5375	3327	2133
4	12115	11006	9684	8959	8745	7892	7210	5247	3285	2090
5	11604	10580	9215	8532	8532	7679	6996	5119	3242	2048
I1	11604	10580	9215	8532	8532	7679	6996	5119	3242	2048
2	11220	10196	9001	8361	8233	7466	6783	4991	3200	2048
3	10836	9812	8788	8191	7935	7252	6570	4863	3157	2048
4	10452	9428	8575	8020	7636	7039	6356	4735	3114	2048
5	10068	9044	8361	7849	7338	6826	6143	4607	3072	2048
J1	10068	9044	8361	7849	7338	6826	6143	4607	3072	2048
2	9556	8660	8020	7508	7039	6570	5887	4437	2986	2005
3	9044	8276	7679	7167	6740	6314	5631	4266	2901	1962
4	8532	7892	7338	6826	6442	6058	5375	4095	2816	1920

Color	IF	VVS1	VVS2	VS1	VS2	SI1	SI2	I1	I2	I3
5	8020	7508	6996	6484	6143	5802	5119	3925	2730	1877
K1	8020	7508	6996	6484	6143	5802	5119	3925	2730	1877
2	7764	7295	6826	6356	5972	5588	4991	3839	2688	1834
3	7508	7082	6655	6228	5802	5375	4863	3754	2645	1792
4	7252	6868	6484	6100	5631	5162	4735	3669	2602	1749
5	6996	6655	6314	5972	5460	4949	4607	3583	2560	1706
L1	6996	6655	6314	5972	5460	4949	4607	3583	2560	1706
2	6826	6484	6100	5759	5290	4863	4522	3498	2517	1706
3	6655	6314	5887	5546	5119	4778	4437	3413	2474	1706
4	6484	6143	5674	5333	4949	4693	4351	3327	2432	1706
5	6314	5972	5460	5119	4778	4607	4266	3242	2389	1706
M1	6314	5972	5460	5119	4778	4607	4266	3242	2389	1706
2	5930	5631	5205	4991	4693	4394	4053	3114	2304	1621
3	5546	5290	4949	4863	4607	4181	3839	2986	2218	1536
4	5162	4949	4693	4735	4522	3967	3626	2858	2133	1450
5	4778	4607	4437	4607	4437	3754	3413	2730	2048	1365

E.G. 0.90 carat VS-2 (clarity) L-1 (color) = $5,460

1.20 carat (120 points)

Clarity

Color	IF	VVS1	VVS2	VS1	VS2	SI1	SI2	I1	I2	I3
D1	69615	54600	47775	36855	30576	22113	18564	12558	8190	4641
2	65520	52894	45386	35831	29757	21772	18359	12422	8122	4573
3	61425	51188	42998	34808	28938	21431	18155	12285	8054	4505
4	57330	49481	40609	33784	28119	21089	17950	12149	7985	4436
5	53235	47775	38220	32760	27300	20748	17745	12012	7917	4368
E1	53235	47775	38220	32760	27300	20748	17745	12012	7917	4368
2	51529	45386	36855	32078	26618	20475	17540	11944	7849	4300
3	49823	42998	35490	31395	25935	20202	17336	11876	7781	4232
4	48116	40609	34125	30713	25253	19929	17131	11807	7712	4163
5	46410	38220	32760	30030	24570	19656	16926	11739	7644	4095
F1	46410	38220	32760	30030	24570	19656	16926	11739	7644	4095
2	43680	36855	32078	28665	24161	19451	16790	11671	7576	4027
3	40950	35490	31395	27300	23751	19247	16653	11603	7508	3959
4	38220	34125	30713	25935	23342	19042	16517	11534	7439	3890
5	35490	32760	30030	24570	22932	18837	16380	11466	7371	3822

Color	IF	VVS1	VVS2	VS1	VS2	SI1	SI2	I1	I2	I3
G1	35490	32760	30030	24570	22932	18837	16380	11466	7371	3822
2	34125	31395	28665	24024	22250	18632	16175	11330	7303	3822
3	32760	30030	27300	23478	21567	18428	15971	11193	7235	3822
4	31395	28665	25935	22932	20885	18223	15766	11057	7166	3822
5	30030	27300	24570	22386	20202	18018	15561	10920	7098	3822
H1	30030	27300	24570	22386	20202	18018	15561	10920	7098	3822
2	28665	26276	23615	21499	19656	17609	15288	10647	6962	3754
3	27300	25253	22659	20612	19110	17199	15015	10374	6825	3686
4	25935	24229	21704	19724	18564	16790	14742	10101	6689	3617
5	24570	23205	20748	18837	18018	16380	14469	9828	6552	3549
I1	24570	23205	20748	18837	18018	16380	14469	9828	6552	3549
2	23546	22113	20066	18428	17609	15902	14196	9555	6416	3549
3	22523	21021	19383	18018	17199	15425	13923	9282	6279	3549
4	21499	19929	18701	17609	16790	14947	13650	9009	6143	3549
5	20475	18837	18018	17199	16380	14469	13377	8736	6006	3549
J1	20475	18837	18018	17199	16380	14469	13377	8736	6006	3549
2	19793	18428	17540	16721	15902	13991	12899	8531	5870	3481
3	19110	18018	17063	16244	15425	13514	12422	8327	5733	3413
4	18428	17609	16585	15766	14947	13036	11944	8122	5597	3344
5	17745	17199	16107	15288	14469	12558	11466	7917	5460	3276
K1	17745	17199	16107	15288	14469	12558	11466	7917	5460	3276
2	17063	16585	15493	14742	13923	12285	11193	7781	5324	3208
3	16380	15971	14879	14196	13377	12012	10920	7644	5187	3140
4	15698	15356	14264	13650	12831	11739	10647	7508	5051	3071
5	15015	14742	13650	13104	12285	11466	10374	7371	4914	3003
L1	15015	14742	13650	13104	12285	11466	10374	7371	4914	3003
2	14537	14128	13104	12490	11671	10920	9828	7166	4846	3003
3	14060	13514	12558	11876	11057	10374	9282	6962	4778	3003
4	13582	12899	12012	11261	10442	9828	8736	6757	4709	3003
5	13104	12285	11466	10647	9828	9282	8190	6552	4641	3003
M1	13104	12285	11466	10647	9828	9282	8190	6552	4641	3003
2	12149	11466	10784	10033	9282	8668	7644	6143	4368	2867
3	11193	10647	10101	9419	8736	8054	7098	5733	4095	2730
4	10238	9828	9419	8804	8190	7439	6552	5324	3822	2594
5	9282	9009	8736	8190	7644	6825	6006	4914	3549	2457

E.G. 1.25 carat I-1 (clarity) H-3 (color) = $10,374

1.75 carat (175 points)

Color	IF	VVS1	VVS2	VS1	VS2	SI1	SI2	I1	I2	I3
D1	127512	98532	85008	69552	57960	42504	34003	21252	12751	7342
2	119301	95151	81627	68103	56994	42021	33617	20962	12655	7245
3	111090	91770	78246	66654	56028	41538	33230	20672	12558	7148
4	102879	88389	74865	65205	55062	41055	32844	20383	12461	7052
5	94668	85008	71484	63756	54096	40572	32458	20093	12365	6955
E1	94668	85008	71484	63756	54096	40572	32458	20093	12365	6955
2	91287	81627	69552	61824	52647	40089	31975	19900	12268	6859
3	87906	78246	67620	59892	51198	39606	31492	19706	12172	6762
4	84525	74865	65688	57960	49749	39123	31009	19513	12075	6665
5	81144	71484	63756	56028	48300	38640	30526	19320	11978	6569
F1	81144	71484	63756	56028	48300	38640	30526	19320	11978	6569
2	76797	68103	60858	54096	46851	37964	30043	19127	11882	6472
3	72450	64722	57960	52164	45402	37288	29560	18934	11785	6376
4	68103	61341	55062	50232	43953	36611	29077	18740	11689	6279
5	63756	57960	52164	48300	42504	35935	28594	18547	11592	6182
G1	63756	57960	52164	48300	42504	35935	28594	18547	11592	6182
2	60858	55545	50232	46368	41055	35162	28207	18354	11495	6182
3	57960	53130	48300	44436	39606	34390	27821	18161	11399	6182
4	55062	50715	46368	42504	38157	33617	27434	17968	11302	6182
5	52164	48300	44436	40572	36708	32844	27048	17774	11206	6182
H1	52164	48300	44436	40572	36708	32844	27048	17774	11206	6182
2	49749	46368	42987	39123	35452	31975	26372	17485	11012	6086
3	47334	44436	41538	37674	34196	31105	25696	17195	10819	5989
4	44919	42504	40089	36225	32941	30236	25019	16905	10626	5893
5	42504	40572	38640	34776	31685	29366	24343	16615	10433	5796
I1	42504	40572	38640	34776	31685	29366	24343	16615	10433	5796
2	41055	38930	36998	33520	30526	28304	23667	16036	10240	5796
3	39606	37288	35356	32264	29366	27241	22991	15456	10046	5796
4	38157	35645	33713	31009	28207	26179	22315	14876	9853	5796
5	36708	34003	32071	29753	27048	25116	21638	14297	9660	5796
J1	36708	34003	32071	29753	27048	25116	21638	14297	9660	5796
2	34679	32361	30622	28594	26179	24150	20866	14007	9370	5699
3	32651	30719	29173	27434	25309	23184	20093	13717	9080	5603
4	30622	29077	27724	26275	24440	22218	19320	13427	8791	5506

Color	IF	VVS1	VVS2	VS1	VS2	SI1	SI2	I1	I2	I3
5	28594	27434	26275	25116	23570	21252	18547	13138	8501	5410
K1	28594	27434	26275	25116	23570	21252	18547	13138	8501	5410
2	27628	26468	25309	24150	22604	20576	18064	12848	8404	5313
3	26662	25502	24343	23184	21638	19900	17581	12558	8308	5216
4	25696	24536	23377	22218	20672	19223	17098	12268	8211	5120
5	24730	23570	22411	21252	19706	18547	16615	11978	8114	5023
L1	24730	23570	22411	21252	19706	18547	16615	11978	8114	5023
2	23860	22701	21542	20383	18740	17678	15939	11689	7921	5023
3	22991	21832	20672	19513	17774	16808	15263	11399	7728	5023
4	22121	20962	19803	18644	16808	15939	14587	11109	7535	5023
5	21252	20093	18934	17774	15842	15070	13910	10819	7342	5023
M1	21252	20093	18934	17774	15842	15070	13910	10819	7342	5023
2	19223	18257	17291	16229	14587	13717	12558	9853	6762	4637
3	17195	16422	15649	14683	13331	12365	11206	8887	6182	4250
4	15166	14587	14007	13138	12075	11012	9853	7921	5603	3864
5	13138	12751	12365	11592	10819	9660	8501	6955	5023	3478

E.G. 1 3/4 carat SI-2 (clarity) K-4 (color) = $17,098

To Thine Own Self Be True
What Kind of Customer Are You?

In my years in the business, I've come across five basic kinds of folks who buy diamonds. Tell me what type you are, and I'll recommend what grade of diamond you should buy.

Customer #1 will tell me the three most important things about a diamond are size, size, and size. The bigger the better, never mind if the stone is yellow and has a few black spots or cracks!

My recommendation:

Weight: 1 carat plus

Clarity: I2

Color: L–M

DIAMOND MYTH

"Diamonds are a bad investment."

Diamonds are probably not a great investment for the average person, but they are not a bad investment for someone who buys wisely and well. Since the diamond crash of 1979, when one-carat, flawless diamonds fell in value from $75,000 to $15,000, diamond prices have increased steadily. That's largely due to the tightly controlled world diamond market.

Customer #2 also wants a big diamond, but size isn't the only thing. A little quality wouldn't hurt. Maybe the diamond can be slightly yellow, but please, no obvious cracks or spots. Maybe some teeny spots that can hardly be seen.

My recommendation:

Weight: .50 carat or bigger

Clarity: SI2 to I1

Color: K

Customer #3 is a balanced kind of person, yin and yang. Size and quality are equal values. The diamond doesn't have to be perfect, but it should be clean to the eye, white, and sparkly.

My recommendation:

Weight: .50 carat or bigger

Clarity: SI1

Color: I(1) to J(3)

Customer #4 demands Quality, with a capital "Q." Everything else is secondary. The diamond must be not only eye-clean, but clean when viewed with a 10X loupe, and bright white without a hint of yellow.

My recommendation:
Weight: .50 carat or bigger
Clarity: VS1
Color: G

Customer #5 isn't getting engaged or buying an anniversary stone. The diamond is an investment to be locked away and later resold for a profit.

My recommendation:
Shape: round (no other!)
Weight: 1 carat or bigger
Clarity: VVS1 to flawless
Color: D, E, or F

Take a look at this chart. Find your type, your budget, and the size diamond you'll be able to afford. This table will help you get the most bang for your buck, whatever type of customer you happen to be.

BUYING GUIDE BY CUSTOMER TYPE

Type					
Budget	**1**	**2**	**3**	**4**	**5**
$250	0.33 carat	0.25 carat	n/a	n/a	n/a
$500	0.45 carat	0.25 carat	n/a	n/a	n/a
$750	0.45 carat	0.33 carat	0.25 carat	n/a	n/a
$1,000	0.50 carat	0.45 carat	0.33 carat	0.25 carat	0.25 carat
$1,250	0.62 carat	0.45 carat	0.33 carat	0.25 carat	0.25 carat
$1,500	0.75 carat	0.50 carat	0.45 carat	0.25 carat	0.25 carat
$1,750	0.80 carat	0.50 carat	0.45 carat	0.33 carat	0.25 carat
$2,000	0.80 carat	0.62 carat	0.45 carat	0.33 carat	0.25 carat
$2,250	0.90 carat	0.62 carat	0.50 carat	0.33 carat	0.33 carat
$2,500	0.90 carat	0.75 carat	0.50 carat	0.45 carat	0.33 carat
$2,750	1.00 carat	0.75 carat	0.62 carat	0.45 carat	0.33 carat
$3,000	1.00 carat	0.80 carat	0.62 carat	0.45 carat	0.33 carat

Budget	1	2	3	4	5
$3,500	1.00 carat	0.80 carat	0.62 carat	0.45 carat	0.45 carat
$4,000	1.25 carat	0.90 carat	0.75 carat	0.50 carat	0.45 carat
$4,500	1.25 carat	0.90 carat	0.75 carat	0.50 carat	0.45 carat
$5,000	1.50 carat	1.00 carat	0.80 carat	0.62 carat	0.45 carat
$5,500	1.50 carat	1.00 carat	0.80 carat	0.62 carat	0.50 carat
$6,000	1.75 carat	1.00 carat	0.80 carat	0.62 carat	0.50 carat
$7,000	1.75 carat	1.00 carat	0.90 carat	0.75 carat	0.62 carat
$8,000	1.75 carat	1.25 carat	0.90 carat	0.80 carat	0.62 carat
$9,000	2.00 carat	1.25 carat	0.90 carat	0.80 carat	0.75 carat
$10,000	2.00 carat	1.25 carat	1.00 carat	0.80 carat	0.75 carat
$11,000	2.00 carat	1.50 carat	1.00 carat	0.90 carat	0.80 carat
$12,000	n/a	1.50 carat	1.00 carat	0.90 carat	0.80 carat
$13,000	n/a	1.50 carat	1.00 carat	0.90 carat	0.80 carat
$14,500	n/a	1.50 carat	1.25 carat	0.90 carat	0.80 carat
$15,000	n/a	1.75 carat	1.25 carat	0.90 carat	0.80 carat
$15,500	n/a	1.75 carat	1.25 carat	1.00 carat	0.80 carat
$16,000	n/a	1.75 carat	1.25 carat	1.00 carat	0.90 carat
$16,500	n/a	1.75 carat	1.25 carat	1.00 carat	0.90 carat
$17,000	n/a	2.00 carat	1.50 carat	1.00 carat	0.90 carat
$17,500	n/a	2.00 carat	1.50 carat	1.00 carat	0.90 carat
$18,000	n/a	2.00 carat	1.50 carat	1.00 carat	0.90 carat
$18,500	n/a	2.00 carat	1.50 carat	1.00 carat	0.90 carat
$19,000	n/a	2.00 carat	1.50 carat	1.00 carat	0.90 carat
$19,500	n/a	2.00 carat	1.50 carat	1.00 carat	0.90 carat
$20,000	n/a	2.00 carat	1.50 carat	1.00 carat	0.90 carat
$25,000	n/a	2.00 carat	1.75 carat	1.25 carat	1.00 carat
$30,000	n/a	2.00 carat	1.75 carat	1.50 carat	1.00 carat
$35,000	n/a	n/a	2.00 carat	1.50 carat	1.25 carat
$40,000	n/a	n/a	2.00 carat	1.50 carat	1.25 carat
$45,000	n/a	n/a	2.00 carat	1.75 carat	1.50 carat
$50,000	n/a	n/a	n/a	1.75 carat	1.50 carat

TOO GOOD TO BE TRUE

Is it actually possible for a diamond to be priced too low? You'd think not, but be careful. The prices in this book are wholesale, not retail.

If the price of a diamond is dramatically lower than the prices in this book—beware! Nobody gives away a good diamond; they discount the stinkers. Notice how much the price of a diamond drops when it's a Class III or a Class IV versus a Class I or Class II.

At least one of the following is most likely going on:

1. The clarity, color, or weight has been overgraded.
2. It's an off-make (poorly proportioned) Class III or Class IV. It is poorly warranted (bad return, trade-in, or breakage policy).

How Much Is a 1 Carat VS1, G?

This may seem like a reasonably easy question for someone in the jewelry industry to answer, but it's actually quite difficult if the quote is to be accurate. In fact, an accurate answer cannot be derived because of a lack of information. Probability comes into play when we don't have the information needed to make an informed decision. When we don't have enough data, all we are left with are "reasonable guesses." Here are just some of the things we don't know: For starters, what type of 1ct are we talking about? A shy, full, heavy, or true? What type of VS1 are we talking about? A hard, lab, bonded, paperless, partial, split, universal, or soft? What type of G? G1, G2, G3, G4, or G5? How well proportioned is it? Class I, Class II, Class III, Class IV, Ideal, Signature, Hearts and Arrows, Eight Star, High-Definition, or Kaplan? If they use one of these titles to advertise the diamond is well-proportioned, what are the specifics in angles, percentages, and ratios of that brand? Once you know the specifics (proportions), do they give you enough measurements to determine if the crown angles and pavilion angles are universal or if the diamond is warped? Please don't forget about fluorescence. Is the diamond fluorescent? If it is, is it strong, medium, or faint fluorescence? Was the diamond annealed, fracture-filled, bleached, assembled, or laser-drilled? What equipment was used to measure the diamond? Was the equipment calibrated before it was used? Does the paperwork that comes with the diamond really match the stone? Where did the diamond come from? Is it a blood diamond? Is it a secondary market diamond? Finally, once you ask every last detail, how can you know what you've been told is factual?

Time for a joke. There are three men on a train—an economist, a logician, and a mathematician. They have just crossed the border into Scotland, and they see a brown cow standing in a field. The cow is standing parallel to the train. The economist says, "Look. The cows in Scotland are brown." The logician says, "No, there are cows in Scotland, of which at least one is brown." The mathematician says, "No, there is at least one cow in Scotland, of which one side appears to be brown."

How much is a 1ct, VS1, G? If you were to ask the economist, he might give you more than one answer. If you were to ask the logician, he would be smart enough to ask what type of 1ct, VS1, G you were talking about. And finally, if you were to ask the mathematician, he would say, "Did you forget about one thing? How much profit does the seller want to make?"

INFLATION BEATERS

According to *Bottom Line Personal* magazine, in the last twenty years, only two categories of collectibles have stayed ahead of inflation: stamps at an average return of 9.1 percent, and diamonds at 7.9 percent per year!

Chapter 3

Ring Settings

ONCE YOU HAVE DECIDED on a diamond, you'll need to select a setting. I mean, diamonds are beautiful, but what good are they unless you can wear them?

There are three basic types of ring settings: the Tiffany setting, bridal sets, and diamond wedding rings.

TIFFANY

The Tiffany Setting, named after the famed jeweler Louis C. Tiffany, is a simple, elegant setting that lets the diamond be the star of the show and be in the spotlight. In a Tiffany Setting, the stone is held by four to six prongs, depending on the shape of the diamond.

THREE BASIC STYLES OF SETTINGS: BRIDAL SET (FAR LEFT), THE TIFFANY (MIDDLE), AND DIAMOND WEDDING RING (RIGHT).

Note: When buying a ring that uses prongs to hold the diamond, make sure the prongs are white gold or platinum. Yellow gold prongs will give the stone a yellow cast.

Bridal Sets

The bridal set is a perennial favorite. It consists of an engagement ring and a wedding band made to fit together to look like one ring.

Diamond Wedding Rings

The diamond wedding ring is large enough to be worn by itself and can serve as the engagement ring and the wedding ring all in one. In many of these settings, there is a main diamond surrounded by several smaller stones.

Accents
Baguettes, Melees, Trilliants

These are small diamonds that are set around the main stone.

Baguettes are small, elongated diamonds usually under .15 carats in weight, either tapered or nontapered. Melees are round diamonds under .20 carats. Trilliants are triangular in shape usually under .33 carats.

Quadrillions under .15 carats cost around $1,850 to $2,350 per carat. Baguettes under .15 carats cost approximately $2,000 to $3,000 per carat. Trilliants under .33 carats cost approximately $3,000 to $4,000 per carat. Melees under .20 carats cost around $1,900 to $2,400 per carat. (Wholesale prices, based on SI1, H through I(3) color grade.)

Adding Color

Of course, diamonds are a girl's best friend, but rubies, sapphires, emeralds, and other colored stones are pretty good pals, too! Many women like to surround their diamonds with colored gems or vice-versa, and your true love might like her diamond accented with her birthstone.

There are some stunning combinations of diamonds and other precious stones. Ask your jeweler to show you some.

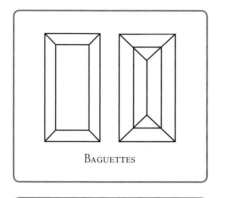

BAGUETTES

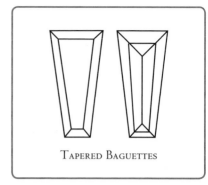

TAPERED BAGUETTES

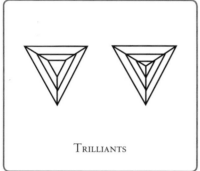

TRILLIANTS

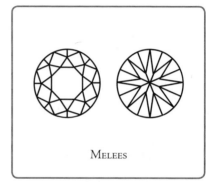

MELEES

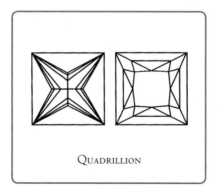

QUADRILLION

A WORD ABOUT GOLD...

Most engagement rings and wedding bands are made of gold. Pure gold is stamped 24K (24 karat), which means it has not been mixed with any other metals. We don't use 24K gold for jewelry because it's too soft and will bend too easily.

18K gold is 75 percent pure gold. Other metals such as copper, zinc, or nickel have been added for strength.

14K gold is 58.5 percent pure gold, and 41.5 percent other metals for strength.

10K gold is mostly other metals and should not be considered for jewelry.

You might see gold jewelry stamped with a number—750 or 585. This is the European system of grading gold. Pure gold is 1000 or 24K; 750 is 75 percent pure gold or 18K; 585 is 58.5 percent pure gold or 14K.

...And Platinum

Platinum is a rarer metal than gold and somewhat harder for a jeweler to work with. As you might guess, this makes it more expensive than gold. It is stronger than gold and therefore holds the diamond more securely—and some women prefer platinum because they feel it shows off the diamond better than gold.

Platinum Doping

The platinum world is being turned upside down, and I thought someone should let you know. But before we get into that, I need to make you a platinum aficionado. So, I went to Google and typed in "what is the definition of platinum?"

This is some of what I got:

- "One of the rarest precious metals, platinum is also one of the strongest and heaviest, making it a popular choice for setting gemstone jewelry and watches. It has a rich, white luster and an understated look. Platinum is hypoallergenic and tarnish resistant. Platinum used in jewelry and watches is at least 85 to 95 percent pure. Many platinum watches are produced in limited editions due to the expense and rarity of the metal."

    "Rare, silvery white metallic element of great strength, weight, and resistance to corrosion. Difficult to alloy, cast, and work owing to its very high melting point. The standard of platinum in the US and most western countries is 95 percent pure and is marked PLAT. From platina, little silver, the word the Spanish gave it when first seen in South America in the eighteenth century."

"Platinum is a white metal, but unlike gold it is used in jewelry in almost its pure form from 85, 90, or 95 percent pure. Platinum is very hard and is extremely long wearing and is very white, so it does not need to be rhodium-plated like white gold. Platinum is very dense making it much heavier than 18k gold. Because platinum is hard it is best suited for setting the large, valuable stones. The platinum prongs for setting stones would be stronger than the setting made with softer gold."

- "A dense (heavy) silvery grey metal, atomic number 78, atomic weight 195.078, used by pre-Columbian South American Indians, and rediscovered in the eighteenth century. Its first use for coins was by Russia in 1828, following the discovery of large platinum deposits in the Ural Mountains in 1822."

Platinum was never less that 85 percent pure under any definition. Well, now platinum is being DOPED! Large metal manufacturers are taking pure platinum and cutting it with copper and cobalt! The product is being sold as 585 platinum. The 585 stands for 58.5 percent pure platinum and 41.5 percent copper and cobalt. The C&C (copper and cobalt) is used as a filler. By diluting the platinum with cheaper alloys, the manufacturer can practically double his profits. This comes at the expense of you, the consumer, if you think you are getting the real McCoy. The large manufacturers that are producing this product tell me that they are not breaking any Federal Trade Commission guidelines as long as they inform the consumer (you) that you are buying watered-down platinum with the 585 stamp inside the ring. The problem comes in when the doped platinum gets sold over and over down the supply chain and less scrupulous vendors decide to remove the

585 and leave just the plat stamp. (This can be done in less than sixty seconds on a polishing wheel.) Then you decide to go online and buy what appears to be a great deal on a platinum band only to possibly find out later (when it cracks, craters, discolors, or your finger breaks out in a rash) that you have been duped by doping!

How you can protect yourself:

- Only buy a platinum ring (or other precious metal ring) from a well-known manufacturer that offers vacuum-poured and vacuum-pressed products and will put in writing and guarantee the platinum content of your ring (90 to 95 percent pure is a good measuring stick with 5 to 10 percent iridium).
- A standard 6mm (1-inch) comfort fit platinum band weighs 12–13grams. A doped platinum ring will come in weighing over 33 percent less at 8.6 grams (approximately).
- The color can also be a dead giveaway; all the pieces I examined couldn't be polished up to hold a true white luster but more of a gray luster. What makes visual identification so difficult is 585 can be dipped in rhodium (a platinum group metal) to mimic the look of real platinum.
- Know the melting point. Because the melting point of true platinum is so much higher than that of doped platinum, the minute a torch touches the imposter, its shell will oxidize (crust with black film). Of course, this test requires a jeweler and a torch, not necessarily things you have laying around your garage.

Let's look at this another way: When does milk stop becoming milk? We all know what it is—a whitish liquid containing proteins, fats, lactose, and various vitamins and minerals. Should there be a point when, if we tamper with its composition, we should no longer be allowed to call it milk? The answer would seem to be no if you go to your local grocer. There is soy milk, 2 percent, low-fat, skim, lactose-free, and whole milk just to name a few. There appears to be no end to the amount of diluting or modifying of milk that will cause the consumer to yell foul. But what if they start marketing a type of milk called "Royal Milk," "Tru Milk," or "Simply Milk" and told you it was "dip your chocolate chip cookie in it" good! It's tasty and more affordable than regular milk. Would you go buy it? What if you discovered that these new milk products were simply one gallon of fresh, cold, delicious milk and one gallon of tap water; does that sound like "Royal Milk," "Tru-Milk," or "Simply Milk"? How much tap water would you allow to be mixed with your precious milk before you simply wouldn't drink or buy it anymore? One gallon? Two gallons? Or would you allow three gallons of tap water with your milk?

A few months ago, I raised my hand (politely) and helped tell anyone who would listen that companies were watering down platinum and I didn't think it was right. I explained all the pitfalls to diluting platinum and how you, the consumer, could protect yourself. Unfortunately, manufacturers are trying to stay one step ahead of all of us. Instead of picking a new name for their product that would easily identify it for what it is, they are riding platinum's coattails and clever marketing to get you to purchase their product. It reminds me of the folks who like to put "low-fat" in front of everything they sell to make you feel better about eating an Oreo cookie. "Low-fat" and "No-fat" are hardly the same thing. Platinum and low platinum aren't either. Introducing products into the market under the brand name "Royal Platinum," "Tru-Platinum," or "Simply Platinum" when they aren't royal, 100 percent true, or just simply platinum is crossing the line. In my last article, I reported how copper and cobalt were being used to dope platinum. Now these pseudo-platinum products are being created by mixing $2,000-an-ounce platinum with $800-an-ounce palladium, then marketing them with a lot of interesting claims: "As good as," "100 percent hypoallergenic," and "Pure precious metal."

If just one person gets a piece of cheap, imitation platinum jewelry and believes it to be the real thing, it is one person too many in my book. Obviously, we all understand what the marketers are trying to do. They are trying to bring platinum to the masses. If the masses can't afford it, we'll just dope it down and dilute it 'til they can. They believe that the average Joe is just too stupid to understand he's being screwed! Guess what? I'm an average Joe and I'm not stupid. I'll write a new article every time someone pulls a fast one. I'll keep you informed. In the meantime, if someone wants to put the word "Royal," "Tru," or "Simply" in front of your platinum, please know it isn't really platinum. Now I've got one more question for you: "Got milk?"

PALLADIUM VP
(THE NEW PALLADIUM)

Readers will recall that when platinum prices started spiking a few years ago, manufacturers were quick to tout alternative metals that could offer all the benefits of platinum (strength, durability, rarity, beauty) at an affordable price. White gold, while always a good standby, still couldn't fill platinum's shoes because of discoloring problems associated with mixing pure gold with pot metal alloys, such as copper, nickel, and zinc.

The industry's "knee jerk" solution was to sell diluted platinum or palladium (a platinum metals group; cousin to platinum) to hit consumer price points that platinum could no longer meet. Doped platinum (585 platinum) had a short life when consumers and consumer advocate groups stood up against the inferior product, and the huge manufacturing plants that invested millions in doped platinum quickly went out of business. Mexican palladium, as it has been so eloquently nicknamed, has proved resilient through vendors such as Kay, Zales, and online discounters looking to make a quick buck without informing the consumer of the downside of manufacturing palladium in an unsterile environment with poor quality control. Consumer complaints of rings breaking, cracking, and just falling apart within the first couple of years are piling up by the thousands.

I previously pointed out the pitfalls of using inferior metals or quality metals poorly melded together. All that said, the top manufacturers of wedding bands have developed a palladium product called Palladium VP (which stands for vacuum-poured and vacuum-pressed.) These gurus found a way to take a mixture that is 95 percent palladium and 5 percent ruthenium and iridium and vacuum-pour it in a sterile environment so neither air or foreign contaminants could enter the mix. Then the product is vacuum-pressed to create the tightest sub-atomic bond possible to produce one tough band! The Palladium VP products are only available in men's and some ladies' wedding bands, but from my vantage point, they have hit a home run! The old palladium problems of being too soft, pitting, and cracking have all disappeared with Palladium VP! They have literally created a product that is hypoallergenic, durable, beautiful, and rare, just like platinum, at half the price! Palladium VP also comes with all the guarantees you'd expect—lifetime sizing guarantees and 100% destruction guarantees! You can run it over with a truck, and they will still replace it for free (guarantees vary from vendor to vendor). Palladium VP fits the gap between $600–$800 white gold gents' wedding band and the $2000–$3000 gents' platinum band, coming in at a comfortable $1000–$1400 price point for an average 6mm heavy comfort-fit band!

The question I keep getting asked is "how do I know if I'm getting sold Palladium VP v. its inferior, south of the border counterpart?" Well, it's simple! Here's what to look for:

- All Palladium VP is stamped Pal-VP.
- All Palladium VP products come with lifetime destruction guarantees and sizing guarantee.

And finally, look at the price! Counterfeiters could take Mexican Palladium and stamp it VP, but they won't be able to sell it at white gold prices ($600–800). If the vendor you're thinking of buying from says they can sell you a 6mm half round heavy comfort fit Palladium VP ring for under a grand, they are probably trying to pull the wool over your eyes. As long as platinum prices are overly inflated, I think it's only natural to look for an alternative. Palladium VP is to platinum what ethanol is to fossil fuel gasoline. It's just a smart way to go!

How Do I Get My True Love's Ring Size?

The simplest way, of course, is to ask her. The only problem with this method is that it might tip her off that you're going to propose. For many suitors, that would be a disaster—statistics show that seven out of ten men shop alone and plan to surprise their intended. The other three take the low-risk route—they propose first, then shop for a diamond with the lady. If you're in the latter group, you can check her ring size at the jeweler's.

Another way is to get your hands on a ring she has worn on her third finger, left hand. Take it to a jeweler, who can quickly tell you the ring size. Don't forget to return the ring promptly!

A third way is to ask her mother. This might be even scarier than proposing, but going to her mom first can be a great idea. It can often tell you three key things: One, your beloved's ring size. Two, how the parents feel about you as a potential son-in-law. And three, the mom can give you a pretty good reading on how your proposal will be received. This way, you'll be a lot more sure of the outcome before you make this expensive purchase.

Gold "Allergy"

Some women, after wearing gold jewelry for a while, will find that it leaves a black mark or smudge on their skin. This is caused by perspiration reacting with the metals mixed with the gold and not from a "gold allergy." Usually, a switch from 14K to 18K gold will solve the problem. But if you are the one-in-a-million who still reacts to 18K, switch to platinum. Your body has expensive tastes!

Chapter 4

Picking the Jeweler

◆━━━━━━━━━━━━━━━━━━━━━━━━━━━━━━━◆

Now that you know what you're looking for and how to look, the next step is to determine where to shop for your diamond. Before you visit every jeweler in the area, "let your fingers do the walking." You'll find lots of jewelers online and in the Yellow Pages under "Jewelers, Retail," and also under "Diamonds, Wholesale." Many merchants advertise in both places. You'll see a variety of information in the advertisements. Some will only mention their "lowest prices." Others will note that the jeweler is a "graduate gemologist" or that they sell "GIA lab-graded" diamonds. To narrow down your search, limit it to jewelers who advertise their GIA and gemologist credentials.

Using the following questionnaire sheet, spend an hour on the phone calling jewelers and screening them to make sure they have the qualifications you're after. Add up the scores and visit the top three on your scoreboard.

Jeweler Questionnaire Sheet (J.Q.S.): A Worksheet

Enter the points earned for each answer.

Score

_____ 1. How do their prices compare to the wholesale prices listed in this book?

At wholesale (75 pts)

10% over wholesale (25 pts)

50% over wholesale (10 pts)

Double wholesale (−10 pts)

_____ 2. Can they supply a guaranteed lab-grading report with the diamond?

Yes (15 pts)

No (0 pts)

_____ 3. Can they provide an appraisal by an accredited gemologist?

Yes (15 pts)

No (0 pts)

_____ 4. Do they have a gem laboratory where the stone can be viewed?

Yes (15 pts)

No (0 pts)

_____ 5. Do they have a calibrated colorimeter for color grading?

Yes (15 pts)

No (0 pts)

_____ 6. Do they have a gem diamond light for color grading?

Yes (15 pts)

No (0 pts)

_____ 7. Do they have an ultraviolet light to check for fluorescence and phosphorescence?

Yes (15 pts)

No (0 pts)

_____ 8. Do they have a 10X 20.5mm triplet loupe?

10X 20.5 triplet (15 pts)

Any 10X loupe (10 pts)

_____ 9. Do they have a gem scope or microscope to view diamonds?

Yes (15 pts)

No (0 pts)

_____ 10. Do they use the GIA-grading scale for color and clarity?

If they use the GIA scale (15 pts)

An automatic disqualification if they do not.

_____ 11. Are the diamonds loose (not mounted)?

If the answer is yes (15 pts)

If the answer is no, this is an automatic disqualification!

_____ 12. Can they provide a Sarin or Megascope report?

Yes (15 pts)

No (−15 pts)

_____ 13. Do they have an electronic scale to weigh the diamonds?

If the answer is yes (15 pts)

If the answer is no, this is an automatic disqualification!

_____ 14. Do they custom-cut diamonds to order?

Yes (15 pts)

No (0 pts)

_____ 15. Do they make their own jewelry on the premises?

Yes (15 pts)

No (0 pts)

_____ 16. How large is their loose-diamond inventory?

$250,000 and over (50 pts)

Under $250,000 (0 pts)

_____ 17. Do they own the inventory, or are they dealing in memorandum diamonds?

If they have their own inventory (25 pts)

_____ 18. What is their trade-in policy?

Equal to what you pay for the diamond (20 pts)

Less than what you pay for the diamond (0 pts)

No trade-in policy (–25 pts)

_____ 19. Do they have a return policy?

If they have a thirty, sixty, or ninety-day unconditional return policy
(20 pts)

For a return policy based on possible misrepresentation, that is, if you
find that the stone isn't exactly what the jeweler said it was (15 pts)

Automatic disqualification for no return policy.

_____ 20. Do they have an unconditional buy-back policy?

Yes (100 pts)

No (0 pts)

_____ 21. Does the store specialize in diamonds (or do they also sell
watches, gold chains, etc.)?

Yes (10 pts)

No (0 pts)

_____ 22. Where is the store located?

If the store is in an office building, such as Boston's Jewelers' Building
(15 pts)

If the store has an ordinary street address (0 pts)

If the store is in a mall (–10 pts)

_____ 23. How long has the store been around?

More than two years (10 pts)

Less than two years (0 pts)

_____ 24. Is the jeweler American Gem Society (AGS) rated?

Yes (10 pts)

No (0 pts)

_____ 25. Do they have a GIA graduate on staff?

Yes (15 pts)

Automatic disqualification if they do not.

_____ 26. Do they see customers by appointment only?

Yes (15 pts)

No (0 pts)

_____ 27. Do they have a breakage guarantee on the diamond?

Yes (40 pts)

No (0 pts)

_____ Total Score

RATING

500–600 points = Superior

460–499 points = Excellent

375–459 points = Good

325–374 points = Acceptable

275–324 points = Marginal

Below 275 = Keep looking!

WHO'S YOUR JEWELER, AND HOW DO THEY CATEGORIZE YOU?

There are three categories of jewelers. A jeweler is either brick & mortar (B&M—has a physical store front); virtual (Internet based—no physical store front); or combo B&M and virtual. I am not including TV vendors for this article because they only deal in commercial quality and costume jewelry.

Within all three categories of jewelers, there are four distinct approaches used in selling based on four customer types: the Discounter, the Bargain Shopper, the Brander, and the Better Thans.

A.   **The Discounter:** The discount shopper isn't particularly interested that an item is top of the line as long as their particular need gets satisfied. They focus on "category needs," not "detailed needs." A discounter buys a car to get from point A to B, not because of how sexy they will look in it or what their neighbors will think. A discounter buys toilet paper, cars, bikes, trucks, and TVs. The rest of us buy Charmin, Lexus, Harley, Ford, and Sony. The Discounter's motto is "Get the job done at the lowest possible price." These are the people that will be in line at 2:00 a.m. outside Best Buy in the frigid cold on Black Friday (day after Thanksgiving) in order to get something for as close to nothing as possible.

B.   **Bargain Shopper:** Walmart has proven that most of us are bargain shoppers—quality merchandise at a low price. Unlike the discounter mentality, the bargainer isn't willing to waste the time and effort that it takes to buy at the absolutely, positively, guaranteed lowest price. They want quality merchandise (generally name brand) but at a savings. Bargainers love to compare notes with other bargainers about what a great deal they got on their new Sony DVD or flat screen. Bargainers will make the effort to visit a few stores until they are reasonably sure they've done well and quit shopping. Whereas the Discounters will only tend to stop shopping when they've been to every store in their area. Of course, with the Internet, it's taking longer and longer to "shop around."

C.   **The Brander:** Like the Bargain shopper, the Brander wants quality, but he's also looking for an emotional connection with the brand. Something that represents him or her. Something that tells the world who they are. Price is less important to Branders than actually having the item that other people have so they can connect with them. That's why celebrity endorsements work so successfully. If an individual sees a celebrity endorse a product, or better yet actually use the product, they form a bond with the product. "Let's see, Robert DiNiro uses the American Express card. If I have an American Express card, then Robert and I have something in common! We're connected in some cool, cosmic way!" Branders want to buy products that other groups tend to buy. These groups are not limited to but include women, men, the wealthy, the affluent, the sexy, the smart, etc. A Brander may not even "need" a product but purchases it anyway because others in their identity group have the same item.

D.   **The Better Thans:** As the title insinuates, the Better Thans honestly believe that on some social, economic, intellectual level, they are "better than" others. There's the right religion, the right political party, the right everything. Naturally, for them to be right, many have to be wrong or "less than." Better Than shoppers only want products that the masses can't have, and if the masses get it, then they don't want it. Yesterday, I was shopping with my wife, and we wandered into Cartier. They had a pink diamond, yellow diamond, and white diamond, tight-knit pave, rolling ring that I could produce for about 5K. They were selling it for $52,000! And you know what? They are selling them! And the reason they are selling them is that they are so expensive. It isn't enough to just own jewelry anymore. The consolidators like Costco, Sam's Club, Walmart, JC Penny's, and Blue Nile burst that bubble. People are hung up on where they bought it, when they bought it (the right season), and what they spent. Louis Vuitton has made a fortune as a mega-successful brand name because of recognition of their line. When people see someone with one of their handbags, every one immediately knows, "Wow! That handbag cost major $$$! They must be somebody!" (Last time I checked, we were all somebodies.) Louis Vuitton even has a new spring and winter line that is only available to their top clients (clients that have spent over 100K with them) that nobody else can buy during that season! In some cases, they will only release ten of a type of handbag and let the socialites and celebrities duke it out for the power purse. I've been accused many times of being a Better Than because of some choices I've made. My Patek Phillipe or Rolex watch is a popular "Better Than" selection. My problem is that in most cases, there seems to be a direct correlation between quality (which is important to me) and the "Better Than" brands. But I'm also the same guy who was at Target this weekend to stock up on toilet paper. Grocery store prices are too high. To Better Thans, the importance price plays in the buying decision is that it has to be priced high enough that most people can't afford it.

The Pitch

Now that I've described the four customer mind-sets, let me outline how the jewelry industry attacks each to get your hard-earned dollar. They know there are many different avenues you can take to buy a piece of jewelry. You can visit a jewelry store that specializes in selling jewelry. This, of course, could be a mom-and-pop store or a national jewelry chain. You can visit a department store that has a jewelry department or even a "superstore" like Walmart, where you can buy a new pair of jeans, a gallon of milk, and a new engagement ring at the same time! There are high-end jewelry stores like Graff, Van Cleef & Arpels, Cartier, Harry Winston (also referred to as guild jewelers); and of course, you can surf the Web. If we set aside Walmart, the top three companies that sell jewelry in the United States are Zales, Sterling, and Finlay. Together, they are responsible for almost 5 billion dollars worth of sales annually out of their 4,375 stores nationwide. In a survey of young, upwardly mobile, professional couples, 93.7 percent told me they would never consider purchasing a major piece of jewelry from a mall jeweler. When I pointed out that there were some pretty high-end stores like Harry Winston and Cartier that happened to be in malls, they commented by a ratio of 4 to 1 that they would not shop at Harry Winston or Cartier either, because you were just paying for a name. When I asked about companies like Bailey, Banks & Biddle; Mappins; Friedlanders; Marks & Morgan; Osterman; Jared, the Galleria of Fine Jewelry; the usual response was "Well, yeah, sure; someone in-between the high-enders and the discounters like Kay; J.B. Robinson; Zales; Gordon's, and such." When I asked what was wrong with Kay or Zales, the general responses from these college-educated, affluent young men and ladies were that they were for people who need to buy in install-ments; the salespeople weren't perceived as knowledgeable; and the décor was, well, in a word, "déclassé."

So it seems people tend to shop where they believe they fit in. Kinda like Goldilocks, the choice has to be just right. However, though people believe they are being given a choice of where to shop, in reality, the deck has been stacked. What the big jewelry retailers did decades ago was buy up most of the mom-and-pop jewelers. These are the same jewelers that spent decades building a loyal clientele and then were bought up by the big corporations, leaving, of course, the original owner's name on the awning so you, the loyal clientele, wouldn't be the wiser. For the first time, I'm listing for all to see the true owners of the jewelry stores you frequent so you know exactly who is getting your money.

Zales Corp.	Store Names	
901 W. Walnut Hill Lane Irving, TX 75038 972-580-4000 fax: 972-580-5336	Gordon's Jewelers	Zales Jewelers
	Mappins Jewelers (Canada)	Zales Outlet
	Peoples Jewelers (Canada)	Piercing Pagoda

Sterling Jewelers	Store Names	
375 Ghent Road Fairlawn, OH 44333 330-668-5000 fax: 330-668-5052 US subsidiary of Signet Group (UK)	Belden Jewelers	J.B. Robinson
	Friedlander's Jewelers	LeRoy's Jewelers
	Goodman Jewelers	Osterman Jewelers
	Rogers Jewelers	Shaw's Jewelers
	Weisfield Jewelers	Kay Jewelers
	Marks & Morgan Jewelers	Jared, the Galleria of Jewelry

Finlay Fine Jewelry Corp.	Stores and Department store locations	
(Largest leased store operator) 521 Fifth Ave. New York, NY 10175 212-551-8300 fax: 212-867-3326 Subsidiary of Finlay Enterprises Inc.	Bergner's	Burdines
	Bloomingdale's	Dillard's
	Elder-Beerman	Bon Ton
	Boston Store	Shaw's Jewelers
	Carson, Pirie, Scott	Macy's
	Gottschalk's	Lord & Taylor
	Herberger's	Kaufmann's
	Rich's	Younkers
	Carlyle & Co.	Bailey, Banks, & Biddle

FULLY BONDED JEWELERS

In every organization, there are always the elite few who stand out in the crowd. In the Army, you've got the Rangers. In the Navy, you've got the SEALs. In the Air Force, you've got the PJs, and in a world filled with ordinary jewelry stores, you have super jewelry stores called bonded jewelers! Why, Fred, are bonded jewelers better than the rest? What are they bonded for? Well, hold on to your hats, and I'll tell you.

For starters, only approximately 20 percent of the jewelers in the world are fully bonded. Only one out of every twenty! "Fully bonded" refers to the fact that they sell fully bonded diamonds, and fully bonded diamonds, my friend, are the way to go if you can afford them. They typically cost 10 percent to 15 percent more than nonbonded diamonds because of the fact that they are better quality. A fully bonded diamond is just a fancy way of describing a fully guaranteed diamond.

This is what you get with a fully bonded diamond

1. All fully bonded diamonds come with a lifetime breakage policy. You bust the stone, the jeweler gives you a new one. (One bust per customer.) This is a wonderful policy because treated stones tend to be brittle and no jeweler would give you this guarantee on an easily broken (and therefore less than 100 percent natural) stone.

2. You're going to love this: All fully bonded stones come with a lifetime buy-back policy. Translation: for the life of the diamond, you can take it back to the jeweler and get 100 percent of your money back! (Mountings and sales tax are not included.) How wonderful this is! If you're not 100 percent satisfied for the life of your purchase, you get your money back. Now you might ask, "How can a jeweler afford to do this?" How can he not? Great diamonds are in demand, very liquid, and easy to resell. Any jeweler worth his salt will be glad to buy back a good diamond. If a jeweler doesn't

want to buy your diamond back, then there was probably something wrong with it in the first place.

3. All fully bonded diamonds come with an unconditional lifetime exchange policy. This is great! If your fiancée ever gets bored with her shape, the jeweler will allow even exchanges. (You have to pay for resetting fees.)

4. Fully bonded diamonds come with a lifetime trade-in policy with a market appreciation rate to keep up with inflation.

5. Fully bonded diamonds come with a market-crash protection policy. If the diamond market ever crashes and your diamond depreciates, the jeweler will refund the difference between what you paid from the new market value.

6. All fully bonded stones are guaranteed to be natural and untreated.

7. All fully bonded stones are guaranteed to be 100 percent conflict-free.

If you can find a fully bonded jeweler, they are the way to go. Dishonest jewelers thrive, knowing that it's possible to take a bad diamond and make it look good. But looking good and staying looking good are two different things. That diamond needs to pop as much on your twenty-fifth anniversary as it did the day you bought it. With a bonded diamond, if the diamond doesn't always meet your expectations or surpass them, you get your money back.

WHO WILL HELP ME NOW?

You've probably already realized there are two components that must be evaluated before you sign on the dotted line: the diamond and the setting that holds it. The funny thing is that more and more people are buying the setting from one place and the diamond at another, which leaves us with some serious questions:

1. Who should set it?

2. Who should be responsible for the diamond during the setting?

3. Who will service the ring after it is set? (Who will size it if it needs sizing? Who will repair it if it gets damaged? Who will do the annual checkup? If you were lucky enough to buy a bonded diamond, is the bonding still in effect if the seller doesn't do the setting?)

The seller of the setting may or may not agree to set the diamond. Many jewelers won't set someone else's diamond because they don't want to be responsible for any chipping or nicks that may result in the setting process. In fact, many jewelers will only set the diamond if you sign a "hold harmless" agreement. The rest of the jewelers, in order to pressure you to also buy the diamond from them, won't agree to set someone else's diamond under any circumstances.

Jewelers carry exclusive lines of designer jewelry no one else in their region can carry to lure you into the store. Their hope is to hook you with the setting and reel you into a diamond.

The reasons the settings are so expensive are because even though the jeweler hopes to sell you their diamond, they are well aware of the commoditization of commercial diamonds and the difficulty of competing against consolidators that are now selling direct. With the loss of the "rock" profit, they must compensate with an overpriced semimount.

I don't blame the jeweler. I wouldn't want to set someone else's diamond unless I had insurance to protect me. Plus, even if I am covered, where is the incentive for me to service some guy who blatantly didn't consider me for the major purchase—the diamond?

As the customer, I wouldn't even ask the jeweler who sold me the setting to set the diamond for one very good reason: He's probably upset with me for not buying my diamond from him, and his setter may take it out on my beautiful new diamond with "torquing." (Torquing is the overapplication of pressure to a prong in order to cause permanent damage to the girdle of the diamond.)

So the answer to who should set the diamond is easy: It's the seller of the diamond. And not just for the setting but all servicing as well.

Furthermore, if the diamond is bonded, the diamond seller's insurance company requires him to set it, or it voids the warranty. If the diamond seller refuses responsibility, then buy your diamond somewhere else.

The Gift of Jewelry

The engagement ring may be the first piece of fine jewelry you buy, but chances are, it won't be the last. A gift of fine jewelry is appropriate at any season of the year and in any season of life. Birthdays, anniversaries, Christmas, Chanukah, the first day of spring, Mother's Day, Valentine's Day—jewelry is always an excellent gift.

You should take as much care buying a birthday gift as you do when you shop for an engagement ring to make sure you get the most value for your loved one and your budget. Whether it's a diamond or some other precious stone, many of the same rules apply. And always keep the recipient uppermost in your mind. Use the Gift Questionnaire Sheet below. It'll help you match the gift to the person and ensure that the gift will be happily received and worn with pride.

Gift Questionnaire Sheet: A Worksheet

Here are some things to think about before you make an expensive jewelry purchase, whether it's an engagement ring, a birthday gift, or a gift for some other special occasion. You may already know all or most of this information, but you probably haven't thought about it in terms of buying a ring. Take the time to fill out this questionnaire, and you're almost guaranteed to be on target with your purchase.

1.   *Birth date:* _____

The birth date tells you the birthstone. Sometimes women like their engagement ring or wedding band to have their birthstone mixed with diamonds. Or, a birthstone ring is a nice gift by itself.

2.   *Height and weight:* _____

You can guess at these if you have to. Sometimes these vital stats will help you make an educated guess of someone's ring size, if you don't know it. It also helps you get a ring that's in proportion with body type. For example, a half-carat diamond may look fine on a person of average build but might look small on a larger person.

3.   *Favorite color:* _____

This is important information! If your true love's favorite color is blue, a diamond set with sapphire accent stones might be perfect. In some cases, the color might be so important she'll want the colored stone as the main stone.

4.   *Personality type:* ( ) Conservative ( ) Traditional ( ) Flamboyant ( ) Contemporary ( ) Trendsetter

The choice of settings is virtually unlimited. The personality type will narrow down the search. For example, if the person is conservative and very traditional, a diamond solitaire in a Tiffany setting might be perfect.

5.   *Ring size:* _____

Very important. The last thing we want to do is take the ring back to have it sized.

6.   *Profession:* _____

Some professionals can't wear jewelry to work or must wear modest jewelry. A ring might actually interfere with some jobs, so the person should be able to remove it easily. In some professions (real estate broker, stockbroker, model), a "knockout" ring is an indicator of success.

7.   *Diamond shape:* _____

Ask if you must but find out what her favorite diamond shape is. Personality type can be an indicator—the traditionalist would probably favor a round stone (65 percent of all engagement rings have round stones) while a trendsetter may like a fancy shape. After round, the most popular shapes are box radiant, standard radiant, princess, emerald cut, oval, pear, marquise, and heart. Don't buy her a heart-shaped diamond unless she specifically asks for it—it's probably the least attractive.

8.   *Carat size:* _____

Ask a woman what size diamond she wants, and she's likely to ask, "How big can I get?" The best way to go about this is to determine your budget and check the price guides in this book.

Size Scale:

>   Average: .38 points
>   Yuppie: Around one carat
>   Ultimate Dream: One and a half to three carats
>   Filthy Rich: Three to five carats

Is the recipient *size*-conscious or *quality*-conscious? You'll need to have some idea to know whether you can trade off a little quality for a bigger carat size or vice-versa.

9.   *Setting color:* ( ) Yellow gold ( ) White gold ( ) Platinum

Three out of ten women like yellow gold, but it's important to be sure. Look at her other jewelry. (Don't forget, on a yellow gold ring, make sure the prongs are white gold or platinum so they don't make the diamond appear yellow.)

10. *Purity:* ( ) 10K ( ) 14K ( ) 18K ( ) 22K

Most jewelry worn by most women is 14K. 18K is a little softer and a little yellower. Platinum is white. Unless she specifies 18K or platinum, 14K is a safe choice.

11. *Other favorite jewelry:* _____

You might want to match the color or style of other favorite pieces of jewelry.

12. *Is there a particular ring she has admired?* _____

Pay attention to your true love, and you'll learn a lot about likes and dislikes, and you may hear her admire someone else's ring or a picture of a ring in a magazine. If you're lucky, she may even say, "That's exactly the kind of ring I'd love to have."

THE NEW YORK DIAMOND DISTRICT
"BARGAINS GALORE" OR "BUYER BEWARE"?

The fabled New York Diamond District, centered on 47th Street in Manhattan, probably has more diamond dealers per square foot than any place on earth. For a couple of bustling blocks, the streets are teeming with diamond sellers, practically hawking their wares as if they were selling hot pretzels. The diamond trade here is dominated by hastening figures who lend the place an unmatched mystique as they shuttle between cutting houses and shops, carrying hundreds of thousands of dollars' worth of diamonds in their pockets and satchels. But is this a good place to buy a diamond?

In my experience, it is probably the most difficult place in America to get a good deal on a good diamond. You have a better chance of winning the lottery or getting hit by lightning than getting a good diamond deal on 47th Street!

The whole place is attitude and hustle. They employ a kind of reverse psychology—here, the dealer doesn't trust the customer! The dealers give you the impression they haven't really got the time or the inclination to deal with you. "You really want a diamond? Okay, hurry up and pick something out, pay me, and please leave. I have more important things to do than sell you one measly diamond. Lab-grading reports? Guarantees? Whaddya want, papers or diamonds? You want to buy—here, take it. You don't want to buy—try the guy down the street. Maybe he has time to deal with papers. I deal with diamonds!"

I bought a diamond on 47th Street one day. Dressed in a business suit, I went shopping, settled on a dealer, and asked for a one-carat, VS1-G. I was given a stone that was said to fit my specs. When I asked for paperwork, the dealer gave me something that fudged on the grades, that said the stone was "VS" but not VS1 and "G–H," not G. Two days later, dressed in jeans, I returned to the same dealer. He didn't recognize me. When I showed him the stone and told him what I'd paid for it, he immediately started berating me, "You got taken! You paid too much for this diamond! You should have come to me in the first place!" When I pulled out my receipt and reminded him I'd bought the stone from him two days ago, he practically pushed me out of the store.

Everyone in New York "knows a guy on 47th Street" who will allegedly give you the diamond deal of a lifetime if you mention the right name. Friends, it ain't that easy.

I've found that if you get above street level on 47th Street, up to the dealers on the higher floors, you can get a decent deal on a diamond if you're a shrewd buyer. Even up there, above the hustle and bustle, dealers pressure you to move quickly on a purchase. Take your time. Examine the stone closely, go through all the steps outlined in this book, *pay by credit card—never cash!*—and get an independent appraisal immediately.

Every major city has its diamond center, and some of them are excellent places to purchase diamonds if you shop for the right dealer and ask the right questions. But the New York Diamond District? Toughest place I know to buy a diamond.

THE REAL THING?
HOW TO TELL A REAL DIAMOND FROM A FAKE

Hands down the number-one question I'm asked online is "How can I tell if my diamond is the real thing?" People want to know if there is some simple test they can do at home or little tricks of the trade to tell if the ring they own is a valuable heirloom or of the Cracker Jack variety.

Without question, the quickest and most reliable method for authenticity would be an independent appraisal. This can be accomplished easily enough by searching for "appraisal (jewelry)" online or in the Yellow Pages. When you call or email to inquire about their services you want to ask three questions:

1. Can you schedule an appointment, or is it first come first served?
2. Ask the fee; $35.00–$75.00 is considered a fair price.
3. Ask if the jewelry will always be in your presence. If the appraiser says they will not evaluate the jewelry in front of you, find another appraiser.

If spending fifty bucks seems a little too steep to uncover the identity of your rock, you can head to your local jewelry store and ask their in-house gemologist to take a peek and give you their opinion. Because opinions are like belly buttons (everyone's got one), understand that in a lot of these quick, thirty-second evaluations, mistakes can be made, especially because most jewelers won't charge you for thirty seconds of their time. (Just like with independent appraisals, don't let the merchandise out of your sight.)

There are some less reliable methods you can try, but there are no guarantees with these:

1. The old "If it will scratch glass, it has to be a diamond." Well, it's true that diamonds scratch glass, but so do a lot of the other fakes on the market. To boot, it's possible to injure your rock even if it's real during your hardness test.

2. The transparency test. If you flip the diamond in question upside down and place it over some newsprint and can clearly read through the stone, it's not a diamond. (The problem with this test is some diamonds are cut shallow and can be read through.)

3. The fog test. This test I like a lot. Put the rock in front of your mouth and fog it like you would try to fog a mirror. If it stays fogged for two to four seconds, it's a fake. A real diamond disperses the heat instantaneously, so by the time you look at it, it has already cleared up. (A downfall to this test is oil and dirt on the stone can affect its reliability, and the test is not accurate at all on doublets where the top of the stone is diamond and the bottom is cubic zirconia epoxied together.)

4. The weight test. The most popular diamond simulant (fake) is a cubic zirconia. CZs weigh approximately 55% more than diamonds for the same shape and dimension. So if you have a carat or gram scale at your disposal, you can see if the imposter tips the scales too much.

5. The UV test. A high percentage of diamonds fluorescence blue when put under an ultraviolet light (black light). Because 99% of all fakes don't, a positive identification of medium to strong blue would indicate a diamond. The bad news is if this method proves you have a diamond, it also proves your diamond is worthless. Diamonds with blue fluorescence are as much as 20% less valuable. Remember, lack of blue fluorescence doesn't mean it's a fake; it could just be a better quality diamond.

6. Under the loupe test. If you own some sort of magnifying lens, there are some things you can look for on the stone that might give away its identity:

A. Look at the rock from the top and see how well the facets (cuts on top of the diamond) are joined. They should be sharp, not rolled.

B. Look at the girdle and see if it is faceted or frosty (a clear sign it's a diamond) or waxy and slick (an indication it's a fake).

C. While you're looking at your stone under magnification, look into your stone to see if you detect any flaws (carbon, pinpoints, small cracks). These are typically clear indications it's the real thing, because it's very hard to put inclusions in a fake.

D. After you examine the stone, focus in on the stamps inside the setting. A stamp of "10K, 14K, 18K, 585, 750, 900, 950, PT, or Plat" indicates the setting is real gold or platinum, which gives a better chance that the stone in it is real as well. While you're looking at the interior of the ring, also look for any "CZ" stamps that would indicate the center stone is not a diamond.

I hope this helps all you Sherlock Holmes that want to know what you got.

DISPOSABLE JEWELRY

Ask yourself a question, "Why do people buy jewelry?" Personal adornment? Possibly beauty? Certainly investment? These may be reasons for some, but the number-one reason for the purchase of jewelry is status. Pure and simple. If I can have something you can't have, I'm better than you. I don't agree with it, but it's a fact. People buy jewelry to impress. If not others, themselves. I've heard more than one woman in my day at a big tenth or twenty-fifth anniversary say, *I deserve this diamond. I've earned it. When I wear it, I feel complete. When I don't, I feel naked. Diamonds make me feel special.* Why doesn't paste or glass or cubic zirconia make a woman feel special? They certainly look pretty. They certainly cover the personal adornment category. So why diamonds? Why gold? Why platinum? Because they are supposed to be valuable. They are supposed to be heirlooms.

They are supposed to look beautiful, be durable, and maybe if we are lucky, we will have something to pass down to our loved ones along with a story of the special day that piece of jewelry came to be. Jewelry is bought and sold every day because it is supposed to be valuable; it is supposed to be worth something. Then it's our job to weave it into the personal folklore that we can pass down through the generations. But what if it's not?

What if all the big retailers put together a lot of pretty, shiny jewelry, ran expensive ads at Christmas and Valentine's Day and Mother's Day, and told everyone to buy this seven-carat tennis bracelet for $1,000.00, buy this diamond drop necklace for $199.00, buy these one-carat diamond stud earrings for $499.00 to make your loved one feel special? And what if that jewelry was junk? Hollowed-out metal, under-carated gold, treated diamonds with no value. Would your loved one feel special then? When the ads on TV say you only choose the best diamonds for your loved ones and it isn't the truth, is it fraud? Is it?

It is! Plain and simple. When someone buys something and thinks it has an inherent value and it doesn't, the vendor is stealing from you. They might as well have stuck a gun to your side at an ATM. But this is worse. These are our mothers, daughters, wives, sisters, our family that is being taken every time a national chain pushes a piece of junk at a low price and has the gall to call it fine jewelry. I don't have to mention these chains' names, because you know who they are, and it's horrendous.

Fine jewelry shouldn't have an expiration date. Paper cups, razors, newspapers, these are things you use and throw away, not jewelry.

For the first time in the history of man, you can buy diamonds with blue-book values so you won't get ripped off. Jewelry should have that same guarantee. I started this section with a question. Now I'll end it with one: Would you buy a piece of jewelry if five years from now it was worth less than 19.7 percent of what you had paid for it? Ninety-eight percent of the jewelry bought today falls into that category. The only question left is are you going to buy disposable jewelry or demand something better.

BUYING DIAMONDS ON THE INTERNET

Seems like yesterday (it was) when companies selling diamonds over the Internet were a novelty, but today there are literally thousands of such sites. This is how it works: You locate a diamond merchant on the Web and look over a selection of stones. Full-color, high-resolution images of the diamonds are displayed on your screen. The diamonds are graded by carat weight, cut, clarity, and color. You select the stone you like, enter your credit card number, and your diamond will be shipped.

My major concern is the quality of the stone's proportions. In my cyber travels, I find lots of "off-makes" (poorly proportioned stones). I could tell they were taking rough stones, which, if properly cut, would have yielded shy-carated diamonds, and creating full-carat stones and in the process sacrificing sparkle for size.

In the process, they offer lots of full-carated diamonds and very few opportunities to "buy shy." If you want a .90ct SI1, I(1), then don't be pushed into a 1ct SI1, G(1), unless you get it for the .90ct price and all the parameters of cut are at least Class II.

In short, you're forced to hunt for the needle in the haystack. Carefully consider the following pros and cons before you decide if it's worth the search.

Cons

1. *The Scams*

   A. *Treated Diamonds:* Every form of treated diamond is detectable by a lab, with the exception of a baked or heat-treated diamond. These are diamonds that two weeks ago might have been yellow but are now miraculously white! Baked diamonds are brittle and can break and, therefore, must be avoided. The only way to avoid being stuck with one is to make the sale contingent on a breakage guarantee and/ or a money-back guarantee.

   B. *Fake or Duplicate Lab-Grading Reports:* Diamonds are popping up all over the country that don't match their lab-grading reports. A lot of people believe that if a diamond has been graded by a third party, there is no need to have it independently checked when you get it. What good is a lab-grading report that says a diamond is great if it doesn't match the diamond? With the technology of today's personal computers, knocking off lab-grading reports has become a piece of cake. Or, a crook can take a good diamond and obtain a lab-grading report two or three times, then take the extra lab-grading report and put it with a similar-looking but lower-quality diamond.

   C. *"Hot" Diamonds:* Another quick hustle online vendors use is selling diamonds they haven't paid for and never plan to pay for. In the jewelry industry, diamonds are routinely handled on consignment. This means the owner loans diamonds to a retailer, with the agreement that he will be paid when the retailer sells the stone. But the dishonest vendor sells the diamond online below his cost to attract a quick sale but never pays his supplier. In a few months, he declares bankruptcy, and the spoils are his. In this case, you might get a nice diamond at an unbelievably low price, but not for long. The FBI is now looking at these cases as interstate theft. How would you feel if in a year and a half, someone knocked on your door, demanding your stolen diamond? You're out the money and the rock!

D. *The Shell Game:* You order a diamond online, get it appraised, and the appraiser says it's a fake! "Cubic zirconia!" You scream foul play, go to the police, and the retailer claims he's innocent. But the police have no way of knowing who the real crook is. Did the seller mail a fake like the appraiser says? Or did the appraiser switch the real diamond for a fake, or better yet, did the customer switch the diamond for a fake before he went to the appraiser? What a mess indeed.

E. *Handling Fees Scam:* Some online jewelers build their profit into handling fees, not the diamond. That way, whether you keep it or not, they just made a sale. Avoid jewelers who charge handling fees that are not refundable.

F. *The Return Authorization Number:* R.A.N. for short. Here's what some "smooth operators" do: They say your satisfaction is the only thing important to them and if you're not happy, you can return your diamond for a full refund. Then they stick it to you by using a R.A.N., which is a way for an outfit to deter or even eliminate returns. These companies make you call back to get an authorization number for return approval, or you can't return the item. This benefits the vendor in two ways:

1.) In most cases, anyone who uses R.A.N.s has limited return policies, usually around thirty days. They know that the more difficult they make it for you to use it or the more procedures you have to undertake, the clock will always be ticking—usually from the very second it was postmarked. If they can stall long enough to make the return policy lapse, they win.

2.) Also, if you want to return something, they shuffle you off to another department. Forget about talking to that nice salesman who sold it to you. You're about to get the gorilla of a salesman on the line who will do everything in his power to talk you out of it. Look, if I want to return something, I don't want to spend an hour justifying my return.

3.) They tell you all returns must be mailed back in the original packaging. Then, they pack it in such a way as to make it impossible to not destroy the packaging and hope you will accidentally throw it away so they can avoid a refund altogether.

2. *Lack of Multiple Stone Viewing:* I've yet to find an Internet diamond company that has said, "Let me mail you a dozen diamonds, keep the one you like, and mail the rest back." Comparative shopping is the American way. How can we appreciate anything without something to compare it to? Unless you're willing to do your comparative shopping locally before buying online, the only other option is to have one stone mailed to you at a time—and that is an enormous waste of time.

3. *Poor Warranties:* The best these companies seem to be able to come up with are thirty- to ninety-day return policies. That's it—period! What if your fiancée breaks up with you after four months and you don't need the diamond anymore? Tough! What if a couple years from now you want to exchange or upgrade? Tough! What if your diamond is chipped or breaks? Tough! What if the diamond turns out to be treated? Tough! Tough! Tough! After the limited return policy is over, if anything goes wrong, you're stuck with a diamond you don't want. Compare that to bonded jewelers that offer lifetime breakage guarantees, lifetime buy-backs, lifetime trade-ins, and exchanges, and online jewelers are outmatched. Who cares how good a deal something is if you don't need or want it? Ask yourself this question: Would you buy a car with only a thirty-day guarantee?

4. *Service:* I need my prongs tightened. I need my ring sized. My ring broke. What's the Internet company going to do for you now? All they can say is mail it back. What about the annual inspection a ring needs? I haven't found one online jeweler that brings this up,

much less says they will take care of it free of charge. When it comes to service after the sale, there is no beating a local jeweler. I know some people live in remote areas and finding a good jeweler is hard, but that should always be the first place you begin your search. Remember, only buy out of town when local jewelers let you down.

5. *Will they be here tomorrow?* According to the *Bloomberg Network*, only 2 percent of online retailers will survive. What are the odds you'll pick the right one? Is it important to you that one of the biggest purchases you'll ever make is from somebody that will stay in business? Look at Levi Strauss—they threw in the towel. They couldn't sell blue jeans online! In the end, they realized there is no way to know a perfect fit unless you try it on. Can't do that on the Internet! So if an American icon like Levi Strauss can't make it on the Internet selling $45 blue jeans, what makes these non-brick-and-mortar cyber peddlers think they will? If I were dealing with an online retailer, I'd be pretty damn sure they had an actual location I could visit and had been around for a while. Because for my money, I want to do business with someone who's going to stay in business.

Pros

1. *Price:* Certainly, the prices on these Internet sites are very appealing. They lure you in like bees to honey. The one thing all these diamond companies must believe is the man with the lowest price wins. They should, however, check their stats. In a recent customer survey conducted by *Jewelers Circular Keystone*, only 35 percent of jewelry buyers said finding the lowest price was their primary concern. Regardless, the frosting on the cake looks very appealing, and I've seen little or no price gouging online.

2. *Selection:* The companies seem to have endless inventories. Walk into your typical jeweler and ask to look at a specific loose diamond

and you're lucky to see two or three stones. In some cases, they don't have any and say they have to bring some in. The one thing I find interesting, though, is on several occasions, I decided to add up these virtual inventories that many companies claim are theirs. In one case, the total value of one inventory exceeded $2.1 billion, and in another case, their inventory exceeded $5 billion. How does a typical start-up Internet diamond seller get billions of dollars worth of inventory with start-up capital of $15–$20 million? That's a nifty trick!

3. *Lab-Grading Reports and Appraisals:* Every diamond bought online has some kind of piece of paper talking about how good it is. Considering there are a lot of jewelers that only hand over a sales receipt with purchase, a third, independent evaluation is a plus.

4. *Sales Tax:* It's hard to overlook, at least for the time being, that buying a piece of jewelry online from an out-of-state vendor can save a lot of money. In Texas, where the sales tax is 8.25 percent in some places, purchasing a $10,000 diamond online would save you $825! It's important, however, to not let shipping charges, credit card charges, and handling fees eat up this legitimate cost-saving feature.

Conclusion
These are still shark-infested waters—unless you have to surf the net, stay on dry land.

Final Thoughts
Well, Fred, are you telling me there is no way you would recommend buying online? No, I'm not saying that, but before I did, these would be my requirements.

1. The retailer would have to be in business, with a brick-and-mortar location for at least ten years. (That way, I would know they weren't going anywhere.)

2. A guaranteed lab appraisal or lab-grading report with the purchase. Also, never accept a lab-grading report older than six months! You never know where that diamond has been or what's been done to it since it was graded. If they are convinced their old diamond is so wonderful, have them regrade it.

3. A bonding document guaranteeing the diamond is 100 percent natural and not treated.

4. Lifetime breakage guarantee to guard against baked diamonds.

5. Lifetime cash buy-back to guarantee against any future customer dissatisfaction.

6. A lifetime exchange policy.

7. A lifetime trade-in policy.

8. A fair, provable price.

9. Free annual service.

10. Knowledgeable salespeople.

11. Good store reputation.

12. Takes all major credit cards.

DIAMOND GUY SEAL OF APPROVAL

Many unscrupulous websites are attempting to make money off my name—Fred Cuellar. When in doubt, if you don't see the Diamond Guy, I have not endorsed it.

FULLY BONDED DIAMONDS

They are the first fully bonded diamond dealer on the Internet. Fully Bonded Diamonds is a subsidiary of Canary Investments, Inc., the parent company of Diamond Cutters International.

HONORABLE MENTION: COSTCO

While generally Costco does not sell the quality diamonds that other fully bonded jewelers do, on occasion I have found a few diamonds that meet my criteria. They are still the first and only major brick-and-mortar retailer to offer an unconditional buy-back policy on their diamonds. Way to go, Costco!

CERTIFIABLE? LAB-GRADING REPORTS
ARE THEY JUST PIECES OF PAPER?

Every day thousands of people go to work in the major gem labs in the United States. They are there to serve the gem and jewelry industry, and above all, the consumer. However, there are limits to what they can do. Can you separate fact from fiction in terms of their capabilities? Here's your chance. Armed with information provided by the experts at Gemological Institute of America (GIA), European Gem Laboratory (EGL), International Gemological Institute (IGI), and American Gem Society (AGS), I developed the following quiz.

Each statement is either fact or fiction. Mark which statement you believe to be true and compare your answers to what the experts have to say at the end of the quiz. Good luck!

1. A lab-grading report isn't a guarantee.

    _____ Fact _____ Fiction

2. All major labs have the consumer's best interest at heart.

    _____ Fact _____ Fiction

3. Grading a diamond can be so subjective some of the labs use four or more graders to get a consensus.

    _____ Fact _____ Fiction

4. Lab-grading reports only represent a snapshot of the opinion of the graders at the time the report was taken.

    _____ Fact _____ Fiction

5. A lab-grading report and a certificate are the same thing.

    _____ Fact _____ Fiction

6. No major labs will do a lab-grading report on synthetic diamonds.

    _____ Fact _____ Fiction

7. GIA does not certify any person, place, or thing.

_____ Fact _____ Fiction

8. At an additional cost, all the labs allow diamonds to be resubmitted for regrading if the submitter is unhappy with the original results.

_____ Fact _____ Fiction

9. All major labs use the same criteria in determining color, clarity, and cut grade of a diamond.

_____ Fact _____ Fiction

10. GIA uses proprietary Sarin and/or Megascope machines to assist in determining the diamond's measurements.

_____ Fact _____ Fiction

11. All major labs calibrate their equipment before each diamond is graded.

_____ Fact _____ Fiction

12. Lab-grading reports could be null and void if a diamond is worn.

_____ Fact _____ Fiction

13. Lab-grading reports are 100 percent accurate within two grades in either direction in clarity and color listed on the report.

_____ Fact _____ Fiction

14. Lab-grading reports lose their purpose (even if the diamond isn't worn) as they get older.

_____ Fact _____ Fiction

15. Physical measurements like weight, dimensions, and proportions are absolutely objective.

_____ Fact _____ Fiction

16. If a lab-grading report "reads" well, the diamond must be beautiful.

_____ Fact _____ Fiction

17. If the lab-grading report "reads" poorly, the diamond must be ugly.

_____ Fact _____ Fiction

18. A lab-grading report tells you everything you need to know to determine the value of a diamond.

_____ Fact _____ Fiction

19. A lab-grading report makes the diamond more valuable.

_____ Fact _____ Fiction

20. The labs can detect all forms of treatment 100 percent of the time, including baking.

_____ Fact _____ Fiction

21. The labs can with almost 100 percent accuracy determine if a fancy color diamond is natural.

_____ Fact _____ Fiction

22. A lab-grading report is an appraisal.

_____ Fact _____ Fiction

23. A fully bonded appraisal based on the GIA grading system is more valuable than any lab-grading report.

_____ Fact _____ Fiction

24. To ensure the diamond is worth what you paid and holds its value in the future, it must come with a lab-grading report.

_____ Fact _____ Fiction

25. A lab-grading report will ensure that the diamond is not a blood diamond.

_____ Fact _____ Fiction

26. All the major labs use colorimeters to be as precise as possible.

_____ Fact _____ Fiction

Answers

1. *A lab-grading report isn't a guarantee.*

Fact: The opening line on a GIA lab-grading report states, "This report is not a guarantee, valuation, or appraisal." No lab wants to guarantee anything or leave you with the impression that they do, because if something goes wrong in the transaction, they don't want to be held responsible.

2. *All major labs have the consumer's best interest at heart.*

Fact: GIA's mission statement: To ensure the public trust by educating and serving the gem and jewelry industry worldwide. As a nonprofit institution, GIA provides knowledge and professionalism that will maintain the long-term stability and integrity of the industry while strengthening and securing consumer confidence.

3. *Grading a diamond can be so subjective some of the labs use four or more graders to get a consensus.*

Fact: In some cases, not even the four graders can agree, so they bring in more people to break the tie!

4. *Lab-grading reports only represent a snapshot of the opinion of the graders at the time the report was taken.*

Fact: Where that diamond came from and what it's been through (mounted, dropped, nicked, etc.) cannot be determined from the date it was graded to the date you receive it.

5. *A lab-grading report and a certificate are the same thing.*

Fiction: A lab-grading report is not a certificate. A certificate would authoritatively confirm the facts and a lab-grading report states a few facts but mostly subjective opinions. It was the jewelry industry (not the labs) that started the slang use of the word "certificate" in reference to lab-grading reports. GIA categorically states that they do not certify any person, place, or thing. In the past, I have often used the word "certificate" incorrectly. To be perfectly accurate, we should all be saying lab-grading report or document if what we are saying is opinion-based. EGL USA does use the word "certificate" on their grading reports, but they disclaim any responsibility for any errors or omissions in the report.

6. *No major labs will do a lab-grading report on synthetic diamonds.*

Fiction: According to Lynn Ramsey, publicist for EGL, "EGL USA is the only lab in North America to certify synthetic diamonds. However, we do not certify diamonds that have been fractured, filled, or any treated stones in which the treatment is known to be unstable under certain circumstances."

7. *GIA does not certify any person, place, or thing.*
Fact: As stated in the response to question #5.

8. *At an additional cost, all the labs allow diamonds to be resubmitted for regrading if the submitter is unhappy with the original results.*
Fact: GIA's response: "There are times when the grade of a diamond is at, or close to, a boundary point between grade ranges. For this reason, we offer services whereby a client may resubmit a diamond to be subsequently examined by additional independent experts, who may or may not render an opinion that differs from the original grading."

EGL's response: "Diamonds may be resubmitted at least two times if the owner disagrees with our grading. After two submissions, the owner can have a consultation with the senior graders."

AGS's Response (Peter Yantzer): "It's very simple. If the customer is not happy with our results and believes we are wrong they can resubmit it for evaluation again."

9. *All the labs use the same criteria to evaluate a diamond.*
Fiction: A.G.S. uses their own in-house system (such as A.G.S. 000) while EGL recognizes an SI-3 grade. In addition, none of the labs agree with each other on one standardized system for measuring proportions.

10. *GIA uses proprietary Sarin machines to assist in determining measurements.*
Fact: Sarin and Megascope machines can be ordered from the factory already calibrated to specific tolerances as requested by the customer.

11. *All major labs calibrate their equipment before each diamond is graded.*
Fiction: "Once a day would be ideal for us, but at least once a week," says Peter Yantzer of American Gem Society. "We fully service them once a year. With hundreds of diamonds being graded a day it is not cost-effective for any lab to calibrate before each evaluation."

12. *Lab-grading reports could become null and void if a diamond is worn.*

Fact: Because a diamond can be damaged during setting and while being worn, in my opinion, any grading report becomes invalid at that point.

13. *Lab-grading reports are 100 percent accurate within one grade in either direction in clarity and color listed on the report.*

Fact: Pinpointing a diamond to an exact grade is subjective, but pinpointing it to a range is not. Example: To say a diamond is SI-1 is subjective, but to say it is not any worse than an SI-2 or better than a VS-2 is objective. The FTC regulations state that a diamond must be within one clarity and one color grade.

14. *Lab-grading reports lose their purpose (even if the diamond isn't worn) as they get older.*

Fact: As was stated earlier, the time frame between the diamond's evaluation and its purchase date is unaccounted for. Lab-grading reports older than six months tell the consumer one of two things: (A) The diamond isn't beautiful enough to be snatched up right away, and/ or (B) The lab-grading report is no longer a legitimate reflection of the quality of the diamond. Old grading reports are a red flag.

15. *Physical measurements like weight, dimensions, and proportions are absolutely objective.*

Fact and Fiction: Leverage gauges, Megascopes, Sarin machines, and scales are temperamental. According to the manufacturers, if (and this is a big if) the equipment is clean and calibrated before each testing, the results are 99.9 percent accurate. If hundreds of stones are tested between calibrations, then measurements may be off plus or minus 3 percent. Because we already know that it is financially infeasible for a lab to calibrate their equipment for every stone, a separate Megascope or Sarin report must accompany or replace the lab-grading report to confirm its physical measurements.

16. *If the lab-grading report "reads" well, the diamond must be beautiful.*

Fiction: No one lab-grading report provides all the vital information. Therefore, it is possible for a diamond to appear to look good (read well) on its lab-grading report when in actuality it is unattractive to the eye.

17. *If a lab-grading report "reads" poorly, the diamond must be ugly.*

Fiction: The lab-grading report may have judgments that are misleading. Also, beauty is still in the eye of the beholder. There are a lot of diamonds that technically return a poor amount of light, are off color and heavily included, but are loved anyway by their owner. Never forget it's what a diamond represents that is its real beauty.

18. *A lab-grading report tells you everything you need to know to determine the value of the diamond.*

Fiction: A lab-grading report is not a guarantee, valuation, or appraisal.

19. *A lab-grading report makes the diamond more valuable.*

Fiction: Don't confuse a bonding document (fully bonded), which does guarantee value, and a lab-grading report. A lab-grading report is an opinion on the overall quality of the diamond and does not increase the diamond's worth.

20. *The labs can detect all forms of treatment 100 percent of the time, including baking.*

Fiction: Nothing is 100 percent, but the labs are probably 99.9 percent accurate on all forms of treatment with the exception of baking, where they are batting .750.

21. *The labs can with almost 100 percent accuracy determine if a fancy colored diamond is natural.*

Fact and Fiction: Fact on all colors except green.

22. *A lab-grading report is an appraisal.*

Fiction

23. *A fully bonded appraisal based on the GIA-grading system is more valuable than any lab-grading report.*

Fact: The fully bonded appraisal is the most comprehensive document you can get on the quality of the diamond. It includes every measurement (taken from a calibrated Sarin or Megascope machine), and a colorimeter reading where grade and type are listed and a consensus of four graders who all must agree on what the worst-case scenario is on the clarity grade. Then it is accompanied with an unconditioned lifetime bonding document to guarantee current market value and secondary market value.

24. *To ensure the diamond is worth what you paid for it and holds its value in the future, it must come with a lab-grading report.*

Fiction: Don't confuse a fully bonded diamond and a lab-grading report. They are two different things. Any quality diamond can come with a lab-grading report, but only about 2 percent of all gem-quality diamonds come with a bonding document.

25. *A lab-grading report will ensure the diamond is not a blood diamond.*

Fiction: The only document in the world that can do that is a country of origin certificate.

26. *All the major labs use colorimeters to be as precise as possible.*

Fiction: Officially, the labs do not use colorimeters at this time. Colorimeters do require constant maintenance and calibration.

Conclusion

Lab-grading reports came into the marketplace to stop widespread misgrading. Did it work? Yes, I think so. However, lately it has become more important what letter or number or percentage shows up on a piece of paper than whether or not that little shiny rock has personality or takes our breath away. It didn't happen all at once; it happened slowly. I see people make decisions on how much they will love their diamond based on what someone else's opinion is. When did we give up our opinion of what's beautiful? When did we relinquish our judgment? Any paper that comes with a diamond can only give you an idea of what you have. Want guarantees? Fine, make sure it's fully bonded. Want beautiful? Make sure it takes your breath away! Make sure every time you look at the rock, it reminds you of why you bought it in the first place; you found love, it found you. You're damn lucky! That rock, regardless of size or quality, is a symbol of that love. It shouldn't be a contest about how big your bank account is or how smart you think you are. Are lab-grading reports or appraisals or documents just pieces of paper? No. They are tools, guides, sign posts. No piece of paper in the world should ever try to tell you how you feel about your diamond. If it talks to you, listen up. It's letting you know that you are loved.

But what happens when you allow a piece of paper to dictate your decision? The following is an example of how in recent years our misplaced judgment planted a seed for corruption.

GIA's Bribery Scandal
By Martin Rapaport

(Rapaport—November 1, 2005) The diamond industry has the right to know: What has been going on inside the Gemological Institute of America (GIA) laboratory?

Have diamond graders and/or supervisors been taking bribes to upgrade GIA diamond grading reports? How long has this been going on? When did it stop? How many graders and stones have been involved? Who are the bribers? What is the GIA doing to clean up its mess?

Before going on, we at Rapaport have a few full disclosure statements of our own to make. Rapaport Group Companies in Israel, Belgium, and India operate GIA take-in windows whereby we accept diamonds for grading by GIA. We handle shipping to and from

GIA laboratories, customer service and payments for lab services as well as marketing and promotion of GIA laboratories. The scale of our operations with GIA is large and financially significant for the Rapaport Group.

Furthermore, this writer firmly believes in the values that GIA has supported these past seventy-four years. GIA's implementation of diamond grading standards, supported by a grading laboratory and educational system, has done more for diamond quality and pricing transparency, fair trade and consumer confidence than anything else in the history of the diamond industry. GIA's education and research protects the industry from fraud as it raises the technical, professional, ethical, and moral standards of our community. The GIA I respect "calls it like it sees it" no matter where the chips fall. It is more interested in "doing the right thing" than protecting its money or saving its reputation.

I believe in the GIA, not because of the buildings, the laboratories or our business with them, but because of the shared values that it supports. This belief in the GIA and our relationship with the GIA is not unconditional. Should the GIA move away from its core values, then we will no longer support or represent them.

So let me make it clear. We at Rapaport define integrity as an unconditional commitment to core values. Our core values include honesty, full-disclosure transparency, fair trade and meeting commitments. Our Group's commitment to integrity means that we are willing to lose money, reputation, and everything or anything else in support of our core values. Therefore, dear reader, we are biased in this report—because we admire the GIA for its history and values. We are, however, not going to pull any punches and, in true GIA tradition, we will "call it like we see it," no matter what the consequences—for Rapaport, the GIA, or the industry.

Background

Max Pincione's April 2005 lawsuit against Vivid Collection LLC, Moty Spector, Ali Khazeneh, and the GIA included a charge that Vivid made payments to the GIA to "upgrade" the quality of diamonds submitted for grading. Pincione presented Exhibit "F," a handwritten page showing details of alleged payments and upgrades. Exhibit F, which appears to be from the year 2000, contains numerous initials and includes the text "To Alina $3,500 For August in Full," "To Alina for September $3,500 paid."

Although the handwritten page allegedly provided to Pincione by an "informant" could have been written by anybody for any reason and may never hold up in court, in my view it looks authentic and like a listing of upgrades and payments for them. Upon information and belief shortly after the lawsuit was delivered to GIA, a GIA employee with a name very similar to "Alina" was suspended. As far as we can tell it looks like "Alina" was allegedly bribed to upgrade the quality of diamonds on GIA-grading reports. Obviously, further investigation and disclosure are necessary.

Rapaport News became aware of the lawsuit in August and published a brief article about it. In September, we began hearing false rumors of an FBI bribery investigation obviously driven by GIA's own internal investigation. Finally, on October 18, the first day of the Sukkot holiday, the GIA issued a press release announcing the completion of their internal investigation and organizational changes that included replacing GIA laboratory head Tom Yonelunas with Tom Moses and firing four employees.

Following the release of the GIA press release and the conclusion of Sukkot, I immediately traveled to New York and spoke with a number of people before writing this article.

While I do not have access to GIA's investigative report, I was able to develop a limited opinion of what is going on. As far as we can tell, the current situation is as follows: No one knows or can guarantee exactly how many, the type, or which lab-grading reports may have been affected by the bribers.

What we do know is that after a very thorough independent—and I believe honest—internal GIA investigation, only a handful of bribers have surfaced and the number of stones known to be affected are in the tens, possibly hundreds, and certainly not thousands. The bribing activity appears to be limited to large stones graded in the New York lab and submitted by just a few firms. GIA is expected to provide all details of its investigation to law enforcement agencies.

Furthermore, to the best of our knowledge and based on our own investigation, no diamonds submitted through Rapaport Group offices have been tainted in any way or were subject to any improper grading. Our policy is that we submit all stones with unique Rapaport numbers and the identity of the actual owner of the diamonds is never disclosed to any laboratory employees. While a highly confidential list identifying our numbers and the owners is provided to GIA management on an occasional basis, to the best of our knowledge, this list was kept entirely confidential and not shared with any lab employees or supervisors who would have an opportunity to change any grades.

Buyers are encouraged to carefully examine all large, expensive diamonds from all sources and to insist on a verification procedure if they doubt the grading standard. While grading reports are, and will continue to be, an excellent basis for trading diamonds, they do not replace the need for independent examination and the need to know and trust your supplier.

Full Disclosure

When an important organization like the GIA makes a mistake, the best and most honest way out of the problem is for the management of the company to take responsibility and make full disclosure of the mistake. Management should also apologize for the damages caused and carefully explain what they are doing to make sure that the mistake never happens again. Full disclosure is not only good public relations in that it enables the reestablishment of trust in the company and its products, it is also good therapy for management. From then on management realizes that they will have to operate in a fishbowl with their actions and reactions scrutinized by their board, the public, and even their competitors.

While GIA's press release provides important information, it is highly disappointing and problematic. It also raises a number of complex ethical issues.

First of all, GIA does not provide full disclosure of what happened— they do not straightforwardly admit that any employees have been caught taking bribes.

They do not name the people taking or giving bribes. While the diamond trade is being concerned, confused, and misled about the number and types of grading reports illegally upgraded, the GIA does not disclose the extent of damage even though it seems likely that only a very limited number of large diamonds graded in the New York lab are known to have been upgraded.

The GIA's refusal to name the bribers is highly problematic. By firing graders and acknowledging the existence of clients who are "implicated" in "improper attempts to influence the outcome of grading reports," the GIA is telling us that members of our trade have bribed the GIA, but they are not telling us who they are.

The GIA is inadvertently casting aspersions on their honest clients, implying that some unknown number of clients are bad apples, but not informing us of how many, who they are, or the types of diamonds that they deal in.

Why isn't the GIA disclosing the names of the bribers? Could it be that when there is a conflict of interest between the financial interest of the GIA and the integrity of the diamond industry, the GIA protects itself at the expense of our industry? Is this how the GIA fulfills its mission statement of "ensuring the public trust in gems and jewelry by upholding the highest standards of integrity?"

When a conflict of interest arrives, is it the mission of the GIA board to protect the interests of the GIA or the public?

GIA undoubtedly has "good" reasons not to practice full disclosure. The threat of damages from the Pincione lawsuit obviously encourages GIA's lawyers to limit public disclosure. On the other hand, the GIA is asking for the diamond industry's trust, and one wonders, what else would the GIA hold back? If bribes were taking place in Carlsbad (California)—would this be disclosed by the GIA or would management, after taking legal advice, take care of it quietly? Can or should the diamond trade trust the GIA?

But what about the GIA board? If the public interest is being damaged and the board knows it—don't they have an obligation to inform the trade and public? Is this to be done through leaks to people that have agendas? Is GIA's board to be exempted from the new zero tolerance policy?

Who makes decisions when there is a conflict of interest between the public, trade, and the GIA? Who has the right to keep secret activities that violate the public trust and/or information that enables the trade to defend itself and consumers against fraud? Are the ethics and morals of the GIA to be governed by well-intentioned lawyers seeking to protect the GIA?

COMPLICATED SITUATIONS

Now that we have provided perspective, communicated our strong words, and made our impassioned pleas, let's take a less emotional, more rational and realistic look at the situation. Other than a possible leaker or two, the GIA board consists of excellent people who really care about the GIA and its public trust mission. They and the GIA are currently in a tough situation. In some instances, whatever they choose is bad and it is extremely difficult to discern the lesser of the two evils.

Frankly, this is not a good time for us to attack the board and insist on idealistic, simplistic solutions to extremely complex problems and situations. Full disclosure is ideal and fair, but it is not a panacea. Applying a full-disclosure policy that is highly damaging to the GIA when appropriate alternative action can prevent abuse may be the wrong course of action. We must recognize that the GIA board has the right and obligation to make decisions that impact not only the GIA, but the industry and the public. We must give the GIA board space to operate and time to do what is right. Heaven knows, they have a hard enough mission as it is.

Having said the above, we emphasize that it is important for the board to carefully consider the full ramification of their decisions on all stakeholders, particularly the diamond trade. As a public trust entity, the GIA's responsibility must be inclusive and sensitive. While a knee-jerk, full-disclosure policy may not be appropriate in the current situation, alternative solutions for the problems generated by partial disclosure must be provided. Ultimately, the GIA must recognize that, with rare exception, what is good for the trade is good for the GIA and what is not good for the trade is not good for the GIA.

Let us now consider the issue of identifying the bribers from a different perspective—a purely GIA self-interest perspective. By now, it is clear that bribers pose a threat to the integrity of the GIA-grading report. If bribers are allowed to go on bribing, they will destroy the credibility of the GIA and eventually force the closing of the GIA laboratory and the GIA activities supported by profits from the laboratory.

If a grader specializing in large expensive diamonds gets paid $X per year, he can be making decisions over the year that directly impact the value of say, one thousand times X. Therefore, dishonest diamond dealers will always have an incentive to bribe graders/supervisors and graders—unless they are angels in heaven—are going to find it hard to resist the persistent and innovative offers of bribers. The more employees in a lab and the closer they are to the dealer community, the more likely it is that the lab will have graders or supervisors taking bribes.

Fortunately, there is a natural way to stop the bribing—deterrence through disclosure. Consider the game theory. If a briber does not get caught, he wins. If he gets caught and the GIA—in order to protect its assets and/or reputation—settles the case in a way that the briber ends up being penalized less then he has gained, the briber wins again and will continue bribing because he is in a win-win situation. By "protecting" its reputation, the GIA is attracting those that seek to destroy its reputation. The greater the GIA's reputation and the more "protected" it is by the GIA, the greater incentive for bribers to attack.

On the other hand, if the GIA—through full disclosure, civil lawsuits, publishing the numbers of suspected reports, or any other way—discloses or causes to be disclosed the identity of the bribers, a different game develops.

The briber suffers huge loss to reputation. The long-term monetary loss from such reputational damage far outweighs the short-term benefit of bribing.

Bribing goes from being a rational, though illegal, activity to an economically irrational activity. The lesson is simple. If we publicly ruin someone's reputation, the potential monetary loss is so great that it just does not pay to bribe (i.e., deterrence). If we don't ruin the reputations of bribers, they will continue to operate and eventually beat the GIA into the ground.

Our goal is not to provide the GIA with specific solutions to all problems, but rather to encourage and plead with GIA's board, management and lawyers to come up with their own innovative solutions. We recognize that the GIA is in a difficult situation. However, sometimes what we think is a solution creates an ever bigger problem. Sometimes our biggest nightmare is when our dreams come true. The bottom line is that GIA's board must consider and take responsibility for the unintended consequences of their actions.

Actions taken with the best of intentions are often the most dangerous.

The trade must also recognize that the GIA is going through a very difficult transitional period. Optimal long-term solutions to the problems at hand will take time to implement. Quick-fix solutions, although apparent, may be unsustainable and nonoptimal.

We in the trade need to make our points, turn down the hysteria, and work together with the GIA to help solve the problems at hand. We must recognize that the GIA will have to take a series of steps as it develops new processes for improving the integrity of its grading reports. The trade should expect and support a process of change that will ensure and enhance the credibility and integrity of GIA's grading reports.

Rest Assured?

The only amusing statement in the press release is that when dealing with the bribers, the GIA tells us "rest assured, they will be dealt with swiftly and decisively." Now I mean no disrespect to GIA, but having grown up in New York, I imagine that these bribers are pretty tough guys. "Swiftly and decisively"?—we are, of course, waiting and wondering. What is the GIA going to do, have their lawyers throw paper airplanes at the bad guys?

Seriously speaking, I doubt that the GIA, who is unable to name the bribers, is capable of "dealing" with them. While we can expect the GIA to forward their investigative report to the appropriate legal authorities, such authorities rarely act swiftly or decisively. Perhaps the GIA could initiate a civil lawsuit that would enable the disclosure of the bribers names and then the diamond dealers could "deal" with them.

The real issue here is why isn't the diamond trade taking responsibility for the rotten apples in our midst? The GIA is the well from which all of us drink.

The New York laboratory provides the 47th Street community with unique opportunities that employ hundreds of people. The GIA enables the entire diamond world to legitimize premium prices for the best diamonds. Bad people are poisoning our well. Clearly, our trade must take immediate proactive protective measures.

The press release issued by the Diamond Manufacturers and Importers Association of America (DMIA) on October 25, 2005, is a good step forward.

We believe that the World Federation of Diamond Bourses (WFDB) and International Diamond and Manufacturers Association (IDMA) should develop a joint resolution at the upcoming Mumbai conference that provides the following:

- Make it a violation for any member to bribe any laboratory employee.
- Make it a violation for any member to knowingly trade in any diamond whose diamond grading report has been improperly upgraded due to bribery.
- Require a five-year suspension for any member found to have bribed any laboratory employee or knowingly dealt in any improperly upgraded diamond.
- Require all organizations to post and/or give notice to all members, the individual, and company names of all those found to have bribed any employee of any diamond laboratory.

Such findings should be based on the conclusion of due legal process by the WFDB, IDMA members, or national court systems. Furthermore, we encourage the WFDB and the IDMA to establish a joint investigative committee that will collect information from members about any irregularities at any recognized laboratories. The committee should also consider publishing advisory guidelines as to the measures that laboratories may take to ensure the integrity of their grading reports.

RAPAPORT CONCLUSION

The Rapaport Group is deeply concerned about "improper attempts to influence the outcome of GIA-grading reports." It is our intention to use our available resources to fully investigate all aspects of diamond grading reports and bribery attempts. To that aim, we encourage members of the trade who have information about any improper behavior related to GIA-grading reports to contact the GIA directly and/or their local Rapaport offices.

Dear friends, what is going on now is not acceptable. Our information indicates that Pincione is planning a more aggressive legal approach and it is only a matter of time before the current controversy is picked up by the general media and the credibility of our industry is put to severe test. Grading report and certificate issues have now captured my personal attention and I will try to write more on this subject next month.

The fundamental foundation of the diamond industry rests on our integrity as a community committed to honesty. This foundation is now under attack. Hopefully, the GIA problem will be limited, but these events and this story must serve as a clear warning that we are in danger of losing the integrity of our industry and our products. Make no mistake about it, if we ignore this problem, it will not go away. Now is the time for all of us who care about our industry to work together and find ways to ensure the security of our grading systems and the integrity of our diamonds.

All rights reserved to the Rapaport Group. (See "Inside the Diamond Business" for more details.)

FINE PRINT
ARE YOU REALLY GETTING WHAT YOU THINK YOU'RE GETTING?

They say that the devil is in the details. If they are referring to the fine print found in contracts, grading reports, catalogs, and bills of sale, they are right. *ABC News* did a week-long special on how consumers are literally signing away their rights when they acquire a new product. Look at the fine print in the stack of papers you sign when you buy a new car or a catalog you receive in the mail. Fine print is everywhere! TV commercials that last sixty seconds give us one second to read the tiny print at the bottom of the screen. Lifetime warranties may have an expiration date (it's in the fine print). Many of us don't read the fine print, and if we do read the teeny-weeny sentences, they don't necessarily make any sense to a layman. They are written with such legalese that even a lawyer could not pin down the meaning.

In summation, people buying products are not getting what they think they're getting. When they eventually figure out they've been bamboozled, there isn't anything they can do about it. You didn't send in the registration card, so there is no warranty, or if you did, they have no record of it, or there is a catch-all phrase that leaves them unaccountable and you holding the bag.

The following thirteen fine-print sentences are the most prevalent and destructive to your rights as a consumer in the world of jewelry, lab reports, and jewelry insurance. If any item you contemplate buying is saddled with one or more of these fine print "viruses," then the potential purchase and subsequent enjoyment of that purchase will likely be compromised.

1. "Original prices may not have resulted in actual sales."

This one kills me! You almost have to read it a few times to understand what they are actually saying. This fine-print statement shows up in many consolidators' websites and in brick-and-mortar store catalogs. It means the price listed as the original price is bogus! Nobody on this planet or any other one ever paid sticker! The price exists to give you a sense of savings when you compare the "sale" price to the "original" price. This is how stores run those fake 50 to 75 percent-off sales and still make a nice profit. Anytime someone says you are getting a sale price, ask them to put in writing the fact that someone in this universe actually paid the original price. If they won't, the asking price is the real price; there isn't a real sale going on, and you need to take your business elsewhere.

2.   "Diamond-carat weights (ct) represent the approximate total weight of all the diamonds in the setting and may vary no more than .07 below the stated weights."

3.   "All total carat weights are approximate."

While the law (Federal Trade Commission) says that any diamond piece of jewelry sold has to weigh within .005 ct of its actual weight, there is an exception. The exception is when stated otherwise. Translation: any jeweler can tell you a diamond weighs any amount regardless of whether it weighs that amount if and only if this fine-print virus is posted on their website, in their catalog, or in any paperwork they give you! If you see it or ask if the weights they sell are approximate and they reply affirmatively—RUN!

4.   "The genuine gemstones in this catalog may have been treated or enhanced by heating."

This one is sneaky! Usually, this paragraph is followed by, "Generally, diffusion (sapphires), oiling or waxing (emeralds and opals), irradiation (blue topaz), or surface enhanced (mystic or twilight topaz)." The key here is generally. By using "generally," they can treat their diamonds with no further acknowledgment than this statement. Translation: you could spend thousands of dollars on a diamond that has actually been baked and is brittle! If you're after quality, stay away from any jeweler that alters their gemstones and hides the fact in the fine print.

5. "This report is not a guarantee, valuation, or appraisal and _____ has made no representation or warranty regarding this report, the article(s) described herein or any inscription described in this report."

6. "_____ Lab and its employees and agents shall not be liable for any loss, damage, or expense for any error in or omission from this document or for its issuance or use even if caused by or resulting from the negligence or other fault of _____ Lab and its employees."

7. "The client declared and accepts that a certificate, drawn up in accordance with the scientific methods applied by _____, cannot as such be disputed before _____, and _____, its appointees or _____ are on no account responsible for possible dissimilarities and/or differences that could appear from repeated examinations or as a result of other methods applied."

8. "All clarity characteristics may not be shown."

These fine-print viruses were all taken directly from lab-grading reports. Lab names have been deleted to protect the guilty. The purpose of a lab-grading report is to offer declarative, objective information that the purchaser can rely on in order to make an informed decision. As consumers, we're looking for guarantees. If we are told it's X, it should be X. We shouldn't be told it's X and then in the fine print find out it might be X and if it's not, the vendor cannot be held liable. Any lab report that has these slimy, small-print viruses should be disregarded as nothing more than propaganda. Any lab report whose opening sentence is "This report is not a guarantee, valuation, or appraisal," is as useful as a college degree purchased on the Internet. A lab unwilling to stake their reputation on what they say in their document serves no purpose. This is why the guild stores like Graff, Van Cleef & Arpels, Cartier, and Harry Winston are all using internal labs where the grading can be quadruple-checked in order to guarantee your purchase. If the labs don't clean up their act and lay down some hard and fast guarantees with their reports, the steroid baseball scandal will seem minor in comparison when tens of thousands of clients realize their diamond doesn't really match the report and their rock is worth less than 20 percent of what they paid.

9. "Diamond grades may vary."

I saw this little ditty in many department store (jewelry department) catalogs and mall jeweler catalogs. "Diamond grades" can refer to the clarity, color, and class of cut, so this little number can create a pandemic of problems. This statement literally allows the vendor to call the diamond any type of quality they want! "Vary" is so subjective that the deceptive jeweler could argue that "vary" means any number of grades off in any direction. Very simple solution here—tell the jeweler to put in writing that they guarantee every single characteristic they are telling you about or giving you in a lab-grading report and if it is disputed by any accredited appraiser, you can get your money back or a replacement—no questions asked. If they blush or hem and haw, get walkin'!

10. "Some styles may contain single-cut diamonds."

Single-cut diamonds only have 16–17 facets (these are usually small diamonds) instead of the standard 58. Little diamonds that don't have enough facets flatten out and fog out very quickly when they get a little bit dirty. No brand new ring should come with single-cut diamonds. If sparkle is important to you in your rocks, avoid these.

11. "Gemstone products are often treated to enhance their beauty. Some treatments may not be permanent and require special care."

This one is horrendous! They are saying that anything under the sun might have been done to your rock (baking, laser drilling, bleaching, etc.) and any side effects are not their responsibility. Not only that, they are stating their "enhancements" might not be permanent (the rock could fall apart) if you aren't careful. Any diamond, I repeat, any diamond that may have been treated needs to be avoided! Period.

12. "Photos may be enlarged and/or enhanced."

Okay, I get the enlarged part, so I can see what I'm buying better. But the enhanced part crosses the line! The whole point of enlarging is to see the fine detail. If the true detail has been altered to look better, then how do I know what I'm getting? Look, if I'm in a chat room and someone emails me a picture of Christy Brinkley and tells me it's her, aren't I going to be a little disappointed when I meet her in person?

13. "If the merchandise is lost, stolen, or damaged, it will be replaced with like merchandise or what it costs us to replace it."

This is known in the industry as the "like clause." Midcap insurance companies place it in the fine print so they don't have to match exactly what you originally had. With some insurance companies, "like" means within one clarity grade, one color grade, ten points of carat weight, and no provisions for class of cut, treatment, or fluorescence. Your half-million-dollar home burned down, and they want to give you a tent to live in, arguing that it is "like" merchandise because it also provides shelter! Any insurance policy with the "like clause" is practically worthless. Premium policies from Lloyds of London or Chubb do not have "like" clauses.

Knowledge is power. Now that you are aware of these fine-print viruses, they'll be easier to find and recognize.

Real versus "Fake" Diamonds
The Bellataire Diamond

"Should Jewelers start warning customers that the diamond they're buying could be treated for color, but there is no way of knowing for sure?"

That's a direct quote from *Jewelers Circular* magazine, September, 1999, page 92. What they are talking about, along with everyone else, is what could be "the greatest gemological crisis to hit the diamond industry!" That's at least what Gemological Institute of America President William Boyajian said at a symposium.

The Bellataire Diamond (formerly known as Monarch Diamond, previously Pegasus) is a nondetectable, color-enhanced, treated diamond that is now on the market and wreaking havoc.

The diamond is the brainchild of General Electric and Lazare Kaplan and is sold through a company called Pegasus Overseas Limited.

In a nutshell, here's what they do: They take an inexpensive brown or yellow diamond, heat it at high temperatures and pressure, and bake out the nitrogen or boron present to make it white. Like a twice-baked potato, with one exception—this one will leave a bad taste in your mouth!

Baked diamonds or annealed diamonds, as some people refer to them, though they are undetectable to labs or independent appraisers, have one major flaw: They are brittle! Moreover, treated diamonds have little or no secondary market value.

Insist your diamond comes with a bonding document to guarantee that it is natural, or you could just wind up buying one of the most expensive pieces of costume jewelry ever.

"FAKE" DIAMONDS

Many customers want to be reassured that their diamond is really a diamond. This should not be a major worry, unless you bought your diamond from a guy on the street. No legitimate jeweler, even one who might try to cheat on color and clarity grades, is going to slip you a piece of glass, a cubic zirconia, or even a synthetic diamond and try to pass it off as a real diamond.

The Yehuda Diamond

The Yehuda diamond, relatively new to the diamond marketplace, is named for Zui Yehuda of Israel. He's the man who developed the process of "filling" a flawed diamond to make it more attractive.

Here's how it works: Yehuda takes a diamond that has cracks on the outside and fills the cracks with clear molten glass. The cracks disappear. Using this process, Yehuda can take a stone with an I1 clarity grade and make it look like an SI2. The advantage of the Yehuda diamond is that you can get a slightly better-looking diamond without paying a higher price.

The disadvantages of the Yehuda diamond:

- You don't know how long the treatment will last. You might be wearing the diamond one day and it will look great, and the next day, the filler will fall out, leaving you with a flawed stone.
- Any repair work on the setting could damage the filler.
- Most people don't like the idea of having a diamond that's not all diamond. If you buy a Yehuda diamond, you might have a very hard time reselling it.

THE FALL OF THE TABLET OF TRUTH

Once upon a time, a long time ago, in a land far away, lived the house of GIA. In this house were the most respected and honorable knights. Every day they went into battle to uphold honor, credibility, and the search for the tablet of truth. Many would come from faraway lands to the house that GIA had built and ask but one question, "Does my rock of honor speak the truth? For if my rock is a mere pebble then I shall send it back from where it hath come and choose another." All were happy in the land of Debeerios until another family built another house that said their knights could find the truth as well. Soon, there were many houses. The houses of IGI, EGL, AGS, HRD, and others all proclaimed that their knights could foretell the truth of the stones of destiny better than the other. The land of Debeerios was in a state of confusion. Does truth have many faces? And if so, which face tells no lies? All the country's men and women were lost.

Then one day a great man rode into Debeerios on a white stallion. His name was King Bonding. Everywhere he went, the villagers would follow. He went to every house and spoke with every knight, and when he was done, he made a proclamation: "There are some knights in all houses that do not speak the truth or hold their tongues and speak only partial truths. To bring honor back to the stones of destiny, I will bless only the mightiest of stones. These stones of destiny that have been blessed by King Bonding will forever be known as the Fully Bonded Stones of Destiny! These stones can tell no lies for the value can never be disputed!" The land of Debeerios rang with happiness and joy, for truth had been restored. No longer could the knights of the houses distort the truth for their own selfish reasons, because if they did, they would never win the final battle with King Bonding.

The Federal Trade Commission requires a jeweler to disclose whether a diamond has been treated. But many jewelers don't have the expertise to know if a stone has been treated and may buy or sell a Yehuda diamond unknowingly.

THE IMPOSTERS

For six months, I slowly and methodically collected data on a group of gemstones I like to call the "Imposters." An "Imposter" is any gem that claims to be as good or better than, just like, as hard, more beautiful than, but cheaper than a diamond. The "Imposters" come in two groups, the simulants and the synthetics. Let's take one at a time.

The Simulants

A simulant is something that looks similar to a diamond but does not have the same properties (weight, specific gravity, refractive index, hardness, etc.). These would include CZs, glass, white corundum, Y.A.G. (Yttrium Aluminum Garnet), Graffs simulant, the Asha, Diamonelle, and Zirconite to name a few. Many of these companies (I won't mention them by name, they know who they are) make some pretty outrageous claims. Some say they have created a supersimulant that will sparkle and last forever. Well, I guess that's true, but for it to be true, you cannot wear it.

It's like those abdominizers that claim you can get rock-hard abs while you use their machine. That's technically true but only if you diet and exercise and use the machine! Most, if not all of these companies will give us a ton of technical data meant to impress us. For example, they will tell us how brilliant and sparkly their fakes are and back them up with Sarin reports, Megascope reports, brilliance scope measurements, and on and on. Look, nobody's disputing that a lot of these simulants are pretty (with the exception of moissanite), but the problem is their hardness.

Vendors brag about how hard their stones are and how they put diamondlike coatings on their rocks to keep them looking beautiful 'til the end of time. Then, they say, if we're wrong, we will give you a new one. So what! If they're wrong, why would you want a new one? If a particular brand of VCR broke every six months, would you be satisfied getting the same product again and again and again? One of the fakes I tested came with a guarantee that actually said, and I quote, "Should your gem ever become chipped, scratched, lose its optical characteristics, or otherwise become damaged as a result of normal daily wear, please contact us to arrange the return of your gem and the defective gem(s) will be promptly replaced. The warranty does not cover damages by another jeweler's work (during setting of the gem, or during repair of jewelry that the gem is mounted in) or damage due to wear during unusual activity such as rock climbing, construction, or other occurrences where common-sense would indicate jewelry is likely to be damaged."

Can you believe this? For starters, who's in charge of deciding what normal daily wear is, and second, where's the commonsense committee that decides when it is dangerous or not dangerous to wear your sparkly new "Imposter"? But you want to know the craziest part? It's the fact that your typical CZ runs just dollars a carat and some companies are selling their super rocks for up to $400.00 a carat! P. T. Barnum was right; there is a sucker born every second and two to take his place.

Most of the prettiest simulants I examined were hand-cut CZs versus machine-manufactured ones. And yes, there are companies selling them for a fair price ($35 to $75 a carat wholesale; $75 to $150 retail). Jewelers Direct and BodyJewels are companies that sell their product at a fair price.

Moissanite is another popular "Imposter" running as high as $500.00 a carat. They are more durable than hand-cut CZs but still no match for the hardness of a diamond. They are made by synthesizing carbon, hence making them doubly refractive. The biggest downside to these is their inability to obtain nice colors. All the moissanite I've seen has a grayish dull overtone.

SYNTHETIC DIAMONDS

In 1954, General Electric produced the first synthetic diamonds. A synthetic diamond is a rock that has all the properties (durability, hardness, refractive index, etc.) of a natural diamond but was made by man. Not to be confused with simulants (those that look similar to a diamond but don't have the same properties) like glass, cubic zirconia, or moissanite. Think about it: Man was able to create in a laboratory what it took Mother Nature one hundred million years (minimum time required for a natural diamond to incubate) to do. I'll tell you something more incredible! What didn't happen in 1955? Can you guess? That's right. No synthetic diamonds in the marketplace! Not in '56, '57, '58, or in the '60s, '70s, '80s, or early '90s! Man figures out how to make diamonds. Then man doesn't do anything with the discovery? Why?

Let's look at the facts. Right after General Electric learns how to synthesize a diamond (which, by the way, wins a Nobel Prize for P. W. Bridgeman of their company), GE is interviewed about the details. They say, "We've only learned how to grow industrial quality diamonds (not sufficient quality to be cut into a gem for a piece of jewelry but rather to be used for drill bits, semiconductors, and such)." It would be sixteen long, painstaking years before man would not only walk on the moon but also create a gem-quality diamond the likes of Mother Nature. GE is interviewed again, and I quote, "We've conquered the next hurdle; we can now produce transparent gem-quality diamonds in an attractive size. There's only one problem. They cost more to grow than to find, cut, and polish." End of story? Hardly! Another quarter century would go by when a little company called Gemesis Corporation would raise their hand and say, "I think I can do it. I think I can figure out how to grow a diamond cheaper than it costs to find one." The problem was very few people were listening, and those who did just scoffed. "If General Electric in partnership with De Beers can't figure out the secret to growing diamonds at a profit, there's no way some little start-up company is going to figure it out!" Know what? They were wrong!

Not only has Gemesis figured out how to grow white diamonds, but they've also figured out how to grow the tremendously expensive fancy colors—the blues, canary yellows, oranges, and even the million-dollar-per-carat reds! I know what you're probably saying, "Fred, if this is true, why isn't it in all the newspapers, on TV, and radio?" Well, the reason is only now have companies like Gemesis grown enough raw diamonds to be able to meet the inevitable demand onslaught! It makes no sense to go public when you don't have enough supply to meet the demand.

THE INTERVIEW

I once had the honor and privilege to talk to Carlos Valeiras (the president and CEO of Gemesis). Here is a portion of my interview.

Question: Mr. Valeiras, I know you've unlocked the secrets to growing diamonds that encompass all the colors of the rainbow, so what will you serve up as a first course to the diamond-buying public?

Answer: While certainly there is a strong demand for the whites, the canary diamonds (yellow) are easier to grow and will offer the best price point to the public. Using your words, that will be our first course along with the oranges.

Question: What kind of price breaks will you be able to offer from the naturals?

Answer: The canaries and oranges will be offered at about one third the going price of the naturals.

Question: You said that you can grow the whites. What's keeping you from offering the whites right now?

Answer: We can currently produce about six hundred carats of rough a month, and we're moving every piece! Since the canaries are more profitable for us and offer the best savings to the end consumer, we're not going to add the whites 'til we can fulfill the demand for the yellows.

Question: How would anybody know they are looking at a synthetic versus a natural?

Answer: All of our synthetics will most likely be laser-inscribed identifying them as lab created. The diamonds will be marketed under the brand name Gemesis-Cultured Diamond.

FINAL THOUGHTS ON SYNTHETICS

Synthetics do not appreciate in value and have no trade-in value. In April 1995, synthetic diamonds became available to the public, selling for about two thirds the cost of natural diamonds. There is no secondary market for these stones, so if you buy one, you're stuck with it forever. If you tried to resell it, you'd get back only 10 percent of your initial investment versus an 80 percent resale average for a good quality natural diamond that was correctly purchased. As of January 2008, it is not profitable to grow or replicate a real natural diamond of any impressive size with a high clarity or colorless grade. Yet if you surf the Web, there are over a dozen companies claiming they are selling lab-created diamonds, synthetic diamonds. Pure fiction. For the latest on synthetic diamonds, go to my website, www.thediamondguy.com.

MAKING THE PURCHASE
A FINAL REVIEW

1. Fill out the Gift Questionnaire Sheet.
2. Call all potential jeweler candidates on the phone and have them answer questions on the Jeweler Questionnaire Sheet.
3. After you've called all the jewelry stores that you're planning to compare and have filled out a Jeweler Questionnaire Sheet on each one, pick the top three stores.
4. If for any reason you cannot find a jeweler in your area that satisfies all the requirements, call my HelpLine for assistance (800-275-4047).
5. Before you visit your jeweler choices, call each one and make an appointment. By making an appointment, you can be assured that you will get individual attention.

6. Once in the jewelry store, look at the diamonds they have to offer. Write down the clarity and color grade of each stone you like and fill out the Proportion Questionnaire Sheet on each stone. Only consider purchasing diamonds that match the carat weight, clarity, and color you like and pass the Proportion Questionnaire Sheet. Their prices should also be close to the recommended prices listed in this book.

Chapter 5

Tricks of the Trade

BLUE DIAMOND BLUES

Some jewelers may try to market a "blue-white" diamond as though it were a white diamond with a hint of blue and more valuable than a plain white diamond. It's not! It's a diamond that fluoresces blue and is therefore less valuable. Avoid it!

THE "50% OFF" SALE

Browsing through your Sunday paper, you spot an exciting ad: a local jeweler is having a "50% Off " sale on diamonds! Wow! You jump into your car, drive to the store, and you make what you are sure is an incredible buy on a one-carat diamond.

You're still patting yourself on the back a week later when you happen to walk past another jewelry store where you see the same size, same quality diamond selling for less than what you paid—*and it's their regular price!* What happened?

You were taken in by a fake sale. Many jewelers run these sales. They'll take a diamond that is worth, say, $1,000 wholesale, and instead of marking it up 100 percent, which is standard practice, they'll mark it up 400 percent and tell you that $4,000 is the regular price—when in fact the regular price for such a stone would be $2,000. Then the jeweler takes 50 percent off the inflated price and sells it to you for full retail, $2,000.

The way to know if you're really getting a sale price is to compare the jeweler's price with the wholesale price list in this book. If the jeweler's regular price is more than double the wholesale price, you're not getting any bargain.

For example, Joe's Jewelry Store has a one-carat VS1, G(1) on sale for $24,868, marked down from $49,736. You look at my price list and see that a one-carat VS1, G(1) wholesales for $16,524. Therefore, full retail should be $33,048. Joe has artificially inflated the "regular" price to trick you into believing you're getting a bargain.

"CERTIFIED": A DIRTY WORD IN TODAY'S MARKET

You see or hear the ads all the time: We sell only GIA, AGS, EGL, etc. "certified" diamonds with a "certificate" to back it up. This should tell you one thing: RUN! "Certified" is a word that is supposed to put you at ease and make you relax so you put your guard down, but in reality, the claim is meaningless.

The lab "certificates" are riddled with disclaimers that specify it is strictly a bought opinion and in no way guarantees anything, making the "certificates" worthless. The jeweler will pretend he bears no responsibility because someone else graded it, so who or what "guarantees" the diamond? Nothing and nobody! Any jeweler tells you that "certified" guarantees quality belongs in the same cell as Bernie Madoff.

Do you know where the safest country in the world to buy a diamond is? Hint: It's not the United States anymore. It's actually India, where jewelers are buying back the diamonds they sell to customers who aren't happy. "They're not just selling diamonds, they're selling security and trust," said Marc Goldstein from Rapaport.* India is the first country whose jewelers stand behind the merchandise they sell with a lifetime buy-back policy.

Currently about 20 percent of jewelers in the United States sell fully bonded diamonds (diamonds with a lifetime buy-back policy). Disgraceful! I'm sick and tired of seeing young couples down on their luck and being forced to sell their diamond to find out that it is only worth an average of 19.7% of what they paid. Their usual response when they find out that they have been taken to the cleaners? "But it was 'certified'"! I can't be more serious about this pandemic that is destroying the integrity of diamonds; please DO NOT buy a diamond from anyone who even whispers the word "certified." Let this be the year that we banish the dirty word "certified" from the diamond business forever and replace it with a fully bonded appraisal (F.B.A), leaving you 100 percent in the driver's seat. By refusing to buy any diamond that is misrepresented and only comes with a thirty-to-ninety-day return policy, you will never find yourself with a diamond you don't want and nowhere to turn. You can help bring back fairness to the diamond industry.

*Goldstein, Marc. *Rapaport*. December 2009. Vol. 32 No. 12. Pg. 49.

BAIT AND SWITCH

This is a term that's been around for a long time, and it's not limited to the diamond business. Bait and switch refers to anyone who runs an advertising special on a particular item just to get you into the store. When you go to the store, however, you're told that the advertised item is sold out. Then they try to sell you something else—invariably, something more expensive. The jeweler hopes that because you've already made the trip to the store, you won't want to go home empty-handed.

Don't be impatient! Many people arrive at the store determined to buy something and get talked into something they don't really want. Take control! Grade the jeweler using your Jeweler Questionnaire Sheet, and if he or she passes that test, stick around and look at some diamonds, using a scratch sheet to check each one. Compare the prices to the wholesale prices in this book to see what kind of deal you're being offered. And for an exact updated price on a particular stone, call my HelpLine, 1-800-275-4047 or 713-222-2728.

Is White Really White?

Jewelers love diamonds that fluoresce blue and will sometimes install special lighting to enhance the fluorescence of their diamonds. The blue masks the yellow color that might be in the diamond and make it appear to be a higher color grade than it really is. Always take the loose diamond you're looking at and place it on a white background to check the color, and make sure there are no spotlights shining on it. Always ask the jeweler if the stone has fluorescence. If he says no, ask him to prove it by placing it under an ultraviolet lamp so you can see if it glows a particular color. If you decide to buy the diamond, get it in writing whether or not the stone has fluorescence.

Grade Bumping/Soft Grades

The Federal Trade Commission requires that a diamond be within one clarity and color grade of what it is originally sold as. Because of this, jewelers tend to "bump" the grade. For example, if a jeweler buys a stone as a VS1(G), he'll bump it up and sell it as a VVS2(F). If you buy it as a VVS2(F) and have it appraised as a VS1(G), the dealer is legally covered, because he sold it within one grade of what it really was.

The Fraction Scam

Some jewelers will list the weights of their diamonds only in fractions, such as 3/4 of a carat. Your next question should be, "Well, is it seventy-five points or not?" Many jewelers will call anything from sixty-five to seventy-five points a 3/4 carat diamond. These same jewelers will call anything from ninety points to one hundred points a full carat. *This is illegal.* A diamond must weigh within *half a point* of its stated weight. You'll notice a jeweler will never round a diamond down—they'd never call an eighty-five-pointer a 3/4 carat stone. Ask the jeweler to weigh the stone in front of you on an electronic scale.

If he says he can't because it's in a setting, you shouldn't be looking at it anyway. Only buy loose diamonds.

THE OLD SWITCHEROO

You've shopped around, rated the jewelers, graded the diamonds, and finally found the stone you want. You lay your money down and order a setting. When you get the ring, you have it independently appraised—only to discover that the diamond in the ring isn't the same stone you purchased! The jeweler has pulled a switcheroo. You go back and confront him, and he accuses *you* of switching stones.

What now? There's really nothing you can do, no way to prove a switch was made. You must prevent the switcheroo before it happens.

When you decide on a diamond, get the jeweler to put in writing the exact weight and the clarity and color grades of the stone. Before the diamond is mounted, have the jeweler show you where the blemishes and inclusions are and plot them on a drawing. Keep this drawing with you, and when you return to pick up the mounted diamond, check it again, looking for the same flaws that are on your drawing. If they match, you have the right diamond.

THE SANDBAGGER

If you've purchased a diamond by following all my instructions, you shouldn't feel the need to go to an independent appraiser to double-check your purchase. But if you do, watch out for the sandbagger! The sandbagger is someone who lies to you and tells you that you've been taken, that your diamond isn't worth what you paid for it. Why would he do that? So that he can recommend where you should buy your diamonds—no doubt at a place which gives him a kickback! Or he may tell you, "You should have bought from me."

THE VANISHING ACT

Now you see it—now you don't! Carbon, that is. There is a laser beam process for removing carbon from inside a diamond. It's called *laser drilling*. A diamond that contains black carbon, visible with a 10X loupe, is zapped with a fine laser beam, which vaporizes the carbon, removing the black spot.

The problem is that the laser beam creates a *tunnel* from the surface of the diamond to where the carbon used to be. You might not be able to see this tunnel with the naked eye, but you'll see it under a loupe. And if a stone has been drilled several times, it can be weakened.

Laser drilling can make a diamond more attractive to the eye, but it can also lower the resale value. The Federal Trade Commission requires jewelers to disclose to consumers whether a diamond has been laser-drilled.

So, you think it's easy to get a good engagement ring? Or do you think you've already got a good one? Better think again. The cards are stacked against you.

THE DIRTY DOZEN

Twelve little facts you probably didn't know:

1. The average person in the United States pays twice what they should for their engagement ring.
2. One out of every three diamonds sold in the United States is laser-drilled.
3. One out of every fifty diamonds sold in the United States is fracture-filled.
4. One out of every two diamonds sold in the United States has been treated to some degree, including doublets, coating, and irradiation.
5. Seventy-eight percent of all round diamonds are cut poorly to salvage weight, resulting in diamonds that lose two-thirds of their potential sparkle.

6. Ninety-eight percent of all fancy diamonds (pear, marquise, emerald cut, etc.) are poorly cut to salvage weight, resulting in diamonds that lose two-thirds of their potential sparkle.

7. The average diamond sold in the United States with a lab-grading report may have been overgraded in quality by two grades to enhance its salability.

8. Two out of every three diamonds have fluorescence (a diamond's reaction to ultraviolet light) that causes the diamond to look oily and milky in sunlight.

9. One out of every five diamonds is weighed incorrectly to increase the profit margin of the jeweler.

10. The average diamond sold in the United States is tinted yellow and will probably never appreciate in value.

11. The average diamond sold in the United States has cracks, breaks, or contains carbon that you can see with your own eyes.

12. If we define a good diamond in general terms as a diamond that is big, white, clean, sparkly, and will hold its value and/or appreciate in value over time, less than twenty out of every thousand diamonds sold in the United States would classify as good.

TORQUING

Webster defines torque as something that produces or tends to produce rotation or torsion and whose effectiveness is measured by the product of the force and the perpendicular distance from the line of action of the force to the axis of rotation. Boy, like that helps. Sorry. To "torque," however, is a slang term in the business for overtightening with the intent of trying to damage the rock. Torquing is kind of like spiking a punch bowl or a disgruntled chef adding a little something to your entrée that doesn't pass the health code. Torquing is usually done by someone you may have purchased the setting from but not the diamond or a jeweler you stopped by for ring cleaning that didn't sell you the diamond. Torquing is the destruction of your property just like vandalism with you as the victim.

The scenario usually goes like this:

Jeweler (The Torquer): Good morning, may I help you?

Happy Couple (You & Fiancée): Nope, already have our ring, just killing some time.

Jeweler: Grrr… (under his breath) Killing *my* time!

Happy Couple: Excuse me?

Jeweler: Umm. I was just admiring your ring. Would you like a free ring cleaning?

Happy Couple: Oh my, that would be delightful! (All right maybe nobody says "delightful" these days, but it's my story.)

Jeweler takes the ring to the back and hands it off to the henchman, I mean bench man.

Jeweler: Give it the "they should have bought it here" special!

Bench Man: No problem, boss. One torque job coming up. He pulls out a pair of tightening pliers and crunches the prongs 'til he hears a high-pitched ping. (The high-pitched ping is the diamond cracking under prongs.)

Jeweler: Good as new!

Unaware Couple: Thank you; it looks lovely.

End of scenario

The mean, bad jeweler has now accomplished two things: One, he's vented his anger out on your ring, and two, he's set up the poor jeweler who sold you the diamond to take the fall when the pieces of the girdle fall off. When that happens, the M.B.J. (Mean Bad Jeweler) will hope that you are mad at the old jeweler and maybe you'll remember the nice guy who cleaned your ring for free for your replacement diamond.

What's the lesson here? Whoever you buy your diamond from sets it, cleans it, tightens it, and does all annual checkups. We want to keep all M.B.J.s out of our lives.

INSCRIPTION DECEPTION

One of the latest crazes is to have your diamond laser inscribed. What I'm talking about is the placement of serial numbers by a laser on the girdle of diamonds for identification purposes.

PERCEPTION

By placing a serial number on the girdle of a diamond that matches a lab-grading report, an independent appraiser can verify if the diamond matches the lab-grading report. Also, if the diamond is ever stolen and recovered, the serial number can be put into a database so the diamond can be returned to you. The inscription is permanent like a tattoo and cannot be removed or altered without a major weight loss or potential damage to the diamond.

REALITY

The only way to be 100 percent sure a diamond matches a lab-grading report is to check its measurements and match up its plotting of inclusions and blemishes. Anybody can take an extra lab-grading report and laser inscribe its number on a diamond that doesn't match it. If some common thug stole your diamond, having a serial number that matches your lab-grading report might bring it back to you, but it is unlikely. All sophisticated jewel thieves have the girdles repolished to remove the laser inscription so the diamond cannot be traced. This, of course, dispels the notion that an inscription is permanent and cannot be removed.

I have to hand it to all those companies that keep trying to come up with some new gimmick to hook us on. But come on; let's put this in the simplest of terms. If we already have the fingerprint (the plotting) of the diamond, we don't need to carve our initials into it to prove it's ours.

PILLOW TOPS

Cushions, Asschers, European, Old-miners, Rose cuts—all diamond cuts that are long gone, like the eras they flourished in. Gone like the flappers and the Roaring Twenties; gone like the Great Depression and the Zoot suits...or are they? Gadzooks, the Pillow Tops are back!

Practically every jeweler from here to Kalamazoo has resurrected Pillow Tops and is selling them as the diamond your "nana" used to wear! Well, guess what? Your "nana" got wise and unloaded it when she realized that the Pillow Tops are the most overweight, chubby, least sparkly, worst value of all diamond shapes! Looks like we have to learn the lesson all over again. The lesson: The rounds are the most valuable, and the Pillow Tops are just for show. If you want to impress for less bucks, then step right up and buy a Pillow Top. If you want to invest in the best, then avoid the inexpensive cushions and buy round. As a nation, we learned these lessons and buried the Pillow Tops over fifty years ago, but just like a bad cold that you can't shake, the Pillow Tops are back.

It kills me to see one customer after another be hoodwinked into buying these diamonds, which should have stayed buried. This resurrection was made possible by hooking celebrities into buying "estate jewelry," which was later copied by the general public. Please, if it's important to you at all that your diamond be worth what you pay for it, leave the Pillow Tops on your mattress and away from your fingers!

THE "TRUE WEIGHT" OF DIAMONDS

One-carat diamonds offered for sale rarely truly weigh one carat if cut correctly.

Let me explain. Diamonds are a lot like people. They come in all shapes and sizes, and just like people, they can carry a little extra weight. In fact, in the community of diamonds, more diamonds are "overweight" than in the community of people: up to 88 percent of all diamonds. The sad part is that it's the diamond industry that is purposely producing all of these chubby diamonds! In 1919, over eighty years ago, a gentleman by the name of Marcel Tolkowsky determined that the diamond industry as a whole was cutting diamonds incorrectly and adversely affecting the diamond's sparkle. Mr. Tolkowsky released a paper on the correct way to cut a diamond so it would have maximum sparkle (light return), no excess body fat. The Tolkowsky cut ended up becoming the American ideal. Subsequently, in the 1950s, a gentleman by the name of R. W. Ditchburn applied the same mathematics in order to trim the fat off the other shapes (marquise, pear, oval, etc.). For decades, if you asked for a well-cut "Ideal" diamond of a particular size, you got it. Then the marketers convinced the public that a one-carat diamond or more was the dream size. That's where the problems crept in. Diamond cutters all over the world started inventing their own criteria for "a well-proportioned stone" so they could fatten up the diamond. Clearly, we have a problem when 75 to 88 percent of all one-carat diamonds are overweight! Just like in the old commercial where there was a whole lot of bun and very little meat, we are running into the same problem today with diamonds that should be one carat but are cut fat so that they will tip the scales over one carat.

The only way the problem is going to be solved is for the diamond-buying public to start asking for the diamond's "True Weight." True Weight is a diamond in which the crown height plus max girdle thickness plus pavilion depth equals the total depth percentage and whose proportions meet class I or class II criteria. I've never met a jeweler who will volunteer to the consumer that the device used to measure the diamond's vitals (Sarin or Megascope machine) also has a button to measure fat content! It's called the recut feature.

Once a diamond has been analyzed, all the grader has to do is enter the recorded data into the recut program, enter the desired results (like a plastic surgeon showing you what your nose will look like after the surgery), and click the mouse. In seconds, the recut program will announce what the diamond should have weighed if it had been cut correctly v. its current weight. Practically every diamond I see is overweight by 20 to 30 percent!

It is the diamond's "True Weight" we should be paying for, not extra love handles left on by the cutter. If enough of us demand to only pay for a diamond's "True Weight" versus its "overweight," then maybe someday the cutters will get the message.

DIAMOND MYSTERIES
THINGS AREN'T ALWAYS WHAT THEY SEEM
Story 1—Mistaken Identity

It was a crisp February morning when Sarah finally got around to going through Gram's jewelry box. She opened the box of memories filled with charm bracelets, add-a-bead necklaces, sterling silver from her turquoise phase, and of course, "the ring." As the only granddaughter, the ring had been promised to her when she had barely learned to walk. She could still hear Gram's words echoing in her head, "Little Sarah, this ring used to belong to my grandmother. Bought on a railman's salary and some day it will belong to you."

With all the sparkling baubles and beads was a neatly organized stack of papers. In that stack of receipts and appraisals, she found the original sales ticket of $629 (a king's ransom in those days) for the ring. It was over one hundred years old. With that were a few appraisals that had been done on the ring, the last one dated Nov. 14, 1929. It valued the ring at over $3,100!

As Sarah slipped the ring on to her finger for the first time, it didn't make its way past her knuckle. Gram had lost a lot of weight over the years, and it had been sized down repeatedly. Gramps always took care of that before he passed away almost a decade ago. The ring would need to be sized again for her to wear it.

Later that afternoon, she went by a popular jeweler she had heard her friends talk about, had her finger sized, and left her heirloom. It would be ready by the end of the week. The next day, Sarah received a phone call that would change her life.

"Mrs. Allen, this is John Stevens. I'm the manager at McKay's jewelry shop. I don't know how to tell you this, but the center stone in your grandmother's ring isn't real. It's a diamond simulant. Something that looks like a diamond but isn't." Sarah practically passed out.

What happened? Was the jeweler telling the truth, and if so, how could that be because she had the original sales ticket and appraisals on the diamond? Also, if the jeweler was innocent, why had it taken him a day to discover the stone was imitation and not when she had brought it in? Is the jeweler the thief or an accidental pawn in a game of the vanishing diamond?

Keep reading to learn the answer to this and the following mysteries.

Story 2—Change of Heart

Michael had been dating Mary Katherine off and on for almost three years. It seemed every time they would get close to a commitment, some monkey wrench would send them back to square one. After a lot of soul searching, it finally dawned on Mike that even though he had told M. K. he loved her, he had never "put his money where his mouth was." So when it came time to clock out on Friday, he headed straight for the mall to buy an engagement ring. This would finally settle once and for all to Mary Katherine and the rest of the world that he wanted to spend the rest of his life with her.

Michael planned to pop the question on the following Friday, but by Saturday, it just slipped out, "Mary ah, M. K., Mary Katherine, will you marry me?" Mike stumbled for the ring that had been in his pocket since yesterday. "Well, just don't sit there, what do you say?"

"Um, ah, sure, wow, how big is it? You betcha."

During the next month things seemed to go the same between Mary Katherine and Michael, but there was something he couldn't quite put his finger on. Something was wrong. And exactly six weeks to the day Mike had popped the question, he found out what: "Mike, look," Mary Katherine started, "I've had some time to think about it, and well, I don't think I'm ready." She promptly handed the ring back. Before Michael could say another word, the woman of his dreams walked out of his life with a hug, a kiss on the cheek, and "Let's still be friends."

It took Michael two weeks before he could bear to look at the ring he had tossed in his sock drawer since the breakup. But with the sixty-day return policy looming, he didn't want to own the ring and not have the girl. So he headed off to get his refund. He felt sure the jeweler would understand.

"Hi, Mike, how's that new fiancée of yours doing? When's the wedding day?" asked Stan, the jeweler.

"Well, the thing is, Stan, it didn't work out. I'm going to need to get my money back."

"Jeez, sorry to hear that. Can I see the ring?"

With that, Michael handed over the little ring box of broken promises when the jeweler said, "Hey, Mikey, I don't know what you're up to, but this ain't no diamond! What are you trying to pull?"

"What am I trying to pull? That's the same stone you sold me! If something's amiss, it's by your doing!" The battle lines were drawn, and out came the sabers! What happened?

Story 3—Double Take

"So how much is the diamond?" asked Allen to the attractive salesgirl at Clark's Department Store. "The tag says it's $850. Got anything more expensive?"

"I believe so, but they're in the vault, and only the store manager, Mr. Peters, can handle that." As much as Allen enjoyed talking and flirting with the curvaceous blonde, he relented.

"Well, I guess I need to meet with Mr. Peters, but you have a fine day with your fine self!" The clerk excused herself.

Within a few minutes, Mr. Peters stepped out of one of the corporate offices. "May I help you?"

"Yes," replied Allen, "I'm looking for an expensive diamond, preferably loose."

"So," Mr. Peters said with a smile, "someone getting engaged?"

"Something like that," Allen replied.

"You said expensive, but how big do you think your future fiancée would like?"

"Let's not worry about her. What do you have in a loose diamond, must be round, 2.11ct?"

"Hmm, let's see, around 2ct, here's a lovely 2.02 VS1, E in a four-prong platinum, Tiffany setting."

"No, no, thank you," replied Allen. "Loose, I want to buy it loose."

"Okay, that's fine, but what kind of setting are you eventually going to put it in?"

"I'll worry about that later," Allen snapped back. "Can I please see some stones now? I'm kinda in a hurry."

"No problem. Let's see what I've got. How about a 2.05; its clarity is—"

"No, no bigger!"

"All right, how about a 2.20?"

"Okay." This piqued Allen's interest. "How much?"

"$55,000 flat," replied Mr. Peters. "It's an SI1 with an H color, ideal cut."

"Wow, that looks pretty good. I'll take it."

"Well, okay, sir." Mr. Peters was surprised; he'd thought this guy was wasting his time. "How would you like to pay for it?"

"Charge it, the American way."

Within fifteen minutes, Allen was on his way with his new diamond. When he got home, it only took Allen a few minutes to retrieve the Yellow Pages he had perused earlier. "Here we go," Allen thought to himself. "While You Wait Appraisals." He called and made an appointment.

"Mr. Richmond will see you now," said the small, soft-spoken receptionist at the appraiser's office.

"Thank you," replied Allen. Mr. Richmond sat behind a small metallic desk surrounded by microscopes, scales, monitors, and things with blinking lights.

"Mr. Allen Ball? How can I help you today?"

"Well, I just bought this diamond a 2.11ct, round, I mean a 2.20 round SI1(H), and I just want to make sure everything is on the up and up." Allen handed Mr. Richmond the small, neatly folded parcel paper that held the loose stone. Mr. Richmond took it, opened it, and let the rock slide out of the paper into an awaiting polishing cloth, where it was quickly covered up and rubbed.

"I'm giving it a good cleaning before we take a look." Within seconds, he opened up the cloth and gently dropped the stone on to a white pad that laid in front of him. There, he picked it up with a pair of tweezers and viewed it under a 10X magnifying lens. "Hmm, oh my, Mr. Ball, I don't know how to tell you this, but this isn't a diamond. It's a cubic zirconia."

"What? That's impossible! I know it's a diamond. All I need for you to tell me is that's not the quality I paid for!"

What happened?

Story 4—Now You See It, Now You Don't

Every day Margaret started her day with the same ritual: shower, breakfast, and a dip. Not a dip in the pool but a dip in the ultrasonic cleaner for her beautiful 2ct VS2 (G) round diamond anniversary ring. The ring was mounted in 18K yellow gold and meant the world to her. Four children, twenty-five years of love and devotion, six relocations, and one grandchild later, this ring was her gold medal.

Today, like all other Thursdays, she met with her gal pals for a roaring game of cutthroat bridge. True to her schedule, right after breakfast, she pulled down the ultrasonic cleaner from the bay window above her sink. Upon looking inside, she realized that she had allowed her ammonia and water solution to evaporate, so she would need to mix up a fresh batch. "Hmm, let's see. Where's that Parsons sudsy ammonia?" she said to herself as she looked under the cabinet. "Ah, here it is! Darn! Empty!" She glanced down at her ring to break the bad news that it might have to skip today's bath when it hit her. "Clorox! I bet Clorox will work. I've got plenty of that!" She ran to her laundry room, grabbed the Clorox, poured it in the ultrasonic cleaner, dropped in her ring, placed the ultrasonic cleaner back onto the bay window, and ran upstairs to get ready.

"Mrs. Williams," called out Maria, the housekeeper. "Mrs. Lawrence is here to take you to bridge."

"Now, Maria," Margaret said, "lock up and set the alarm. After that string of robberies in the neighborhood, I want you to be safe." Maria locked the front door behind Margaret and pressed the four-digit code to the alarm of the house.

As Margaret sat down to shuffle the cards to start the game, she realized she had forgotten to retrieve her ring from the ultrasonic cleaner. "A few hours of extra cleaning will do the ring some good," she thought. "Anyway the house is secure, and Maria is there for safekeeping."

The ninety-second warning signal for the alarm beeped when

Margaret opened the front door to her home. Within seconds, the alarm was disabled, and Margaret headed straight to her kitchen. She could still hear the ultrasonic cleaner running when she pulled it down only to discover her ring was gone! "Maria, has anyone besides yourself been in this house today?" she asked.

"No, Mrs. Williams, nobody, just me."

"Then where's my ring?"

"I don't know." At that moment, Margaret's husband Roy was returning from his day at the golf course and was soaking wet with perspiration; it had been almost 102 degrees that day.

"What's all the commotion Marg?"

What happened?

Story 1 Answer

There could be a lot of finger-pointing here. For starters, the jeweler should have looked at the ring under a microscope and determined its authenticity before Sarah left the store. Sarah should have insisted on a plotting (a mapping of what the interior of the stone looked like under magnification) of the stone to make sure she would get the same thing back. Both Sarah and the jeweler did a poor job of protecting themselves. Also, what about all the ring sizing that Gramps had done? Was it possible some other jeweler along the way had done the switching? Things aren't always what they seem. There was a very interesting clue that was right under Sarah's nose from the beginning. It was the date on the last appraisal: November 14, 1929. During the previous two weeks, the stock market had crashed, losing over thirty billion dollars in its assets. Was it a coincidence that as the United States entered the Great Depression, Gramps suddenly decided to get the ring appraised? No, it was no coincidence. During the court case against the jeweler, Sarah found a pawn ticket dated November 14, 1929 in her grandfather's chest! Apparently, times had gotten tough, and he had to sell Gram's diamond. I'm sure he had always planned to switch it back before anyone found out, but he died before he had had a chance. Jeweler innocent.

Story 2 Answer

In this little mystery, you've got three potential suspects, maybe more. For starters, the jeweler could have certainly sold a fake versus the real thing, but if he were smart, he would have plotted the diamond to prove he had sold the real McCoy. Also, if the customer had immediately appraised the diamond after the purchase, he would have known instantly if the jeweler had been up to no good. Also, what happened to the ring while his good little girlfriend had it? Could she have been devilish enough to have made the switch herself? Or was the culprit Mike himself? Finally, let's not forget the ring was in an insecure sock drawer that many people had access to. In the end, the jeweler had made the mistake of not plotting the stone to prove or disprove the jeweler's innocence or guilt, and the case went off to court.

Jeweler sued by customer, customer countersued by the jeweler. It wasn't until almost a year later and thousands of dollars in legal fees that old Mary Katherine confessed under threat of a subpoena she had actually switched out the stone. I repeat again, things aren't always what they seem. All the litigation would have been avoided if the jeweler and the client had done a better job of protecting their own self-interests.

Story 3 Answer

Believe it or not, this one isn't as easy as it might seem. Sure, the jeweler himself may have switched the stone when he had sold it (not likely, because if a jeweler gets even a hint of scandal of selling fakes, he's out of business), or we might quickly blame the appraiser for switching the stone when he had it hidden in his cleaning cloth.

Or how tough would it be to accuse the customer of setting the whole thing up himself? These should have been your clues; for starters, the customer purchased the diamond quickly, no negotiating and no asking for documentation. Allen was also obsessed with talking about a 2.11ct diamond, once when buying the 2.20 and again a Freudian slip with the appraiser. During the sale, Allen didn't want to discuss either the setting or the girlfriend, which should have made the jeweler nervous rather than anxious to sell. Everything here, from Allen flirting with the first sales girl to his reaction at the appraiser, points to Allen being up to no good. How else could his final statement to the appraiser be, "I know it's a diamond. I just want you to prove it's not the right quality?"

Here's what really happened: Allen had bought, using cash, a 2.11ct from another jeweler, a very poor quality but real diamond valued at $11,000. His plan was to buy a good one for $55,000, get the poor one appraised representing it as the one he had just bought, then act surprised when it wasn't the SI1, H 2.20 he had paid for. Then he'd call his credit card company, act shocked that the diamond had been misrepresented, stop payment, and leave the poor, honest jeweler with a 2.11ct piece of junk. A perfect plan but with one hitch. When he took the 2.11 to get appraised, he never thought the appraiser would switch it for a fake! In this instance, two people had their hand in the cookie jar.

Story 4 Answer

Surprisingly or not, the maid was arrested for the theft of Mrs. Williams's ring. However, in the end, she would be proven innocent. The ring had disappeared of its own accord, and as it turned out, Mrs. Williams would be shown to be the unwitting accomplice.

Here's what happened: As we already know, Margaret kept her ultrasonic cleaner in a glass bay window. We also know that it had been a very hot day. Combined with a Clorox solution, which should never be substituted for ammonia, all the elements were there. The sun through the bay window heated the Clorox, boiling the solution until the 18K yellow gold setting did the only thing it could do, and that was dissolve. When Margaret looked into the ultrasonic cleaner, her ring wasn't gone. It had just been destroyed. The only things that were left were her three diamonds that appeared transparent in the cleaning solution. Margaret became an accomplice to the disappearance of her own ring when she poured the solution with her diamonds down the drain.

As unbelievable as this all sounds, it's all true. I was the expert that was brought in at trial to testify to the value of the ring. When I heard about the Clorox, I put two and two together and got the maid off. Oh, if you're wondering how I proved my theory, it was when the plumber came in and removed the elbow of the drain under the sink and found Mrs. Williams' three little sparklers!

IN CONCLUSION

For practically two decades, I've done my utmost to be the best consumer advocate in the purchase of a diamond. I've told consumers about the tricks of the trade, fracture-filled diamonds, baking, and every dishonest thing a bad jeweler could do to take your money and leave you holding the bag. But with these handful of true stories, I wanted to show you how easily it is for the shoe to be on the other foot.

Every time a customer walks into a jewelry store, the jeweler is not only concerned with the hopes of making a sale but the fears his wish will come true and it winds up being the first step in a scam against him! Even as we saw in the first story, an honest jeweler got pulled into court because he had his guard down while he was trying to do someone a favor by sizing a ring he never sold in the first place.

The lesson here is, "I do believe that in the heart of man is goodness," to quote a great man and innovator in the retail industry, L.L. Bean. And we shouldn't be too quick to judge and cast the first stone. Even on the darkest days, there's always at least one light that shines in the distance, and it's the light of truth. Sometimes difficult to find, sometimes difficult to see, but it's always there. All we have to do is look for it. And please remember, things aren't always what they seem.

Chapter 6

Common Myths about Diamonds

◆━━━━━━━━━━━━━━━━━━━━━━━━━━━━━◆

1. A DIAMOND IS FOREVER

A diamond will only be forever if you take care of it. If you don't, a diamond can chip, fracture, or break. Even a diamond should come with a care instruction tag.

2. DIAMONDS ARE VERY RARE

Nope! There is more of a man-made shortage than a natural shortage. The distribution of the number of diamonds put on the market each year is highly regulated. There are really enough diamonds to give each man, woman, and child in the United States a whole cupful.

3. WOMEN ARE MORE SIZE-CONSCIOUS THAN QUALITY-CONSCIOUS

This one is almost true but not quite. Even though most women believe that bigger is better, there are still quite a few women out there that will sacrifice size to get a better quality diamond.

4. A DIAMOND IS THE MOST EXPENSIVE GEMSTONE

The truth is there are quite a few more expensive gemstones on the market. For example, a top-quality ruby can be worth over thirty thousand dollars a carat.

5. A LARGE DIAMOND IS ALWAYS WORTH MORE THAN A SMALL DIAMOND

Size is only one criterion by which a diamond can be judged. A small, high-clarity, high-color diamond can cost more than a large, low-clarity, low-color diamond.

6. AFTER A DIAMOND HAS BEEN CUT, LITTLE DIAMONDS CAN BE CUT FROM THE SHAVINGS

Usually, there are no shavings, only dust. Most diamonds are ground down, and there aren't any little pieces left over to cut anything else. Most people believe a diamond is whittled, not ground down. This is another myth.

7. A FANCY-SHAPED DIAMOND IS MORE DIFFICULT TO CUT THAN A ROUND DIAMOND

All diamonds, to a certain degree, are difficult to cut, and some very large diamonds take more time and effort to cut than smaller diamonds do. But one diamond is not harder to cut than another just because of the shape.

8. DIAMONDS ARE GOOD INVESTMENTS

Webster's dictionary defines investment as "an outlay of money for income or profit." Because most people purchase diamonds to be worn and not to be resold, diamonds are not a good investment. Only through proper education and training could diamonds become a good investment. For the average Joe, I would recommend buying a diamond for the enjoyment and prestige it brings and wouldn't be too concerned about making a buck.

9. A DIAMOND SHOULD BE BOUGHT STRICTLY ON ITS VISUAL APPEARANCE: "IF IT LOOKS GOOD, BUY IT"

A lot of people believe "what I can't see can't hurt me!" Well, we all know that blind ignorance will only lead to disaster. Practically any diamond looks good in a jewelry store. The jeweler spends quite a bit on spotlights to make any quality diamond sparkle. But unless you plan on carrying a spotlight with you everywhere you go, you'd better check the four Cs, or you might purchase a diamond that only looks good in a jewelry store and is lifeless everywhere else.

10. AN EMERALD-CUT DIAMOND IS THE MOST EXPENSIVE SHAPE OF DIAMOND

I don't know why some people believe this. I constantly have clients tell me that they like emerald-cut diamonds but know that they are the most expensive and can't afford them. This is crazy! The emerald cut diamond is one of the *least* expensive of all the shapes. You see, it is the shape that is most like the natural shape of the rough, so there is a little bit less waste during the cutting process. If you like emerald cut diamonds, enjoy them, don't avoid them; they are not any more expensive.

11. DIAMONDS ARE BAD INVESTMENTS

Diamonds may not be a good investment for the average person, but they certainly aren't a bad investment. If a diamond is purchased at the right price, it will most certainly hold its value. Since the diamond crash of 1979, when D flawless diamonds fell in value from $75,000 to under $15,000, the price of diamonds has been increasing constantly.

12. NO DIAMOND IS PERFECT

The definition of a perfect diamond would be a diamond free from inclusions and blemishes when viewed under 10X loupe (flawless), with no trace of color (D-color), and perfectly proportioned. Even though they are rare, there are such diamonds around.

13. IT IS DIFFICULT TO TELL THE DIFFERENCE BETWEEN A DIAMOND AND A CUBIC ZIRCONIA

Any good jeweler can tell the difference immediately. A cubic zirconia has more of a plastic look. There seems to be a light blue cast throughout the entire stone. One sure way to determine the difference is by weighing the cubic zirconia. A cubic zirconia will weigh 55 percent more!

14. DIAMONDS ARE EXPENSIVE

Some are, but some aren't. It depends on their quality. Believe it or not, it's possible to get a one-carat diamond for as low as three hundred dollars if it's junky enough.

15. DIAMONDS ARE A GIRL'S BEST FRIEND

This one would have stumped me, too. I've always believed that all women like diamonds. It wasn't until recently that I learned there are some women out there that very much dislike diamonds and think they are a waste of money. I guess for them maybe a dog is their best friend.

16. A DIAMOND WITH A LAB-GRADING REPORT MUST BE A GOOD DIAMOND

I can't even count how many jewelry stores I've gone in to and asked a jewelry salesperson if a particular diamond is good, only to hear, "Sir, it must be good. It has been graded by Laboratory XYZ! And only the best diamonds in the world can come with this lab-grading report!" Give me a break; any lab anywhere in the world will grade any diamond sent to them. Purebred or rabid dog, it doesn't make a difference to them. The labs just want their fee.

17. An ideal cut diamond is ideal

In the 1960s, jewelers tossed around the term "perfect" like they were passing out candy: "Sir, this is a perfect diamond." "Ma'am, this is a perfectly fine diamond." Or "Heck, this diamond is just plain perfect!" The FTC eventually stepped in and said the term was just plain misleading. Jewelers argued that they should have the right to call anything perfect that was perfect in their opinion.

They were overruled; the FTC passed a guideline that said only a D flawless, well-cut diamond could brandish the label of "perfect." The jewelers changed their pitch. Forty years later, we are hearing the same thing: "Sir, this is an ideal-cut diamond." "Ma'am, this is an ideally fine diamond," and finally, "This diamond is exactly cut; it is ideal!" Only one problem, FTC hasn't stepped in yet. And until they do, there will be over one hundred interpretations of ideal. But don't be fooled. It's easy to identify the scammers. They are the ones who insist that total depths can exceed 61 percent for rounds and nonrectangular fancies. They are the ones that insist on tiny tables for rounds and giant tables for emerald cuts. They insist that these measurements are ideal, and I guess in some respects they are ideal in increasing the weight of the diamond so their bottom line goes up. Want ideal? Be more specific and ask what class of cut a diamond is. In that arena, there are hard and fast rules.

18. Great symmetry equals great proportions

For the most part, symmetry refers to the arrangement of the facets on the diamond, length-to-width ratios, out of roundness, and inline culets. Symmetry, excellent or otherwise, does not infer great proportions or the relationship between crown and pavilion angles. If any salesman tries to imply that just because the symmetry on the lab-grading report is good or better means it must be a well-proportioned stone, it's time to leave.

19. ONLY DIAMONDS CAN CUT GLASS

There are a number of things that can cut glass. From synthetic diamonds to glass itself. Anyone who suggests that the best way to prove a diamond is real is to rub it against glass should have their head examined. This wives' tale should stay just that.

20. A JEWELER WILL TEND TO MOUNT HIS BEST DIAMONDS IN READY-TO-GO SETTINGS

On the contrary, a jeweler will always premount his worst diamonds in settings. That way, he can hide any chips under prongs and make it impossible for you to get an exact color and weight measurement. Always remember a jeweler's best diamonds are in his safe, and the only way to see them is to ask for them to be brought out.

EXPOSÉ

The Rock Talks

He's been described as a girl's best friend, socialite, movie star, tough guy, and he's been the subject of over six hundred books. He has been known to hang around royalty from Queen Elizabeth to as far back as Henry VIII. His list of friends past and present are the who's who of not only Hollywood (Marilyn Monroe, Elizabeth Taylor, Julia Roberts, to name a few) but of professional athletes like Ruth, DiMaggio, Jeter, and Chamberlain. His movie credits include *The Pink Panther, Gentleman Prefer Blondes, Diamonds Are Forever, Marathon Man,* and

---

hundreds more. He's been described as the silent type, but insiders have told this reporter that he loves to talk to women. We've finally been able to corral Mr. Diamond in this once-in-a-lifetime exclusive interview where he talks with such clarity and honesty this reporter had to dry his eyes more than once.

Reporter: Mr. Diamond, thank you for taking time from your busy schedule to talk to me today.

Mr. Diamond: Please call me "Ice." My friends call me Ice.

Reporter: Thank you. Ice it is. Tell me, what was your first big break?

Mr. Diamond: Break is probably a poor choice of words, but I dig where you're coming from. But nevertheless, let's call them opportunities. Without question, there isn't a success story that would happen without people who stuck their neck out for you. Friends who support and believe in you like Agnes, Charles VIII, Mary of Burgundy, the Duke of Burgundy, Oppenheimer, De Beers, Gerald, and so many others, too many to name in this interview.

Reporter: Ice, I'm familiar with a few of the people and organizations you mentioned. Perhaps you could give our listeners a rundown of how these select few deserve a mention.

Mr. Diamond: I'd be glad to. Agnes Sorel was the first person ever to believe in me. In the fifteenth century when she hung around Charles VIII, she became the first woman to wear diamonds in public. I had been a shut-in until then. I wasn't very good with people, a little shy.

Reporter: Shy? You? I don't believe it!

Mr. Diamond: Yes, it's true. Agnes believed in me enough to push me out of my nest and into the public's eye.

Reporter: What about Mary of Burgundy, daughter of Charles the Bold, Duke of Burgundy. What's your connection here?

Mr. Diamond: Agnes taught me to believe in myself, face the world, and not be afraid to be me. Mary, oh sweet Mary, taught me about love. Nothing in this world matters if you have love. She was the first person to wear a diamond engagement ring.

Reporter: And Oppenheimer, De Beers, and Gerald. I'm assuming you're referring to Gerald M. Lauck, past president of N. W. Ayer Advertising agency in New York?

Mr. Diamond: Of course I am, but let's start with Oppenheimer, chairman and CEO of De Beers. Oppie, even though not my first agent, was my best. He represented me like my father. He knows everybody and put me in the right circles. It was through Oppie's effort in 1939 that led to the introduction to Gerald Lauck. It was Oppie and G that hatched the plan to introduce me to movie stars and literally put me in the movies.

Reporter: Were you nervous?

Mr. Diamond: Maybe a little, but when Marilyn Monroe sang, "Diamonds Are a Girl's Best Friend," any butterflies I had went away.

Reporter: How do you account for the fact that in the 1920s, less than 10 percent of women in the United States wore diamonds compared to the almost 70 percent today?

Mr. Diamond: Because they didn't know me then, not the real me. Before Oppie and G started their publicity campaign, people thought I was aloof. I guess I deserved that because I only hung out with royalty, but I wanted the world to know that there was something more to me. That I had something to offer everybody.

Reporter: And what is that?

Mr. Diamond: If something grown from carbon can make something of himself, then the dream is alive in all of us. Nothing is impossible. We are all capable of grand things. If a rock can make it, so can you.

Reporter: Nice message.

Chapter 7

After the Purchase

◆━━━━━━━━━━━━━━━━━━━━━━━━◆

ONCE YOU OWN THE ring, you have to take care of it as you would take care of any major investment.

INSURANCE

As soon as you get home with the ring, take steps to get it insured. If you don't already have an insurance company, start shopping for one. Many insurance companies will only insure personal jewelry if you have a homeowner's or renter's policy with them. If you have to shop for an insurance company, use this questionnaire.

1. Name of company: _____

2. Will they insure jewelry? Yes ❏ No ❏

3. If yes, under what conditions will they insure jewelry?

    _____

4. What is the cost of the insurance per year per $100 of value?

    _____

5. Do they need an appraisal, or will the sales receipt do?

    _____

    _____

6. Do they need a photograph of the jewelry?

    _____

7. Does the policy cover loss, theft, and damage?

---

8. Does the policy cover replacement value at the time of the loss?

---

9. Following a loss, does the insurance company pay the insured amount or replace the lost article with a new one?

Dirty Diamonds
A dirty diamond knows no class

Regardless of what anybody tells you, the maximum light return for any diamond in any shape is 91% (give or take .1). Class 1; A.G.S. 000; American Ideal; Kaplan; EightStar; Hearts on Fire; or High-Definition; 91% is all you get. In the end mathematician Tolkowsky's numbers for rounds hold up, and mathematician R. W. Ditchburn, PhD, proved in his monumental book *Light* that the same concepts could be applied to any shape diamond. In simplistic terms, you need three things to appreciate the sparkle of a diamond:

1. An observer
2. A diamond
3. A light source

Remove any one, and you're left pondering does a tree that falls in the forest make a sound if there is no one there to hear it? Or better said, how much beauty can a diamond possess in the dark or how well received can a diamond be if never viewed?

I've spent the better part of my adult life helping people critique, evaluate, and eventually choose the best diamond for them. With each passing day, the diamond-buying public is becoming more savvy. However, many of you are buying magnificent diamonds, then allowing them to gather so much soot, dirt, oil, hand lotion, soap, hair spray, and grease that any benefit from buying a well-proportioned, white, eye-clean, gigantic rock is negated. Please remember this fact: A dirty diamond knows no class! Repeat it again, A DIRTY DIAMOND KNOWS NO CLASS. It doesn't make a difference whether you have a well-proportioned Class 1 versus a poorly proportioned Class 4 if you don't keep it clean. If you as the wearer of a new diamond aren't prepared to clean your diamond every day, day in and day out, religiously, then throw my book away or anybody else's book that you have read on diamonds! It won't make one bit of difference what clarity or color grade you have if you don't keep it clean! And I'm not talking once-a-week clean or clean-it-when-it-gets-dirty clean. I'm talking EVERYDAY clean! Take sixty seconds of your day to drop your ring in an ultrasonic cleaner. If you're not willing to do that, you've flushed a lot of money away.

If you're a man reading this and you're about to plunk $9K down for a one-carat diamond and you know your fiancée-to-be can't keep her own car clean much less a new diamond clean, then stop! Reevaluate your purchase. When the only benefit of a good diamond is increased light return (when clean), then don't purchase a good-quality diamond if the diamond can't be properly maintained. At the end of any given day, even the 91% diamonds will have only 67% light return because of the oil and dirt that accumulates from normal wear. Within a week, the diamond will look like a tropical depression has moved in, hazy and foggy with poor visibility. For off-makes (poorly proportioned stones), the effect is more rapid; within two days, lifeless city! But in the end, if neither the cheap, half-price Class 4 nor the expensive sparkly dynamo is cleaned, they will look the same!

I tell my clients every day a great diamond is like a battery-operated toy at Christmas. It's fun and exciting as long as you've got working batteries in the toy. Allowing a diamond to get dirty is like removing the batteries from the toy. Please keep your diamonds clean, and if not, trade them in for crummy ones and pocket the savings.

Remember, a dirty diamond knows no class.

DOS AND DON'TS

- *Don't* let people touch your diamonds. People seem to have an overwhelming desire to touch a pretty ring. Politely tell them look but don't touch. Oil from their fingers will quickly dim the brilliance of the stone, and the oil makes it easier for airborne dirt to stick to the diamond.
- *Do* clean the ring *daily*! Diamonds just don't look good when they're dirty.
- *Don't* wear the ring in the bath or shower. Soap scum gets trapped under the prongs and can make the diamond look dull. Also, it's too easy to whack the ring against the tub or shower stall, possibly damaging the ring or loosening the diamond.
- *Don't* be tempted by jewelry store window offers of "Free Jewelry Cleaning." Never leave your jewelry with a jeweler you don't know and trust. Unfortunately, there are jewelers who would use this opportunity to switch your diamond for a fake. Or they might not know what they're doing and damage your jewelry accidentally while cleaning it.

SOME FINAL SUGGESTIONS

1. Don't make an engagement ring a birthday or Christmas gift. First, if on the off chance she were to break up with you and the engagement ring was a birthday or Christmas gift, then she would be able to keep the ring. Second, the giving of an engagement ring should be on a special day all by itself—for example, on the one-year

anniversary of your first date. The more thought and preparation you put into this, the more it will be appreciated.

2. Once you've purchased the ring, as tempting as it might be to want to show off your purchase to your friends and family, don't. The showing off is for your girlfriend to do once she gets the ring. What you don't want happening is for everyone to say, "Oh, yes, that's pretty; we've seen it before!" One of the most exciting parts about receiving an engagement ring is showing it off and watching your friends and family's reaction to seeing it for the first time. Don't take that away from her. Once you purchase the diamond, don't show it to anyone. That will be her job.

3. If you can't follow rule two and break down and show the ring to someone and it happens to be a lady, don't—I mean don't—let her try it on. Some women are very superstitious about being the first and sometimes the only one to wear the ring. You don't want your wife-to-be to run into this person and have her say, "Oh, yes, I saw it last week and tried it on and told your fiancée that if it looks good on me, it will look good on you!" You're a dead man if this happens, and all the money you spent on the ring will go down the drain!

CLEANING YOUR DIAMOND
AND OTHER JEWELS

You can keep your jewelry sparkling clean at home with a little time and effort, but you should also take your jewelry to your jeweler twice a year for a professional cleaning and to have the stones checked to make sure the setting is tight.

A popular method of home cleaning is ultrasonic. An ultrasonic cleaner sends sonic waves through a cleaning solution to literally vibrate the dirt off your jewelry. Every morning you can place your jewelry into the cleaner, and in ten minutes, the jewelry is ready to wear. You can buy an ultrasonic cleaner for under $50 in specialty stores.

JEWELRY CLEANING

Philips has invented an ingenious product called the "Sonicare Flexcare" toothbrush. This amazing product can simulate over thirty thousand brush strokes per minute. The technology is so powerful that you do not even have to touch the bristles to a surface to clean it; as long as you are within 2mm of the cleaning surface, the pure vibrations of the bristles can do their magic. I really love this product.

If it does wonders getting to the crevices and cracks of your teeth, imagine what it can do for your diamond! Here's how it works: You soak the bristles and jewelry in a sudsy ammonia solution and then apply the brush to your jewelry. Sixty to ninety seconds later, ba-boom: jewelry is clean! Forget about having a big, bulky ultrasonic cleaner on your countertop. These toothbrushes take up a fraction of the space and do a much better job. It's the best of both worlds.

Not all ultrasonic cleaners are safe for all gemstones. Read the directions to be sure yours is safe for your jewelry.

You can also clean your jewelry by hand. Purchase a plastic container with a lid (24 oz.), a bottle of household ammonia, and a medium toothbrush. Fill the container with two parts water, one part ammonia. (Keep the lid on this solution—the fumes are pretty strong!) Each day, place the jewelry in this solution and let it soak for at least ten minutes. Take the jewelry out of the solution and scrub it with the toothbrush, making sure you scrub *underneath* as well as on top. Rinse with warm water, shake off the excess water, then dry with a lint-free cloth.

Jewelry Care Guide

Gemstone	Recommended	What to Avoid
Amethyst	Any ultrasonic; bristle brush*	Nothing
Aquamarine	Some ultrasonics**; bristle brush	Some ultrasonics
Citrine	Any ultrasonic; bristle brush	Nothing
Diamond	Any ultrasonic; bristle brush	Sharp blows
Emerald	Warm soapy water; bristle brush	Jewelry cleaner; household chemicals; treated cloth; sharp blows; extreme temperature changes; some ultrasonics
Garnet	Some ultrasonics; bristle brush	Jewelry cleaner; household chemicals; treated cloth; sharp blows; extreme temperature changes; some ultrasonics
Onyx	Any ultrasonic; bristle brush	Sharp blows
Peridot	Some ultrasonics; bristle brush	Jewelry cleaner; household chemicals; treated cloth; sharp blows; extreme temperature changes; some ultrasonics
Ruby	Any ultrasonic; bristle brush	Nothing
Sapphire	Any ultrasonic; bristle brush	Nothing

Gemstone	Recommended	What to Avoid
Tanzanite	Some ultrasonics; bristle brush	Jewelry cleaner; household chemicals; treated cloth; sharp blows; extreme temperature changes; some ultrasonics
Topaz	Some ultrasonics; bristle brush	Jewelry cleaner; household chemicals; treated cloth; sharp blows; extreme temperature changes; some ultrasonics
Tourmaline	Some ultrasonics; bristle brush	Some ultrasonics
Tsavorite	Some ultrasonics; bristle brush	Jewelry cleaner; household chemicals; treated cloth; sharp blows; extreme temperature changes; some ultrasonics
Zircon	Some ultrasonics; bristle brush	Sharp blows; some ultrasonics
24K Gold	Any ultrasonic	Treated cloth; sharp blows; scratching

** *I recommend a medium toothbrush.*

** *Some ultrasonic cleaners may damage certain stones. Check the directions that come with your cleaner.*

Chapter 8

"Will You Marry Me?"

THOSE FOUR LITTLE WORDS form what may well be the most important question you'll ever ask. The rest of your life flows from that question. It joins two families and begins a new family and determines everything from what you'll eat for dinner to where you'll spend your holidays to what your children will be like.

In other words, this question is a BIG DEAL! Too big to treat casually. You don't want to just pull out the ring box while you're watching TV and say, "Oh, yeah, I thought you might like to, uh, y'know... would you?"

Make it a moment you'll both remember forever!

She will remember it, every tiny detail of it—the weather, what she was wearing, what you were wearing, the time, the place, *everything*. She'll remember who she told first and what they said and how her parents reacted and how your parents reacted—everything. So take the time and make the effort to plan it and make the details come out right. Why spend a lot of time and money getting the perfect diamond only to have the big moment turn out to be a flop? The diamond is just one part of the perfect proposal. It takes thought, planning, loving attention to detail, and occasionally teamwork to create the kind of fireworks that will leave a lasting glow on your lives together.

Planning the Perfect Proposal: A Worksheet

Attire   Will you wear a tux? Maybe a gorilla suit to say that you're not monkeying around? Make a statement with your wardrobe.

Budget   Do you rent a plane or a limo? Take her to the most romantic restaurant? Feed her champagne and caviar? Determine what you can afford to spend on a once-in-a-lifetime occasion.

Location   *Very important!* The observation deck of the tallest building in town? A hilltop under the stars? On the deck of a sailboat? On a moonlit beach? Don't forget, it can be a "combo": first a restaurant, then the beach, for example.

Day & Time Pick a day that's special to you, such as the anniversary of your first date, or an evening when a full moon rises over the lake.

Food   Taking her to the first restaurant you went to together can be fun. Cooking her a meal is a sure winner!

Flowers   Absolutely! Whether it's great bouquets of flowers or a single red rose, flowers are a must for romantic moments.

Candy   Find out what her favorite is and present it as a treasure wrapped in gold paper and tied with a bow, even if it's a Snickers bar.

Accessories Take along a cellular phone so she can call her mother or her sister. She'll be bursting to tell everyone! If you can, set up a video camera to record the moment.

Scrapbook   Write down all the details of the moment—details that you (and your children) will savor in years to come. Include newspaper headlines from the day you got engaged.

FIVE PROPOSAL STYLES

Over the years, I've come across five basic styles of proposals. Which best describes your situation?

THE TOTAL SURPRISE

She doesn't know it's coming—not a clue, not a hint. You've never even discussed it. This is gutsy! It reminds me of the school dances of my youth, where all the girls were on one side of the gym and all the boys stood on the other. You'd finally get up the nerve to make that long walk across the floor to ask a girl to dance. If she said, "No," and they often did, the walk back across the floor was very, very long.

I figure fewer than 10 percent of all proposals are in this category. It's like doing a high-wire act without a net. Most guys drop hints first or get hints from her that indicate which way the wind is blowing. But there are the big risk-takers, the guys who live on the edge who just go out and buy the ring and make the dinner reservations and GO FOR IT! Hurrah for them, but—*I have to tell you I don't recommend popping the question "cold."*

SHE KNOWS

You've talked about getting married. You know you both want to get married and spend your lives together. You've talked about having kids. You've pledged your undying love. The only thing she *doesn't* know is when it's coming.

Men, the time between when she knows you'll give her a ring and the moment when you actually give it to her can be one of the greatest times of your life. Have some fun! Keep her guessing, plan the moment well, and when she least expects it, spring your wonderful surprise.

LET'S ELOPE!

"Will you marry me? Right now? Tonight?"

Wow! This one makes no sense to me unless:

- The pregnancy test came up positive.
- *America's Most Wanted* is profiling you tonight.
- It's her fifth marriage, your seventh.
- You don't want to give her a chance to change her mind.
- World War III has broken out and you've been called up.
- You love her so much you just can't wait.

IT'S NOW OR NEVER

Way to go—you've waited so long she's resorting to threats: "We're getting married, or I'll find someone who'll appreciate me!" Fish or cut bait, guy. If you love her, get off the fence and show her you can't live without her. If it's come to the threatening stage, you have to be extra, extra romantic to make up for her long wait. Use my proposal planning guide on page 208 and make it a great one!

Ringless

You and your true love are in each other's arms, caught up in a rising tide of passion. The dialogue goes like this:

"Honey, I love you!"

"I love you, too, sweetheart."

(Kiss, kiss, smooch, kiss)

"I can't live without you!"

"Oh, baby, you're the only one I'll ever love!"

(Smooch, kiss, smooch, kiss)

"Will you marry me?"

"Yes! Oh, yes, yes, yes!"

But does Romeo have a ring in his pocket? Nooooooo. So where do we go from here?

Don't think this lets you out of getting her a ring! Get that thought out of your head right now!

A lot of ringless proposals lead to a couple shopping together for the ring. Or, you could revert to the "she knows" proposal and keep her guessing. *Either way, the ringless proposal shouldn't be ringless for long.*

Soul Mate or Cell Mate?
Miss Right

She looks like an angel, she walks like an angel, she talks like an angel, but she's a devil in disguise! Oh yes, she is a devil in disguise! If these words sound familiar, it's because they're from an old Elvis Presley song, but they still ring true today. How can a fella know when he's got a catch or needs to throw her back? Sometimes it's difficult to tell, but the rejects will always tip their hand before the dealing is done. Let me share a few of my favorite stories about when some women dropped their guard to reveal their true intentions.

Story 1: Woody Allen and the Playboy Bunny

"Mr. Cuellar, your next clients are here. Shall I bring them back?" asked my assistant.

"Bring away," I replied as I quickly made an attempt to clean up my perennially messy desk. When I looked up, I saw one of the most striking, intriguing couples I had ever seen. She was a bombshell, a Marilyn Monroe type with an hourglass figure, tight, black leather pants, and a purple tube top that defied gravity. He, on the other hand, was ten years her senior and about five feet, six inches tall with a comb-over and Woody Allen glasses. He probably weighed about ninety-eight pounds dripping wet and was wearing a short-sleeved baby-blue shirt with a pocket protector and charcoal gray, shiny polyester pants hiked up so high that they were looking for a flood. She was attached to his arm like an extra appendage and kept repeating, "Oh, baby, oh, baby, I love you. I love you so much."

As I asked them to be seated, I couldn't stop wondering what this guy's secret was. Genius? Wealth? Was he a lover extraordinaire? Who cares! This looked like the real thing. She hung on his every word and laughed at every corny joke. I was impressed. Love is blind! It conquers all boundaries. Good for Woody! Good for all men who aren't tall enough, buff enough, or handsome enough! This was a victory for geeks and freaks everywhere. Until…

"Mr. Cuellar," he said.

"Call me Fred."

"Can you point me to the restroom?"

"Sure. Go out of my office and take your second left."

"I'll be right back, honey!"

"Hurry back, love muffin. I'll be here," she replied.

As I returned to my seat after I let my new hero out, Marilyn's demeanor changed instantly. "So how long you been in this diamond biz?"

"Most of my life," I replied.

"Must be raking it in, huh?"

"I do okay," I replied.

"Look, I can break free from the doofus in a heartbeat. Let's hook up."

"What? You're here getting an engagement ring. What the hell are you talking about?"

"Ah, I'm just here getting the ring. Then I'm splittin'!"

"Mr. Cuellar, can I let your client back in?" Lesa rang in on the intercom. Within seconds, the couple was reunited, and the game began again.

"Oh baby, you was gone so long! You know better than to leave honey bunny so long," she said as she gave me a wink and a smile.

How your woman acts when she's not around you is probably more important that how she does when she's with you. Always look at both sides of the coin.

Story 2: Big Rock or I Walk

When I returned from lunch, my next clients were already seated in my office, waiting for me. "Hi, guys, how's everything going? I'm Fred Cuellar."

"I'm looking for a three-carat, round, VVS1, D diamond and not a bit less," she snapped back.

"Well," I said. "The lady knows her diamonds! How does that sound to you, sir?"

"It doesn't make a difference to him. He's just here to write the check!"

"Sounds like the rough part," I replied. He smiled; she didn't.

"Well, I guess we'd better get down to it. Let's pull out some diamonds." I reached into my drawer, pulled out a lovely two-carat diamond, placed it in a mounting, and handed it over. "Here you go, a beautiful three-carat, round, VVS1, D diamond, just like the lady ordered!"

She smiled, but it would be the last time. "You see, now that's a rock. That's what I'm talking about!" she said.

"Really?" I asked. "Do you think you could be happy with that?"

"Oh, yes," she replied. "It fits my hand like a glove."

"Well, that's wonderful, because you'll be glad to know it's really a two-carat, not a three-carat, and that should save you over $10,000!"

Again, he smiled, but she didn't. "What!" she bellowed. "You said it was a three-carat!"

"I lied. I just wanted to see if you could tell the difference, and since you can't, you might as well save the money."

"Look, I don't know what you're up to, but either I get a three-carat, or I walk."

It was probably wrong of me to stick my nose where it didn't belong. Maybe I should have pulled out a three-carat from the get-go and let this couple be on their way. But she angered me. Because I had spoken with the man on the phone previously, I knew going in that this wasn't a man of great wealth. He was thirty-nine, never married before, and was going to have to get a loan to purchase the ring. So when she started spouting demands, I guess I lost my cool. What's the lesson here? Love doesn't come with a price tag.

Story 3: A Class Act

"Miss Ward is on the phone," chimed my assistant.

"Any idea who she is?" I asked.

"Says her fiancé bought a diamond from you and she would like to talk to you."

"Put her through…Fred Cuellar here!"

"Hi, Mr. Cuellar. I…I…don't know where to start," Miss Ward said and began to cry.

"Calm down, calm down. Whatever the problem is, I'm sure we can fix it. Just start at the beginning."

"Well, you see, last night, my boyfriend proposed to me, and it was so wonderful. Dinner, dancing, and your beautiful ring!"

"Sounds pretty good so far. What's the problem?" I said.

"He can't afford it. I know he can't. He's between jobs, and he just went overboard."

"Well," I said, "have you told this to him?"

"Oh, no. He's so proud of my diamond, how he researched it, shopped around—it would just crush him!"

"Well, what can I do?"

"I'd like to give you some money, then have you call him and tell him you overcharged him and need to return some of his money. You see," she said, "he has a job interview coming up, and he needs a new suit. With the money he gets back, he can get the suit and hopefully get the job. The diamond is pretty, but I have to take care of my man."

The good ones always pick you up when you fall; the great ones don't let you fall at all.

MR. RIGHT

Tall, dark, and handsome? Knight in shining armor? Or is the dude a dud? Ladies, now it's your turn. For every woman playing games, there are probably ten men who have mastered the art of deception. Here are my stories.

Story 1: The List

One late Friday afternoon, I sat down with a man I affectionately call the List Maker. Not really different from most of the anal retentive men you've ever met, with the exception that this man had gone too far. His life had become a list—a list of pros and cons, check and balances, pluses and minuses. Every action had been carefully scripted according to a plan that must have been meticulously thought out over and over.

"Mr. Cuellar, it appears it's time for me to get married, so I'm going to need a diamond."

"Congratulations. Who's the lucky lady?"

"Don't have one," he replied, "but I will."

"Wait a minute. Don't you have this backward—first you find the girl. Then you get the diamond?"

"Nope, the girl will be the easy part. There are plenty of women looking to be a homemaker. But to get her, I'm going to need a diamond."

"Do you mind if I ask you a question?"

"Shoot!" he said.

"Where does love fall into all of this?"

"Haven't you heard?" he replied.

"Heard what?" I said.

"Only fools fall in love! Marriage is a partnership, a legal agreement to share responsibilities. You know, two heads are better than one. Love is nothing more than a fancy word for convenience."

Don't want to be lonely? Get a pet. Need a homemaker? Hire a maid. Love is not convenience. Love is magic.

Story 2: What She Doesn't Know Won't Hurt Her

"Good morning. What can I do for you two today?"

"Well, my name is Max, and this is my fiancée. We're getting married at the end of the year, and whatever kind of diamond my lady wants, she gets."

"What size would you like to start with?" I asked.

"We want a big one because the best deserves the best. Let's try five carats."

"Oh, honey!" she exclaimed. "I don't need a big diamond! In fact, any size will do."

"Nope," he said. "The best deserves the best! Price is no object."

Within thirty minutes, they had chosen a lovely six-carat platinum and diamond ring for $82,000. He pulled out his platinum American Express card for the deposit, and they were on their way. I don't think I had ever seen a smile as wide as hers was when she left. About an hour later came the phone call.

"Fred?"

"Yes?"

"This is Max."

"Oh, hi, Max. Any questions that need answering that I didn't cover?"

"Nope, just one adjustment."

"What's that?" I said.

"Please exchange the diamonds out for cubic zirconias. What she doesn't know won't hurt her."

Not everything we see should be believed, and not everything we believe can be seen. It's okay to trust people, but be sure to cut the deck.

Story 3: The Shoe Box

Mr. Schwartz stood all of five feet, four inches tall. By the age of sixty-four, he had been married forty-two years, had two daughters, and four grandchildren. He had been an industrial engineer (garbage collector) since he had dropped out of high school to marry his childhood sweet-heart, who would soon be having their first child. I still remember the first day I met him. I commented on his Members Only jacket that had been all the rage in the '70s. "Oh, this old thing? You'd be surprised what people throw away. Sylvia, that's my wife, just sewed up a torn pocket and bada bing, bada boom, good as new."

The second thing I noticed was an old tan shoe box under his arm. When he laid it down on my desk, I saw that the words "Rainbow's End" were scribbled on the top in pencil. "You're wondering what's inside, aren't ya, son?" he asked me.

"Maybe a little bit," I replied.

"Well, let me tell you. It's the vacation we never took, the fancy meals we passed up, and a lifetime of bottles and cans that these two hands dragged home. That there is the one-carat-diamond ring I told her she would get someday," he said, pointing to a ring in the case. "Go ahead—count it up and be quick about it. My wife's waited long enough for her diamond rainbow."

A new, good quality, one-carat diamond was going for over $6,000 those days. I thought that this box must be filled with thousands of dollars—more than enough for Sylvia's dream diamond. But as I started counting the cash, there were more tens than twenties and more ones than fives. At the end of my count there was exactly $2,231.55. He was short—there would be no one-carat diamond, not with what was in the box. Maybe in the late 1950s, this would be more than enough for the diamond of their dreams, but not in today's market. The best they could get would be a half carat.

"Well, son, do I have enough? When can I pick up my one-carat diamond ring?"

"Let's see. $2,231.55. That will just cover it. You can pick up the ring tomorrow."

A good man keeps his promises even if it takes a lifetime; if you're ever in the position to save a dream, do it.

Note: *All the stories here are true with the exception of name changes.*

CRACK THE CASE ON YOUR BOYFRIEND'S PROPOSAL PLANS
TOP TEN SIGNS HE'S ABOUT TO POP THE QUESTION

1. He's cleaning his closet: If your boyfriend is finally tossing out that "private" box of mementos from former girlfriends, he is letting go of his past and is ready to focus on the future with you.

2. He's sizing you up: Your favorite ring is missing, and your best friend has been asking the size of your finger. Chances are your boyfriend is doing some investigating before visiting the jeweler.

3. He's cutting costs: Dates have gone from gourmet dining to drive-through dinners—if your boyfriend is suddenly a miser, he may be saving up for the special day.

4. He goes for the gold: You spot your boyfriend flashing a shiny new gold card—many men open credit cards with higher spending limits to make the expensive ring purchase and snag some frequent flyer miles in the process.

5. He's on the "we" channel: If his conversations no longer start with "my" but with "our," he is definitely ready to move out of singlesville.

6. He's family-oriented: Your boyfriend is enthusiastically organizing a get-together with both of your families. An anxious interest in "meeting the parents" is a true sign he's ready for the next step.

7. He's watching weddings: You attend a friend's wedding and are shocked at your boyfriend's commentary on the music, flowers, and food. Even more surprising—he encourages you to catch the bouquet!

8. He's letting go of "the bachelor" inside: He's sold his scooter and canceled his weekly poker games—a mature lifestyle change means marriage is sounding more meaningful to him than ever before.

9. He's a man with a plan: Your socially laid-back guy suddenly insists on prior plans, and instead of waiting until Friday night to plan your weekend, he's making arrangements Tuesday or earlier… he may have a certain social "engagement" that he doesn't want you to miss.

10. He's your dad's new golf partner: If a close connection has developed between your dad and your boyfriend, it's more than likely that they've had "the talk."

FOR MEN ONLY

Many a man in a fit of rage has blurted out, "What in the name of God does my woman want?" "I give and I give and I give, and she's still not happy!" I can relate. I've been trying to figure women out my whole adult life. Heck, even the better part of my adolescence was spent on the question. And it was always the minute I got close to the answer that I'd be sent blindly into a black hole of confusion. Women are a lot like golf swings: Just when you think you have mastered them, your next ball slices off the fairway. Women by definition equal confusion or that which lacks explanation. So, hand-in-hand with the search for the meaning of life, I ventured out on this crusade to answer the one question that seems to defy logic. What do women want?

At the beginning of my search, I had to accept the possibility that the question may not even have an answer. I mean certainly not all women think the same, so how in heaven can they all want the same thing? A single gal can't possibly have the same needs as a married gal. A career woman can't possibly relate to a homemaker. A teenager can't crave what a thirty-year-old might or, for that matter, what a senior citizen desires. Women are different, so they must want different things. Right? Well, kind of yes and kind of no. There are, if you look carefully, some common things all women want. How do I know? I asked them. Here are my results.

Women want it all or none of it. They want to be understood but not typecasted. They want to be happy but allowed to be sad. They want companionship but don't need someone to be happy. They want honesty but seldom the truth. They want equality while being placed on a pedestal; and most of all, they want respect. Respect for who they are, where they've come from, and where they are going. Don't pity them or coddle them. Today's woman is a woman of diversity and contradictions. What she wants today is not what she will want tomorrow because she is setting new goals. Men can't figure women out because they are a masterpiece in progress. A woman doesn't grow old; she just gets better. Wonder why you can't put lightning in a bottle? Because it just moves too quickly. Just like women. Ask your average man what 2 + 2 equals, and he'll say 4 every time. Ask a woman, and she'll say "looks like a little get-together." Women are always one step ahead and always will be. If we are to keep up, there are a few key ideas we need to survive.

1. Listen.

2. Listen.

3. Listen. See a pattern here? Men do a lot of hearing and not enough listening. Want to stay out of trouble? Listen. Want to be the man of the house? Listen. Want to have a long, loving relationship? Listen. My God, listen 'til the blood drips from your ears; listen until you want to scream out a solution; listen until she has nothing left to say; and when she's done, shut up and listen some more. Most women are the caregivers, and if you want her to give, you'd better do some caring.

4. Hug her. Hug her in the morning; hug her before you leave for work; email her a hug; and hug her ten times when you get home. A woman is a fire. Want to keep her burning? You have to fan the flames. You do that with hugs.

5. Don't lie. Don't white lie, and don't sugarcoat the truth. Tell it like it is. A woman can forgive a lot of things, but she won't put up with a snake-in-the-grass liar. If you screw up, lose your Christmas bonus at the track, forget to take out the trash, stare at another woman—give it up. Take your licks and move on. I repeat, a woman can forgive almost anything, but she will not allow herself to be disrespected. Lie to a woman, and you are dissing her. Tell the truth, you live to play another day.

6. Every woman I talked to listed structure in their top three needs. A woman wants stability, balance, and a sense of order. She wants someone she can rely on. You say you're going to be home at 6:00, you be home at 6:00. Running late, call. The hardest thing for us guys is to differentiate between support and total control. Creating

a foundation and stability doesn't mean trying to solve all the problems to the point that you disempower the one you love. Your love is not a crutch but a bond. A bond where dependability is synonymous with trust.

7. Love them. Love them most of all. Let it all out. Let it all out every day, every minute, every second of every day. Be love. Crawl up inside of it and approach every problem with the question: What would love do now? If you do this, fear will never enter your life.

What do women want? They just want to be happy like us. They just have a different way of showing it. Learn their language; listen when you'd rather speak; hug instead of walk away; tell the truth until it hurts; be a man she can depend on; and love her like you love yourself. You'll no longer ask what women want. They'll be asking you what you want and giving it to you.

When Is It Time to Get Married?

When I was a teenager growing up, there was a rock group I listened to called Three Dog Night. For those of you who haven't heard of them, they had over a dozen top-ten hits like "Joy to the World," "One," "Old-Fashioned Love Song," "Black & White," and "Never Been to Spain." One of my favorites was "One." The opening lyrics are:

> *One is the loneliest number that you'll ever do*
> *Two can be as bad as one*
> *It's the loneliest number since the number one*

I used to love that song and believed its message; nothing can be lonelier than being by yourself. Two can be as bad as one, or being with someone else can be as bad as being by yourself, but clearly, there is no hope for being alone. So when I ask the question, "When is it time to get married?" it almost implies a rite of passage we must undertake if we are to be happy. I mean, who would ask the question, "When is it time to stay single?" Naw, that makes no sense because the song clearly states two is the only number that has a chance. But is the song right?

After a lot of reflection, I realized that we live in a society where "one" gets a bad rap. Think about it. If a male or female friend of yours is single and getting up in age, nobody says, "Good for him, Mr. Independent!" No, everybody says, "What's wrong with him?" "Doesn't anybody love him?" "At least he has his friends." Or God forbid a woman! Turn thirty and she should be sent to a nunnery or off to spinster preschool. We are brought up believing in soul mates and not being completed 'til Mr. Right or Miss Right comes along. And you know what? We are wrong! Two may be less lonely, but two doesn't equal joy.

For example, have you ever been with someone so long that you want to pull out your hair and if pushed hard enough, you'd scream out, "Look, I just have to have my own space!" I bet you have. Look at the Buddhists. Inner peace and happiness comes from within when we find our center, our purpose, our reason to get out of bed in the morning. Look, I'll repeat the question, "When is it time to get married?" Or put a much better way, "When is it time to share your life with someone?" That answer is simple. When you know who you are, know where you're going, and have some idea of how to get there. Then you can figure out if someone is headed in the same direction and wants to share the ride of a lifetime.

Thirty-four Percent

A recent survey of women ages eighteen to fifty-four asked, "What was the single most important factor in choosing a marriage partner?" Thirty-four percent responded personal wealth. Personal wealth? What in God's name does money have to do with love, soul mates, and forever? As males, should we be mortified that one in three aren't looking for a sparkling personality or a winning smile? Or on the contrary, should we be happy that at least the numbers are in our favor? We have a two-out-of-three chance that who we are matters more than our purchasing power!

When I first read this statistic in a magazine, I couldn't help but take notice, 34 percent! To me, it seemed high. In an age when Destiny's Child has a number-one hit with "Independent Women," and Jennifer Lopez belts out "My love don't cost a thing," who the hell are these 34 percent, and how can single guys stay away from them? Now I guess if you see yourself as a nerd or a wannabe sugar daddy in training you might not care. But it seems to me that the rest of us want to know who this 34 percent is. Maybe we could get them to wear buttons. You know, something catchy like "You can't have this ass without some cash!" No, they'd never go for that! Maybe "With some money, you'll get lucky!" That's a little better.

On second thought, it just hit me that they don't want us to know because if we did, we'd pack up our gear and head upstream. Nope, sadly, the 34 percent are destined to be secret agents. Only when it's too late will their true identities come out.

Is the secret to act poor and then reveal we're loaded when they fall for us? Or try to borrow money for a month from them and see how they react? Nah, I doubt it. I think man's only ally is time. Don't rush it, take it slow, and be yourself. I imagine these 34 percent aren't very patient ladies (and I say that loosely). Yup, that's it. Take your time and see if your relationship turns to wine or dies and withers away on the vine. Yeah, that should be our motto.

COMATOPIA

More than a few decades ago, I was born in Kittery, Maine, the second child, the first and only son. My dad, a pilot in the U.S. Air Force (later a wing commander), brought me up with a code of ethics that I still use today. "If a job is worth doing, do it right the first time." "Be a man of your word." "Be a gentleman." There are a lot of life's lessons he taught me, but he never told me about "comatopia." True, it's a made up word, but it does have its origin. It comes from the word "coma" (unconscious, can't wake up) and "utopia" (a country of perfection). The irony is that "comatopia" is a perfect place to live, but you can't appreciate it because you're out like a light.

"Comatopia" is a land that every man, young man, or schoolboy will visit, is visiting, or is stuck in right now. We were not forced there against our will. We volunteered gladly. Let me explain: When a man/boy meets a woman/girl, his brain goes through an almost instantaneous checklist:

Face

Breasts

Booty

Legs

Then a quick addition followed by a question that, if answered "yes," is a weekend pass into "comatopia."

"WOULD I DO HER?"

The minute a man asks and answers this question to himself, he not only has entered "comatopia" but will be stuck there 'til he gets kicked out, takes a cold shower, or rounds third base.

"Comatopia" is a state of mind where a man says and does things purely for the possibility of a booty call. Is she smart? Who cares! Is she kind? Who cares! Are you compatible? Who cares! Who cares! Who cares! I'm in combat mode: get the booty, get the booty. Women, most of them, are more evolved. They have the capability of not just evaluating the book by its cover; they'll even skim a few chapters. Women make educated decisions. Men make "comatopia" decisions. There are very few women who will sleep with a man they don't like, but ask any man from "comatopia" the same question, and he'll snap right back, "What do liking somebody and sex have to do with each other?" I'm not proud that "comatopia" exists or that I've even visited there more than once. What I'm trying to do is make all men aware of it so they will stop making fools of themselves for superficial reasons.

1. You don't go out with a girl just because she passes the extremely low, low bar of "I'd do her."

2. Realize that big breasts do not compensate for character flaws.

3. Ask yourself if this new person in your life meets the standards of going from an unknown to an acquaintance to being your friend before you even consider how hot she is or isn't or whether you should do the horizontal shuffle.

4. I know trying to act like 007 may be fun, but women can see through a phony in a heartbeat. Be yourself; at least if you're shot down you won't spend the rest of your life wondering if she hated the real you or your poor James Bond impression. It's true that the truth can hurt sometimes and it may be brutal, but without it, we can't make adjustments at halftime to be a better person.

The key for men in finding "Miss Right" versus "Miss Right Now" is to fall for who she is and what she believes in, not how she fills out a swimsuit. If on top of all that she's beautiful too, you truly are a lucky man. But you know what? If you do allow yourself to get to know and fall in love with the person inside first, I guarantee the book cover won't matter. Just look at us. How many Robert Redfords and Brad Pitts are among us? Not many, but we're loved anyway. We can learn a lot from women and very little from "comatopia."

FOR WOMEN ONLY

The following articles are targeted at explaining, understanding, breaking down, and excusing what might be one of the toughest nuts to crack—the male species. Why he does what he does, why he doesn't do what he should, why he says one thing and then another, why some are scoundrels and some saints. We'll dive into the male psyche to hopefully shed a little light on what makes a guy tick.

Having been a guy my entire life and played the game, it's now time for someone to call a time-out and share with you gals the locker room's secrets most men would take to their grave. Enjoy!

SECONDHAND MEN

I went to an antique store to browse the other day. As I walked in, I saw a line of beautiful mahogany curio cabinets, a chest of drawers, and a rolltop desk that would have taken anyone's breath away. As I continued my stroll, I saw an eighteenth-century, four-poster canopy bed, hand-carved and meticulously taken care of, shining under a chandelier. "Looking for a bed, mister?" the spunky, old saleswoman asked.

"Nope," I said, "just looking around."

"You know that bed has quite a history behind it," she replied.

"Oh, really?" I said. "Fill me in."

She was delighted that she had piqued my interest. "Rumor has it Roosevelt himself slept on it!"

"No kidding? How do you know that?" I asked.

"His initials are carved into the headboard," was the quick reply. Sure enough, once she pointed it out, you could easily pick out the T. R. amongst the scrolled pattern. "Also take a look at this. You see the slight cracks in the wooden support slats that held the mattress?"

"Yeah, I sure do," I said.

"Well, that about cinches it, don't you think?"

"Why is that?" I asked.

"Hell, sonny, everyone knows he was a rough rider!"

I fought hard against breaking out into laughter but lost the battle. "No, no, that's OK, maybe if you just let me look around."

"The bed goes for $25,000," she whipped back, "but I'm willin' to deal."

"No, ma'am, that's OK, just let me…excuse me, what's all that stuff under the must-go sign?"

"That's junk nobody wants. Can't give that stuff away," she sniffed.

"Mind if I take a look?"

"Go ahead. It's all 75 percent off."

As I stumbled through the broken rockers and silver-plated candleholders, I saw something that caught my attention. "Whatcha want for the lamp?"

"It's broke. Don't work. Fifty bucks, and I'll wrap it up myself."

"Seems like a lot for a broken lamp."

"OK, OK, $35, but you wrap it yourself."

The lamp was probably a knockoff and would need rewiring, but I figured, what the heck. The leaded glass dragonfly pattern was pretty. "Okay, I'll take it." As it was being rung up, I noticed a curious, rusted, old stamp underneath the base of the lamp: Tiffany Studios. The lamp was later appraised for $80,000.

I tell this story for a reason. Most assuredly, Teddy Roosevelt didn't sleep in that bed, and a broken-down lamp in a junk pile can shine again and be worth a fortune. Men are no different. To some degree, we are all secondhand men. We have pasts, futures, and stories to tell. None of us comes to the antique store new. The question for the woman is, which of our stories are false and which ones are true?

The Scarecrow, the Cowardly Lion, and the Tin Man

All men—not some men—are either one, two, or all of the above. Knowing which one you have and how to deal with him will either make or break your relationship.

Let's start with the scarecrow. Unlike his title, the scarecrow is brave, loyal, and trustworthy. He would fall on a brushfire if it meant saving a life. Scarecrows are so kindhearted that their mates always take top priority. Scarecrows remember birthdays, anniversaries, and special occasions. Their downfall lies in self-maintenance. Their stuffing is always falling out. Their organizational skills are poor at best, and matching the right tie, sports coat, and slacks can sometimes be disastrous. Scarecrows are generally considered loners that avoid large crowds and will stay introverts unless forced out of the nest. Most scarecrows think they lack the brain power for success, but they're generally geniuses. If you don't mind a man with maintenance problems, who is probably a little sloppy, scarecrows make great husbands and can be molded with little or no extra effort. Don't get me wrong, scarecrows aren't wimps. They're just guys who are too smart to know how smart they are.

Cowardly lions are direct opposites of scarecrows. They are boisterous, loud, sometimes obnoxious, and very macho. They are extroverts to the third power. They are the athletes, the lawyers, and the salesmen. You see, to a cowardly lion, the "cowardly" is silent. To them, they are just lions—kings of the jungle. But the sad part is that it's just an act—partly for their benefit, partly for others—but it is still just an act. You see, ladies, men are a nation of opposites. If he acts macho, he's really shy. If he's shy, he's a conqueror, and hidden inside of every cowardly lion is a man that thinks if he acts tough enough and talks tough enough, maybe he can convince himself he's tough enough. Cowardly lions can make great husbands, but they are tougher to tame. If you don't get through the machoman act, you're doomed. Until the cowardly lion realizes he doesn't have to act tough to be a man, you'll never get anywhere. By the way, some cowardly lions are smart, but very few. Unfortunately, they spend much more time thinking about themselves than they do others. A cowardly lion's favorite saying is, "What's in it for me?"

The Tin Man, if you recall, was looking for a heart. That's probably the best way to describe a tin man—a man in search of emotion. Tin men can be accountants, engineers, even architects. Usually, they are great men—overachievers, men of logic, cause-and-effect fellows. The biggest problem with tin men is that they overanalyze everything and can be extremely anal. They have a sense of perfection that must be a standard for all others to live up to. Quite frankly, most tin men end up living very empty lives. They get left behind because they can never learn the art of compassion and the voice of the soul. Want to be a wealthy wife? Find a tin man. He'll be a great provider. Want to live a glorious life? Teach a tin man how to feel, how to touch, how to love. Give the tin man a heart, and you'll have a love affair that will never die.

Now don't get me wrong. Not all men are just one of these characters. Some are combinations—heck, there's even a Dorothy or two out there. But what you should get from this article is that there is no one definition of a man. We are all different, and if you're going to want to get to know your man better, it might be a good idea to know whom you are talking to.

SUPERMAN SYNDROME

Big boys don't cry. If you want a job done right, you have to do it yourself. Survival of the fittest. The boy with the most toys wins. A real man solves his own problems. Behind every good man is a good woman. Young boys are told a lot of things growing up. Stereotypes are created at a whim to please society and the world around us.

Superman Syndrome is the fallacy that a man ain't worth two cents if he's not a good provider and problem solver. Ever hear the expression, "I wonder who wears the pants in that family?" It stems from ignorance bred by the idea that a real man is head of his family and makes all the final decisions. It's that ignorance that turns young boys into men who think every time their family or their wife has a problem, they're expected to be supermen and solve the problem.

Real men solve problems—that's what we're told our entire lives. That's why I think men get confused when our mates tell us about their day, and instead of listening to understand and sympathize, the superman in us listens to fix, solve, and save. Most men don't understand that women don't need saving anymore. I don't know if they ever did. Women just want to be heard. Not solved or fixed, just heard and understood. Nothing has meaning until we give it meaning. A problem is not a problem until we label it one.

I don't know what women do when they sit around and share ideas. But I do know what men do when they group together. They tell war stories: battles won, problems solved, questions answered. We puff ourselves up, I think not so much out of ego but to help each other garner a little more confidence to take on another day.

You see, deep down, we know we aren't supermen and we can't solve all the problems, but that doesn't stop us from trying. Maybe this article should be targeted to men, telling them to stop labeling everything out of a woman's mouth as a problem and trying to fix it. But there is also a message here for women: Try to understand that when we don't have something to fix, we feel useless. I don't know how to make men better listeners, but if I could make one request, maybe once in a while when you do have a problem to solve, even though you can probably solve it yourself, you could be Lois Lane and let your guy be Superman. Because even if we can't save the world, we still want to be heroes.

Sophomore Jinx

In baseball when a pitcher is doing well (striking everyone out), they say he is in a zone. His fastball, curve ball, split finger, and slider are all probably working for him! He can do no wrong. He's got the right stuff. When a pitcher is getting lit up (hit on), they say he's lost his stuff, no zone, throwing up junk. He typically gets pulled for a relief pitcher. But if a pitcher does get lucky enough to stay in a zone for nine innings, twenty-seven batters, twenty-seven outs, and no walks, they say that pitcher has pitched a perfect game. In the history of baseball, few pitchers have ever thrown a no-hitter. Even fewer have ever pitched a perfect game, and no pitcher has ever pitched two consecutive perfect games in a row. Never. Ever.

For some men, perfection can be a curse. A ghost they end up chasing for the rest of their lives. Others just quit rather than face the certainty of constant disappointment. Without question, the quest to the top of the pyramid is certainly much more enjoyable than defending the crown. Consistency in achievement on or off the field can be paralyzing to men. The bedroom is no different.

At the beginning of every relationship, a man is attempting to throw his good stuff. He goes all out. He stands up on the mound, winds up, and tries to put one over home plate. Right in the pocket. Flowers, dinner, massage, foreplay, doubles, triples, home runs. Sometimes, and I mean rarely, it's magic, euphoria, time stops, and even the gods give a standing ovation. For that moment, the man is perfect. The perfect lover! Now keep in mind the male is proud of himself, but somewhere deep inside, regardless of how happy he is with his performance, anxiety quickly sets in. "Oh, my God! What if she thinks I can pull this off every time? What if she thinks this is just my run-of-the-mill, day-to-day stuff? I'd kill myself if I had to try to pull this off again!" Panic has taken over. He has become his own worst enemy. "Why in God's name did I have to set the sexual bar so high? Should

I run or confess? No, better that she think I'm a sex god than admit I'm human. I'll run."

You know what happens next? Nothing. The phone doesn't ring; the man doesn't call. If it's the beginning of the relationship, it becomes the end. The confused gal whose world was rocked thinks she was just played when, in reality, the man just has sophomore jitters or is afraid of a "sophomore jinx." All men know that no pitcher has ever thrown two perfect games, and the likelihood he's going to be the first is slim and none. The sad part to this story is that this couple actually did have magic, did make time stop, but now it's lost because most men who care about a woman's feelings at some level are insecure. It's that insecurity that allows boys to be heroes, fight wars, become scholars, become dads, become men. Men do great things to squelch insecurity, and as we get older, it gets smaller; however, it never goes away entirely. If as a woman you can see through our bravado, there might be a few relationships you can save before it's too late.

If you're dating and perfection shines on you in the bedroom, make a point to let him know as a reward next time he gets to sit it out while you take charge. Men, whether they admit it or not, love to be made love to. We don't always need or want to be in control.

If you're in a relationship already and you sense signs of performance anxiety, take the bull by the horns (literally) and relieve a little tension. Men don't get headaches in the bedroom. It's just sometimes they don't feel like going nine innings. It's your job to be the relief pitcher every now and then.

SNUGGLERS' BLUES

I'll be the first one to admit my wife has snugglers' blues. Snugglers' blues is when a snuggler marries a nonsnuggler and feels deprived. You see, there are a lot of us men who are two-pillow men. When we go to sleep at night, we have one pillow to hold and one under our heads.

Snugglers want us to nix the snuggle pillow and snuggle them instead. Here's the problem:

1. The dead arm: When we enter into an official snuggle (spooning position), inevitably a man's arm gets pinned under his mate's body, where it quickly falls asleep, becomes numb, and goes into shock.

2. The inferno: A man is generally carrying around a few extra pounds of insulation, and when his body comes into contact with another body, he heats up. Look, bears go into hibernation because they're cold, which then allows them to get a good night's sleep. Heat up a bear, and he won't be able to sleep. A man is no different. Some of the biggest fights my wife and I have are over what temperature to keep the thermostat in the house at.

3. Incapacitation: Men need to alter between three positions during a good night's sleep (side to side, belly flop, and flat on the back). If a snuggler ambushes a nonsnuggler during one of these positions, he feels trapped—trapped in a position that at any moment he may decide needs to be changed—and will find himself unable to escape. Trapped position equals no sleep.

Now it may appear to the average observer that, being a nonsnuggler myself, I'm trying to defend my position (no pun intended), which is true. But I am not unsympathetic to the snuggler who equates snuggling with intimacy and nonsnuggling with being a jerk. Look, we nonsnugglers are just trying to get a good night's sleep. Obviously, there needs to be a compromise, so I think I've concocted a plan: Fifteen to thirty minutes of snuggle time prior to lights out, then break to separate corners. Or set your alarm thirty minutes early in the morning and snuggle then.

I want to live in a world where snugglers and nonsnugglers can come together as one and live as happy people. I want to live in a world where a man is not judged by the color of his skin. Oh, wait a minute, I'm getting carried away. How do you solve snugglers' blues? Compromise.

Will I Marry a Cheater?

If you're married, you'll probably remember the words, "I, (fill in your name), do take (fill in his name) to love, honor, and cherish through sickness and health, through good times and bad, forsaking all others 'til death do us part." Or maybe you were more creative and wrote your own vows. Either way, I'll bet my bottom dollar monogamy and "'til death do us part" were part of your vows. If your man said these words or is going to say these words, you can stop reading this article right now. You have married or are going to marry a cheater. I don't know whose idea it was to put boundaries on love and death in the same sentence, but the person was an idiot. The quickest way to drive a man to cheat is by putting boundaries on him or bringing up his own mortality. That's why so many middle-aged men run off with another woman—because 'til death do us part pops up in their head and they feel they have to leave their current relationship because it's only heading one place: Deathville.

Statistically, 99 percent of all men will cheat on their spouse during their marriage. The other 1 percent doesn't exist. It's just there because no statistical average is 100 percent accurate and the survey has a 1 percent error ratio. That's right. That's what I'm saying. All men cheat, are cheating, or will cheat. Now don't get me wrong. Not all men's mistresses are women. In some cases, it's football, golf, sports in general, work, money, or possessions. Heck, men can cheat on a woman with a television set. Cheating can be anything that makes a woman feel lonely, depressed, taken advantage of, or replaced. Ever feel jealous of something your boyfriend or husband is doing or has done? Then you've allowed yourself to be cheated on.

Want to know what I believe are the two reasons most responsible for divorce in this country? Jealousy and boundaries. Tell a kid he can't have a cookie, and I promise you will catch him with his hand in the cookie jar. Even Adam and Eve, who had everything, blew it the minute someone (who will remain nameless) said you can eat everything but don't touch the apples. Come on, the nameless one was practically begging them to take a nibble. Men as well as women tend to want what they are told they can't have. Want a forever-lasting relationship? Loosen the reins. The tightest relationships are the ones with the loosest reins. Remove jealousy, remove boundaries, and you'll remove cheating.

I think if I could write the perfect vows, they would be, "I'll always try to do my best, but if there are times when I am weak, you'll allow me to speak and not judge me for my thoughts." Want to blow a man's mind? Tell him, "Honey, just because we are getting married, you don't have to give up your other interests. Just always be honest with me. Tell me the truth. Loving me doesn't mean letting go of others or the things you love." Do you know the number-one reason women give for leaving a man if he cheats on her? It isn't the other women—it's the deception.

So if you're a man reading this article (and you really are a man) and you're thinking of letting something else come between you and your spouse, be at least big enough to be honest with your woman and tell her. And if you're a woman reading this, make your man understand that you can be loving and understanding of just about anything, unless he disrespects you or is dishonest.

Why Won't the Question Pop?

Benjamin Franklin once said that the only two things that are certain in life are death and taxes. I think either of these absolutes could be argued, but that's for another discussion. If, however, I could add one more absolute, it would be the search for happiness. I think it's fair to say that we all want to be happy. In fact, I'd even say that some people spend their entire lives trying to achieve that state. Some people believe money, friends, or family will make them happy. Some believe that when they find the perfect mate, happiness will blossom. Then, when that perfect mate pops the question, they'll have someone to share their life with forever and ever. That sounds good, doesn't it? No loneliness, just sharing, loving, and joy. But I'm getting too far away from the title of this article.

Why won't the question pop? If you're in a relationship and have exchanged I love yous, why won't he jump over the broom and pop the question? Does time have something to do with it? Maybe a lack of commitment? Maybe he hasn't cut the apron string from his mother. Maybe he was in a bad relationship and needs time to heal. Maybe he's never been in a relationship and doesn't understand the rules. Maybe he's saving up for a big rock and doesn't have the last payment yet. Or maybe the question was never supposed to pop in the first place. Ever hear the saying, "A watched pot will never boil?" Love doesn't come with a rule book. In fact, if it did, I probably wouldn't play. Love doesn't wait for anything or anybody. Love just is. Love isn't a question, an answer, an agreement, or a proposition. Love just is. Are you wondering when your man is going to pop the question? Well, maybe you should stop worrying. If your man has to think about whether he wants to spend the rest of his life with you, he's not the one. And if you think a ring on your finger is going to somehow magically change your love for each other, you're wrong. The question you should be asking yourself is, "Am I happy when I'm with him? Does he build me up when I'm feeling down? Does he help me smile when I'd rather frown?" Love isn't a question. Love just is.

Now I'll be the first to admit that life equals change and relationships must change as well. We must reinvent ourselves every day to show the world who we are and what we represent. But does a woman need a man? I hope not. If you ask the rich, the famous, and the philosophers, they will probably tell you happiness is not found in possessions or even a person. Happiness is found in sharing, not needing! Let me repeat that again, happiness is found in sharing, not needing. If you need a man, you'll push him away. If you need a job, you'll lose it. If you need money, you won't have it. The act of needing admits to the world you are without. Instead, try sharing yourself, sharing your love, sharing your happiness. You cannot share something you do not possess.

Why won't the question pop? If you need it to, it won't. Strong relationships are built on sharing, not dependency. Show your man you can stand on your own two feet. Then you can ask the real important question, "Why should he be asking the question anyway?"

NECESSITIES

I think we can all agree that there are some basic necessities we all must have to survive: food, water, clothing, and shelter. Now whether your food of choice is caviar or a burger and your beverage a beer or Don Pérignon has a lot to do with your value system and personal taste. Personally, I'm a blue jeans kind of guy, but I have enough Giorgio Armani suits hanging in my closet to keep my wife happy. It's so easy to get caught up in a race of one-upmanship—keeping up with the Joneses. I've seen men motivated by a lot of things. Fear of loss certainly is a big motivator in our society. As a couple creates a union, there are some things I think had better be ironed out before the knot is tied, and that's necessities.

Before I ever got serious with a woman, my list of necessities was actually quite small. An apartment seemed just as good as a house and a couple pounds of bologna, a few loaves of bread, and Kraft macaroni and cheese could sustain me for weeks. I remember that at one time, I ate nothing but Taco Bell tacos for dinner for six months straight. (My God, do you know that to this day, you can still get two tacos for ninety-nine cents?) What to wear, how to look, what to eat seemed like decisions low on the totem pole of life compared to striving after my real passion: work. Success consumed me, not the trappings but the winning. There are many men who are no different. Einstein wore the same slacks and shirt practically every day of his life. Now he had many pairs of the same pants, but he'd made a conscious decision that certain choices weren't worth worrying about day after day. What's for dinner? What am I going to wear? If it weren't for women, there would be a lot of men living very happy lives in huts.

Women change all that for a man. For the most part, women raise our necessity bar to a new level. Women add humanity to men. Women create necessity. I think most women by nature have an appreciation for beauty that most times has to be taught to us (cave)men. When a man loves a woman, he'll want to lasso the moon for her. That's a task I've tried many times only to fail. I think it's important that when a woman makes her lists of needs and wants, preferences and wishes, she does so very carefully. Preferences can turn into needs and needs into necessities so that a man can become overwhelmed very quickly. And when possessions take priority over your relationship, you've lost the war. Necessities are necessary, but please don't make the list too long, or you may get what you desire but lose us in the shuffle.

"Possessions usually mean less once possessed," a famous man once said. So don't stray too far from the truth. It's one thing to have a house as a home, but does a palace have to be your roof? If a couple can't see eye to eye on what are priorities and what are preferences, they're in for a rocky marriage. Not every man wants to be a multimillionaire, and not every woman would sacrifice time with her husband to live in a mansion. The road map to a successful marriage lies in two people wanting to end up in the same place. So you'd better make sure you're on the same page and, for that matter, reading the same book.

Newlyweds' Prayer

Lord, watch over us as we venture into uncharted seas.

Protect and guide us to live in your glory and be an example of your love.

Watch over our families that have become one through our union.

Give us patience and understanding to weather the storms that test every alliance.

Be our shelter when we are homeless and our compass when we have lost our way.

Lord, let us be always be forever grateful for the gifts you have bestowed upon us so that never a day goes by that we take for granted the love we share now.

And let the everlasting love we will share together always fill our hearts.

Chapter 9

Buying Your 2nd, 3rd, or 4th Diamond

◆————————————————————————◆

THERE'S A VERY GOOD chance that the diamond engagement ring won't be the last diamond you buy! Perhaps you're already looking for your second diamond. In my experience, there are five main reasons people shop for another diamond: Remarriage, Replacement, Upgrade, Trade-in, and Special Occasion.

NEW MARRIAGE

Marriages end, sad to say, by death or divorce, but love can bloom again! New love at any age brings springtime back into your heart, and pretty soon, you find yourself gazing into jewelry store windows. Now I'm going to give you one piece of advice that will spare you a lot of grief.

Love is beautiful the second time around—but a ring isn't! Never recycle or even duplicate the ring from your previous marriage.

God forbid you should ever recycle a ring that you gave to a former fiancée or an ex-wife. Never!

DIAMOND FACTOID

The country that produces the most diamonds, both by weight and by number, is Australia (forty million plus carats)!

Your new love wants to feel special, wants to know that there's never been a love such as her. You'll shatter that feeling if you give her a ring from a previous relationship.

Of course, the exception is a family heirloom, perhaps your mother's or grandmother's ring—but not if it was also worn by your former wife. If you do give your beloved an heirloom ring, she's entitled to a new setting if she wants one. It's only the diamond that's forever. If your family has a problem with a setting change, it might be best to leave the heirloom in safe deposit and purchase a new ring.

REPLACEMENT DIAMOND

If her first diamond is lost, stolen, or damaged, you'll be shopping for a replacement. Don't assume she'll want an exact replica! Some women love the original so much they will want exactly the same thing if the original is gone, but other women will be ready for a change. Tastes do change over time after all, so talk this over. Be diplomatic and give her the option of change. Say to her, "Honey, I know your old ring meant a lot to you, and it meant a lot to me, and I'd do anything to bring it back, but it's gone. And since we're doing (a little)(a lot)(tons!) better than we were then, I want this ring to be all you want it to be. So I'll be happy to get you a duplicate of the old ring or a new one that's bigger, better, or just different. The choice is yours—I just want you to be happy." You'll be a hero!

If the old diamond was damaged so that the clarity grade has dropped by two grades or more, the insurance company should cover the cost of replacement. If your damaged diamond was not insured, maybe you can still use it as a trade-in.

DIAMOND UPGRADES

This can be an upgrade in size, quality, or both. Many women are happy with their original ring but would still like to have a bigger one.

An anniversary is an ideal time to make this upgrade. This is another time to be practical and talk things over together. Does she want to trade in the original or want to keep the original and get a new one? Many women treasure their original engagement ring, and even if they get a bigger diamond later, they want to keep the original and wear it as a pendant or save it for a child's future engagement. Or some women will take a more practical approach and use the trade-in value of the original to get an even larger new diamond.

Fred's advice: Never trade in her existing engagement ring without her knowledge!

TRADE-INS

Diamonds for trade-in can come from a lot of places. Your wife's old engagement ring, a ring from a failed engagement or former marriage, or a family heirloom. The keys to getting the most for your trade-in are as follows:

1. Get an independent appraisal of the trade-in diamond and ask the appraiser for the Rapaport value of the stone. "Rapaport" is a price sheet all appraisers use to determine a diamond's wholesale value. The Rapaport value equals wholesale price; retail is 2X Rapaport. You should always be able to buy a diamond at its Rapaport price and receive credit on a trade-in at Rapaport.

2. After you get the appraisal, you can visit your jeweler, knowing what you should get for the trade-in. Don't be lazy and let the jeweler appraise the diamond. A lot of jewelers might undervalue your trade-in.

3. Jewelers hate trade-ins, so always negotiate your new purchase *before* you indicate you have a trade-in. If you tell the jeweler up front that you have a trade, he'll just jack up the retail price.

    - Determine what type and grade of diamond you want.
    - Negotiate the price, using the guidelines in this book.

- Show your trade-in, telling the jeweler you've already gotten an independent appraisal.
- Make sure the trade-in amount equals the appraised wholesale value.
- Subtract the trade-in value from the price you negotiated for the new diamond, and that's your bottom line.

Example:

You're buying a .90ct SI1-I1, Class 2, no fluorescence.

Price: $7,679

Your trade-in is a .50ct VS1-J1

Appraised value: $2,730

You pay: $4,949

SPECIAL OCCASIONS AND GIFTS

As time goes by, you'll want to add to her diamond collection with gifts for a birthday, Christmas or Chanukah, an anniversary, or some other special day. This might mean diamond stud earrings, a diamond tennis bracelet, a pendant, or an anniversary ring. The number-one question I'm asked about these purchases is, "Do I get the same quality as the engagement diamond?" Well, my friend, how important is the purchase to you? Most people see the engagement ring as something they'll treasure for a lifetime. Is that how you view this new purchase? If so, don't waste your money on second-class merchandise. If not, get a cubic zirconia or costume jewelry.

The decision is yours.

TRUNK SHOWS

Many jewelers offer what are known as "remount trunk shows." These are basically marketing events at which they offer hundreds of settings and where jewelers try to entice you to replace or trade in your old diamond. The problem with a trunk show is that all the diamonds

---

have been mounted in settings, so it's impossible to check their weight, clarity, and color. And don't ever trade in your old diamond at these shows—they'll probably undervalue it.

Fred's advice: Never buy a diamond in a prefabricated setting for more than $2,000 unless the jeweler will let you view the diamonds loose.

Chapter 10

How to Sell a Diamond

◆————————————————————————————————————◆

I KNOW THIS BOOK is called *How to Buy a Diamond*, but let's face it: Not all diamonds are forever. There may come a time in your life when you want to sell a diamond or two for one reason or another. It may be an engagement ring from a previous marriage or a pair of diamond studs from an ex-boyfriend. It may be a family heirloom or just a diamond you don't wear anymore. Rather than let it gather dust in your safe deposit box, you'd like to convert it to cold cash. Here's what you need to do. And remember, patience is a virtue! If you rush into a sale without doing your homework, you'll get burned. Follow these steps:

STEP 1: APPRAISAL

Have the diamond appraised. You need to know what you have, and a qualified appraiser can tell you. Find one by calling the Appraisers Association of America, 386 Park Avenue South, 20th floor, New York City, NY 10016, at (212) 889-5404. Tell them where you live and ask for a list of appraisers in your area. They won't tell you over the phone, but they'll send you a few recommendations—it'll take about a week. If you can't wait, look in the Yellow Pages under appraisers. Check the appraiser's affiliations. The top three groups are:

- *Appraisers Association of America, www.appraisersassoc.org*
- *American Society of Appraisers, www.appraisers.org*
- *International Society of Appraisers, www.isa-appraisers.org*

Membership in any of these is a good indication the appraiser is okay.

STEP 2: RAPAPORT VALUE

Ask the appraiser for the Rapaport value. Rapaport is a wholesale price sheet published in New York that tells jewelry stores all over the country the prices they should pay for diamonds. The Rapaport prices are wholesale, based on class-three-cut diamonds. *The price the appraiser gives you will be the highest price you can get for your diamond.* For example, if your diamond is a one-carat, round, VS1-G, Class III cut with no fluorescence, the Rapaport value would be $10,700. (Note: Class IIIs are discounted 25–50 percent from Class IIs.) That's the most you'll get for it. That same diamond would sell for more in a jewelry store, but you're not a jewelry store! Anyone who buys a diamond from an individual who gives no guarantees or warranties is simply looking for a good deal.

STEP 3: BUYERS

Find a buyer. There are a number of possibilities here, but I'm going to firmly guide you away from most of them. In my mind, the two best choices are (1) family or friend and (2) a jeweler.

A. FAMILY OR FRIEND

This is my top recommendation hands down. I've seen people try every which way to sell a diamond or piece of jewelry, then finally discover that a family member or friend would love to buy it. Before you go to strangers, look close to home for a buyer. You'll always make your best deal with someone who knows you, loves your jewelry, and wants to own it, while a liquidator just wants to resell it for a quick buck.

B. Jewelry Store

Yes, but be careful! Never let the jewelry out of your sight—you don't want someone pulling a "switcheroo" on you. Before the jeweler starts a spiel about how poor your diamond is, show him the appraisal. At that point, the jeweler will probably make you an offer that is below "dump value." Dump value is a trade expression—it means 60 percent to 80 percent of the diamond's Rapaport value, and it's the lowest price a diamond should ever sell for. If the jeweler offers you *below* 60 percent, don't take it. He's going for a fast buck, because he knows he can resell the stone overnight to a dealer at regular dump value. But if the jeweler offers you 60 percent to 80 percent of the Rapaport value, he's actually being fair. Remember, to make any money from the deal, he'll have to find a new buyer for the diamond, and who knows what expenses he'll incur to do that?

Let's take our one-carat VS1-G, Class III cut diamond from step two, which has a Rapaport (wholesale) value of $10,700. Dump value would be 60 percent to 80 percent of that or between $6,420 and $8,560. Try to negotiate the best price, of course, but don't feel insulted if the jeweler's offer is 5 percent below the low dump price. He's just trying to make a little money for handling the deal. But if he offers you only 40 percent or even 50 percent of wholesale, tell him NO DEAL!

Now let's talk about some options that I do NOT recommend.

C. Newspapers

The premise is simple: You take out an ad, a buyer calls you and gives you money for your diamond. But it's never that simple. I have seen the classified ads work but not often. In fact, I did a little survey on my own and found only an 11 percent success rate. You can do better than that in Las Vegas! Furthermore, placing an ad exposes you to all sorts of people, including crooks who want to steal your jewelry. You'll make appointment after appointment with "buyers" who don't show up. Even if you attract a legitimate buyer, he'll drag you back to the appraiser and then make a ridiculous offer. I would avoid the classifieds. It's not worth putting yourself in danger.

DIAMOND MYSTIQUE AT WORK

The diamond weighed forty carats. It was discovered in Lesotho, South Africa, and had been cut into a Marquise shape and mounted as a spectacular ring. The clarity grade was high—VVS—but the color was only M or N, and at wholesale, the diamond would fetch perhaps $260,000. But when the ring sold at auction in April 1996, the winning bid was $2.58 million—ten times the wholesale value! Why? Because this was the ring Aristotle Onassis gave to the widow of President John F. Kennedy as an engagement ring, and bidding at the Sotheby's auction of the Jacqueline Kennedy Onassis estate was a feeding frenzy by the well-heeled who wanted to touch and own a piece of Camelot. For the high bidder, Anthony J. F. O'Reilly, the ring had a special appeal. His wife, Chryss, was a Goulandris, a member of a powerful Greek family that had been an archrival of the Onassis family in the shipping business.

D. ON CONSIGNMENT

A jeweler might say, "Hey, why not leave your diamond with me and I'll sell it on consignment and make big money for you?" DON'T DO IT! NEVER leave your jewelry with anyone unless you're paid up front. He can promise you the moon, switch your good diamond for a piece of junk or a cubic zirconia, then call you in a couple of weeks to tell you to pick up your jewelry because he couldn't sell it!

E. PAWNSHOPS

They should be called "prawn shops," because they'll dip you in cocktail sauce and eat you alive. On average, pawnbrokers will offer you only 10 percent of wholesale. STAY AWAY!

You may have heard of *Diamond Dealer Clubs*; however, these are only for the trade, and unless you're in the trade, you won't get within ten feet of these places.

Another option for high-end jewelry only is an auction house. Two to consider in the United States are:

Christie's
20 Rockefeller Plaza
New York, NY 10020
(212) 636-2000

Sotheby's
1334 York Avenue
New York City, NY 10021
(212) 606-7000

ANTIQUE OR "ESTATE" JEWELRY

Many people love to shop for antique jewelry in hopes of finding a beautiful and unique piece of jewelry softly glowing with the patina of time and enhanced by the mystique of history. Fine, but remember that buying previously owned jewelry is a lot like buying a used car. Be smart enough to get a trained mechanic to look under the hood—that is, get an independent appraisal and follow the guidelines in this book just as if you were buying a new piece of jewelry.

There are two things to be careful of. One, a lot of antique diamonds are Old Mine or Old European cuts. These styles, popular in the late 1800s and early 1900s, are cut very high and deep and allow a lot of light to leak out the bottom. They really are nothing better than a Class III or Class IV cut diamond. If you're buying an antique diamond with one of these cuts, expect a 50 percent to 60 percent discount off the prices listed in this book.

The second caution is, "Watch out for fairy tales!" Dealers know that a diamond with a fascinating history is going to sell faster and for a higher price than one without a history. Don't be mesmerized by tales of Russian princesses or Arab sultans. Listen politely and smile but then say, "That's great, but it's still a VS1-G, Class III cut!"

Chapter 11

Anniversaries and Occasions

◆————————————————————————————◆

IF THERE'S ANY MAN out there who believes that his jewelry-buying days are over after he purchases the bridal set, let me dispel that notion here and now! The fire in that first diamond always ignites a burning desire for more. "My engagement ring is lonely," she'll say. "It needs diamond earrings to keep it company." Or a tennis bracelet or a pendant—the list goes on.

Anniversaries are perfect times for gifts of jewelry, gifts that say "you'd marry her all over again," to quote from the advertisement. Never make the mistake of getting your spouse a practical anniversary gift like a new toaster or a vacuum cleaner. Anniversaries are occasions to celebrate and renew your love for each other, and only a personal gift such as jewelry is right for the moment.

Here's a traditional anniversary gift list.

Anniversary	Gift
1	Clocks
2	China
3	Crystal, glass
4	Electrical appliances (Yuck!)
5	Silverware
6	Wood
7	Pen & pencil set
8	Linen, lace

Anniversary	Gift
9	Leather
10	Diamond jewelry
11	Pearls or colored stones
12	Textiles, furs
13	Gold jewelry
14	Watches
15	Silver hollowware
16	Furniture
17	Porcelain
18	Bronze
19	Platinum
20	Sterling Silver Jubilee
25	Diamond
30	Jade
35	Ruby
40	Sapphire
45	Golden Jubilee
50	Emerald
55	Diamond Jubilee

Here's a gem anniversary list developed by several trade associations:

Anniversary	Gift
1	Gold jewelry
2	Garnet (all colors)
3	Pearls
4	Blue Topaz
5	Sapphire (all colors)
6	Amethyst
7	Onyx
8	Tourmaline

Anniversary	Gift
9	Lapis
10	Diamond jewelry
11	Turquoise
12	Jade
13	Citrine
14	Opal
15	Ruby
16	Peridot
17	Watches
18	Cat's Eye
19	Aquamarine
20	Emerald
21	Iolite
22	Spinel (all colors)
23	Imperial Topaz
24	Tanzanite
25	Sterling Silver Jubilee
30	Pearl Jubilee
35	Emerald
40	Ruby
45	Sapphire
50	Golden Jubilee
55	Alexandrite
60	Diamond Jubilee

January	Garnet	A red, lustrous stone that occurs mainly as crystals.
February	Amethyst	A clear purple or bluish violet variety of quartz crystal.
March	Aquamarine	A transparent beryl that may be blue, blue-green, or green in color.
April	Diamond	Need we say more?
May	Emerald	A rich green variety of beryl, highly prized.
June	Pearl	Dense, lustrous layers of nacre formed around a foreign object within the shell of oysters and some other mollusks.
July	Ruby	A rare red corundum, sometimes worth $30,000 per carat.
August	Peridot	A deep yellowish-green olivine stone.
September	Sapphire	A rich blue transparent corundum gemstone.
October	Opal	A hydrated silica gemstone noted for its iridescent play of colors.
November	Topaz	A silicate of aluminum, usually a transparent yellow to brownish-yellow.
December	Turquoise	A sky-blue copper aluminum phosphate, highly prized.

Conclusion

◆————————————————————————————◆

CONGRATULATIONS! YOU HAVE FINISHED *How to Buy a Diamond.*
You've learned about the four Cs, how to grade diamonds, how to
select a jeweler, and how to get the best diamond for your dollar. You
have your questionnaire sheets to guide you. Now I want you to ask
yourself two more questions:

Do I really want to marry her?

Does she really want to marry me?

If you don't answer these questions immediately and emphatically
"YES!" then maybe you should think this over before you make a serious investment in a ring that says "forever." Marriage is a magnificent
institution for two people in love who have no doubts about whole-
hearted commitment to one another. Please be sure you're in that
category before you visit the jeweler.

Also, I believe there are good reasons to buy a diamond and also
reasons you should avoid taking the plunge. I'd like to share them with
you now. They're called Diamond Values: What Giving a Diamond
Should and Shouldn't Represent.

I.   Give from the heart, not out of fear.

II. Give through knowledge, not out of ignorance.

III. Give to create joy, not because of intimidation.

IV. Give to celebrate commitment and success, not to impress others.

V.   Give what you can afford to give; don't overextend yourself.

And please remember one more thing: Any diamond can make a good
first impression, but only a good diamond will keep your attention.

I hope you've had as much fun reading this book as I have had writing it. I know that buying a diamond can be one of the most expensive and nerve-wracking purchases you'll ever make, but it can also be one of the most exciting and rewarding—if you apply the lessons you've learned in this book. Follow my advice, and you should be able to get the right diamond at the right price. And isn't that what it's all about?

My final words of advice are:

- If a deal seems too good to be true, it probably is.

- Truly good diamonds are more expensive or just not available and are not being discounted.

- The "labs" experiment failed when we decided to trust the fox guarding the henhouse.

- A diamond is only worth what somebody else is willing to pay for it.

- If it's not fully bonded, it's probably full of bologna.

Happy diamond shopping!

Inside the Diamond Business

$\blacklozenge$————————————————————$\blacklozenge$

Blood Diamonds

Blood diamonds are synonymous with conflict diamonds. The term is designed to dramatically emphasize that behind the glamorous image of diamonds lies a web of corruption, influence peddling, and brutality in some parts of the diamond-producing world.

Consumers began clamoring for assurances that the diamonds they desired were not being used to finance conflicts. To that end, an alliance of government, civil, and industry groups created the "Kimberley Process" to clean up the trade in rough diamonds.

First, in 1998, the United Nations (UN) initiated action that culminated with the establishment of the "Kimberley Process." However, the UN's definition of the term blood diamond or conflict diamond is very narrow and was designed to get everyone on board. The definition reads as follows:

> *A blood diamond (conflict diamond) refers to a diamond mined in a war zone and sold in order to finance an insurgency, invading army's war efforts, or supporting a warlord's activity.*

Next, in July 2000, the World Diamond Congress in Antwerp passed a resolution blocking the sale of blood diamonds. The resolution installed an international certification system on the export and import of diamonds. Countries could only accept sealed packages of diamonds with an official seal, and criminal charges would be levied against anyone and everyone trafficking in blood diamonds.

Six months later in January 2001, the top elements of the diamond industry formed a new organization—the World Diamond Council. They drafted a process whereby all known diamond rough could be "certified" as coming from a nonconflict zone. Thus, the "Kimberley Process" was created and approved by the UN in March 2002. The United States followed with the Clean Diamond Act in April 2003, and the "Kimberley Process" became law in the United States.

According to the "Kimberley Process" website, there are now forty-six members blessed by the Kimberley experts. Only the Ivory Coast (Africa) has rebel forces that control diamond production, but less than 0.2% of the industry.

Our narrative could end here, but I have a much broader definition for a blood diamond. Here is my definition:

- Any diamond that was mined using oppressed labor in unsanitary working conditions.
- Any diamond whose oppressed labor force was victimized in the form of rape, mutilations (loss of arms or legs), beatings, verbal abuse, unconscionable working hours, and below-poverty wage structure.
- Any diamond that was mined or is controlled by a company that is part of a monopoly.
- Any diamond that funds wars or corporate greed where profits supersede human life.
- Any diamond that is used to oppress any human life or the extinction of any race, tribe, or subculture.
- Any diamond that is purposely graded incorrectly and marketed for corporate profits instead of consumer satisfaction.
- Any diamond that is sold at a price above its secondary market resale value, forcing the consumer to take a significant loss if it was to be resold.

So, what percentage of diamonds sold in the world today are blood diamonds? Well, maybe the question should be what percentage of diamonds are NOT blood diamonds.

GIA: FIRES FOUR
BY JEFF MILLER

(Diamonds.net, Rapaport News—October 18, 2005) The following press release from the Gemological Institute of America (GIA) details results of its internal investigation and action, following charges filed against GIA by Max Pincione. (Read the court case below.) The GIA stresses that they have "zero tolerance" for misconduct and have made some organizational changes, one of which was to appoint gemologist Thomas Moses as the new head of the GIA Lab, with the title of senior vice president, GIA Laboratory and Research.

GIA COMPLETES INDEPENDENT REVIEW, ANNOUNCES ORGANIZATIONAL CHANGES

Carlsbad, Calif.—Oct. 18, 2005—The Board of Governors of The Gemological Institute of America, Inc. ("GIA") announced today that a Special Committee of the Board has completed a comprehensive review of the policies and practices currently in place at the GIA Laboratory. The review was initiated as a result of a lawsuit filed in the spring of 2005 by Max Pincione, which named GIA as one of four defendants. GIA is continuing to defend itself vigorously in that litigation.

Ralph Destino, Chairman of GIA's Board of Governors, said, "The Board was deeply disturbed by the claims asserted in the complaint, and we felt that we had a responsibility to ourselves, our clients, and the public to not only look into them but to also thoroughly examine all lab practices. That is precisely what we have done."

Four-Month Independent Review

In May, the Board formed a Special Committee to investigate the allegations in the lawsuit and any related business practices. The Special Committee, in turn, engaged the law firm of DLA Piper Rudnick Gray Cary US LLP ("DLA Piper") to conduct the review under the leadership of Thomas F. O'Neil III, a partner based in Washington, DC, who chairs the firm's Government Affairs practice group and who served as an assistant United States Attorney for the District of Maryland.

"Tom O'Neil has an outstanding reputation as a thorough and tough investigator. We knew we were in good hands," said Mr. Destino.

Mr. O'Neil said, "We conducted an extensive four-month review, during which we interviewed dozens of witnesses and reviewed tens of thousands of documents, including thousands of diamond grading reports. From the outset, the Board embraced the important guiding principles of self-policing and zero tolerance of misconduct.

"The investigation revealed that, although GIA had undertaken to fortify various facets of the grading process during the past decade, additional measures are warranted. Accordingly, we have presented for the Board's consideration a number of possible enhancements of, and supplements to, existing policies governing the grading process and compliance in general.

"The Board already has decided to implement a number of our recommendations, including the appointment of a Compliance Officer in the laboratory who will report to the general counsel and will oversee the enforcement of the Institute's compliance policies," added Mr. O'Neil.

Board Action

The Board has appointed an Operations Review Committee to assess, and implement as appropriate, the recommendations of DLA Piper.

Mr. Destino said that, "As a consequence of the investigation, GIA has made a number of key personnel changes including:

- Four employees of GIA's New York lab have been terminated;
- Thomas M. Moses, G.G., a distinguished gemologist with a stellar reputation around the world, has been named the new head of the GIA Lab, with the title of Senior Vice President, GIA Laboratory and Research; and
- Thomas C. Yonelunas, former head of the GIA Laboratory, while not implicated in any violations of GIA's Professional Ethics and Conduct Compliance Statement, has tendered his resignation, effective December 31, 2005, to ensure a smooth transition of leadership."

ZERO TOLERANCE POLICY

Mr. Destino said, "We have zero tolerance for any misconduct by employees of the laboratory. They undermine confidence in GIA's ability to serve the diamond industry and ensure the public's trust in gems and jewelry. Going forward, all GIA employees will be obligated to report all suspected violations of the Institute's compliance policies to the new Compliance Officer.

"At the same time," added Mr. Destino, "our policies apply with equal force to lab clients. We, therefore, will not tolerate any violations of our code of ethics by clients of the lab, most particularly improper attempts to influence the outcome of our grading reports. We have identified a small community of lab clients who are implicated in such actions and, rest assured, they will be dealt with swiftly and decisively."

GIA MUST BE "BEYOND REPROACH"

GIA President William E. Boyajian said, "I want to thank the Board of Governors for their strong leadership in this sensitive matter. Because of GIA's important position in the industry and in the public eye as the leading authority in gemology, we take very seriously the need for our practices, procedures, and employees to be beyond reproach."

Mr. Boyajian continued, "That is why we are so pleased with the appointment of Tom Moses to oversee the laboratory. Tom Moses is a man of unquestioned integrity and professionalism, as he has demonstrated over his 23 years of outstanding service to the Institute. His leadership will be essential in bringing a serious, systematic approach to our efforts to strengthen our organization even further. At the same time, I want to thank Tom Yonelunas for his many years of service to GIA and the entire industry."

COURT CASE: *PINCIONE VS. VIVID, GIA*
BY JEFF MILLER, POSTED 8/26/2005 3:57 PM

(Diamonds.net, Rapaport News—August 26, 2005) Judging from the emails and phone calls into Rapaport this past week, there is great concern within the diamond industry about a pending court case related to alleged payments in exchange for upgraded diamond certificates dating back to the year 2001.

What follows in this article is a summary of the full court documents in the case of Max Pincione (a New York diamond dealer) vs. Vivid Collection LLC, and the Gemological Institute of America (GIA). This information is provided as a courtesy to Rapaport readers. All parties continue to negotiate and those negotiations are not a matter of public record.

Furthermore, defendant responses are not part of this court document. Quotations are direct phrases from the plaintiff's court filing. Other statements are paraphrased from the court documents to net-out the history and the pending case.

On April 21, 2005, attorneys for Pincione filed complaints against Moty Spector of Vivid Collection, Ali Khazeneh of New York's Upper East Side, and Bill Farley, acting agent for GIA in New York, in the Supreme Court of the State of New York in the county of New York.

The Plaintiff

Under oath, Pincione established that he is the plaintiff and is a dealer in fine gemstones, including "extremely rare and valuable diamonds." He states that he earned an international, "unparalleled, untarnished, and enviable" reputation for "dealing and honesty in the diamond and rare gem trade" whose principal client is listed as the "Royal Family of Saudi Arabia." Through an agent [Medad] for the Royal Family, orders were placed with Pincione.

The Defendants

Vivid Collection engages in the business of selling diamonds. Spector (as officer of Vivid) and Khazaneh are in the business of dealing and or selling diamonds. GIA is an expert business in evaluating the quality of diamonds presented for evaluation.

The Complaints

Pincione says that he received two pieces of jewelry from Vivid, both of which were certified by GIA. The first piece was a platinum round shape diamond ring of 37.01 carats, H-VS2; the second piece of jewelry was a diamond pendant with a 103.78 carat Pear-shaped, D-F.

On May 22, 2001, Shaer & Spector shipped to Cimabue of New York City a diamond ring and cufflinks, green emerald earrings, and a necklace for $16,930,000 on memo. The diamond grading report dated October 3, 2000, shows a Pear Modified Brilliant, 103.78 carat, 56.3 percent depth, 48 percent table, medium to thick faceted, large, excellent (polish), good (symmetry), flawless (clarity grade), D (color), with No fluorescence. [The diamond ring certificate is not in the copy, only described by name in text.] Pincione offered the ring to the Royal Family, and he said that the transaction was made with a "very good profit" to himself, Vivid, and Spector. The Royal Family had the ring inspected, and returned the ring to Pincione without explanation, but did ask for the return of payment. Pincione says it was the first time his client returned a purchase and demanded refund. He said he refunded the Royals their payment.

On March 23, 2005, Capt. Mohammad Hesham Ali Amin, general manager of Medad (a company owned by a member of the Royal Family) submitted a letter on behalf of Pincione "in lieu of my appearance." He writes that in May 2001, Pincione hosted an exhibition of diamonds and jewelry "to which members of the Royal Family" and others attended.

Hesham Al Amin writes, "A member of the Saudi Royal Family purchased the 37.01 [carat] round diamond ring in the amount of" $1.2 million and "the diamond was inspected and was found not to be as purported and returned to Mr. Pincione."

Later, Hesham Ali Amin negotiated the transaction of the diamond pendant for $14 million. The pendant was returned after purchase and Pincione said he was banished from doing business in the kingdom.

"After review by a member of the purchaser's group, it was determined that the stone was not as purported," Hesham Ali Amin wrote.

The plaintiff was told that the diamonds were not of the quality stated in the GIA-grading reports. "That the plaintiff by offering said stones with grading reports containing falsified information unbeknownst to plaintiff at the time, risked by his innocent acts, incarceration and punishment in Saudi Arabia, in accordance with their laws," the documents state.

He explains that in Saudi Arabia acts of fraud are punishable by imprisonment, and "I was forced to intercede into the matter so as to prevent Mr. Pincione from being incarcerated."

"As we personally know Mr. Pincione for many years, we do not believe he was involved in any deliberate act to misrepresent the stones." Hesham Al Amin states that Medad's reputation "has been marred" and that no members of the Royal Family "or other related clientele can conduct business with Mr. Pincione, as reputation and trust are two characteristics that can never be restored when destroyed."

In January 2005, Pincione learned for "the first time of the fraudulent actions and conspiracy of the defendants, from information and documents shown to the plaintiff."

The quality of the diamond ring sold to the Royal Family was "not HVS2 as represented to the plaintiff by defendant Vivid and certified to the plaintiff by defendant GIA, but was in reality of J-quality."

The quality of the diamond pendant was "not D Flawless as represented" by Vivid and GIA, but "was in reality E-VVS2 quality."

The 2002 Defamation Suit

In 2002, Pincione charged that Vivid, Spector, and Khazaneh "had groundlessly accused" him of "theft of a diamond and communicated the false accusation to Harry Winston, Inc.," Pincione's former employer. Pincione took action (defamation) against Vivid and Spector, which was settled out of court with payment of $750,000 to Pincione along with letters of apology from Spector and Khazaneh.

Settlement agreement between Pincione, Spector, and Vivid was signed on December 20, 2002. Vivid agreed to pay Pincione $750,000 in total, in exchange Pincione "forever" releases and discharges Spector, Vivid, Martin Klien, Abraham Klien, Julius Klien Diamonds, Inc., Khazaneh, and Rima Investors Corp, from claims, debts, demands, agreements, etc. And all defendants forever release Pincione from same. Each party also agreed to "refrain from accessing, discussing, copying, disclosing, or otherwise using confidential information…concerning any of the parties."

Vivid releases that "they are unaware and have no knowledge directly or indirectly of any misappropriation, conversion, or any sort of theft at any times of jewelry by Pincione" from any, "but not limited to Harry Winston, Inc. Nor are said releases aware of any other business improprieties of which they participated in directly or indirectly."

On July 8, 2002, Spector wrote in a notarized letter that "you might have heard a rumor created by me whereby I wrongly accused Max Pincione of misappropriating a diamond from me, in excess" of $300,000 while "Pincione had been employed with Shaer & Spector."

Spector apologized to Pincione and "fully retract my previous statements," and declared that Pincione had "nothing to do with such a loss."

Khazaneh wrote on December 20, 2002, that at "sometime during the year 2000, I, Ali Khazaneh, of Rima Investors Corp., communicated the following information to Harry Winston, Inc.: 'On August 27, 1999, Mr. Pincione presented an .83 carat Pink Trillion Diamond to Rima Corp'" and inquired if Rima was interested in having the diamond cut.

Khazaneh withdrew his remarks, saying "Pincione was never at my office on August 27, 1999," and that the plaintiff "never approached me or my company in regards to re-cutting a Pink Diamond or any other diamond for that matter."

NEW CHARGES IN APRIL 2005

The decision to settle the defamation suit "out of court" was "part and parcel of an elaborate, fraudulent scheme, to have the plaintiff enter into a release which by its terms would, unbeknownst to the plaintiff, eliminate and prevent the discovery of additional, substantial, and serious fraudulent actions of the defendants herein…"

In 2002, the agreement said that Pincione would "deliver to Vivid" any property in his custody pertaining to Spector, Vivid, or Abe [Abraham] Shaer of Shaer & Spector, Inc., or documents given him by Mark Blickman.

This agreement, Pincione says, was drawn to "conceal a conspiracy between the defendants herein, to make money illegally, by obtaining from the defendant GIA false records, thereby attempting and succeeding to sell lower quality diamonds falsely certified as higher quality…"

Pincione states that due to the prior "untarnished" reputation of GIA, he had every reason to "rely on the material representations made by the defendants, jointly and severally, about the quality of the gems and the diamond grading reports relating thereto."

Had Pincione been aware of the "falsification of entries in the diamond grading reports" he would "never have settled his defamation action or signed the release set forth herein," the court documents report.

The suit argues that the 2002 defamation suit agreement is null and void "because of said fraud, and said actions were made with actual intent to hinder and impede existing and future claims by the plaintiff."

Six Causes of Action in 2005

1. The 2002 case settlement was "drawn" with the intent "to conceal their [defendants] conspiracy and their procuring false diamond grading reports from the defendant GIA." For "bad faith" Pincione requests a declaratory judgment wherein the "release should be declared non effective and non-operative as to any causes of action against the defendants arising out of their fraudulent actions."

2. The plaintiff's reputation was ruined and the good will between Pincione and his clients was destroyed. By offering the diamonds to his clients "with falsified entries in the diamond grading reports, risked by his innocent acts, incarceration and punishment in Saudi Arabia..." and seeks $50 million in damages.

3. Vivid "breached its contract" with Pincione by supplying "gems of quality certified honestly by defendant GIA." Subsequent loss of business is set forth in damages of $50 million.

4. Defendants "jointly and severally breached their fiduciary relationship with the plaintiff by misrepresenting to him the value of gems submitted..." for sale to Pincione's clients, "thereby injuring the reputation and destroying the good will developed by the plaintiff

after years of hard work." For this, the plaintiff has been damaged in the sum of $50 million.

5. The court document says that Khazaneh executed the 2002 settlement agreement and release along with "a letter of apology, said defendant has been and continues to slander the plaintiff, by stating to various friends and customers of the plaintiff, that: 'I cannot understand why Pincione is not in jail, in that he has stolen so much' (paraphrased)." It is stated that Khazaneh was "warned" to cease and desist "in his slanderous statements."

   The court is asked to void the settlement agreement and release between Pincione and Khazaneh due to "slanderous statements." The plaintiff has been damaged in the sum of $50 million.

6. Khazaneh has "caused the plaintiff to be threatened," in that the plaintiff states a man "who has identified himself as defendant Khazaneh's brother to make telephone calls to the plaintiff threatening the plaintiff with statements including but not limited to: 'If I were you, I would sleep with an eye open,'" and "Dr. Nuchbacker a friend and spiritual advisor to (Khazaneh) has many followers and they would kill for him in a blink..." Cited as "malicious acts" in the statement, the plaintiff says it was "part of a plan of action by defendant Khazaneh to put the plaintiff in fear of his life, and were acted upon with malice," has caused emotional distress, and in so seeks damage in the sum of $50 million.

DAMAGES

Pincione demands judgment against the defendants of "rescinding the release in full" and demands five "cause of action" complaints in the sum of $50 million each; and "altogether with punitive damages against the defendants, jointly and severally, in the sum of $150 million, and the costs and disbursements of this action."

All rights reserved to the Rapaport Group.

Apollo has Landed?

Foreword

On September 9, 2003, *Wired* magazine broke an incredible story about a new type of synthetic diamond that would, in theory, revolutionize the way people buy diamonds and at what price.

Assertion

Mr. Bryant Linares (president of Apollo Diamond, the company that has invented the technology) stated in his interview that Apollo has patented a process to grow diamonds. The tagline for this new product is the C.V.D. diamond. C.V.D. stands for chemical vapor deposition. The idea, according to Mr. Linares, is "you must first determine the exact combination of temperature, gas composition, and pressure—a 'sweet spot'—that results in the formation of a single crystal." Apollo states that they have discovered that "sweet spot." The *Wired* magazine article goes on to paint a picture of $5.00 per carat, nondetectable, synthetic diamonds soon to be on the market. The article continues this could potentially break the iron grip that De Beers has had on the diamond industry for over a century and awake us from our slumber to affordable diamonds for everyone! Happy ending? End of story? Not quite.

Reality

Not mentioned in the article by Joshua Davis from *Wired* magazine is that the product they are producing is averaging only two millimeters thick! That's the exact thickness of a nickel—a far cry from the typical size diamond preferred by the diamond-buying public.

Unless you've got a craving for a 1/20th of a carat engagement ring, there is no utopia here or expected any time in the near future. Another thing not widely reported is that when they are able to get slightly larger crystals, they tend to be brown. The American buying public is primarily a buyer of whites. Apollo's solution to the brown color is to anneal (bake) the diamonds after step one and bake the nitrogen and boron right out like a ring around the collar. Apollo also likes taking credit for discovering the "sweet spot" when in reality chemical vapor deposition of carbon atoms from hydrogen-rich, carbon-containing gas was invented in the 1980s. The process has been used to deposit thin polycrystalline diamond films on cutting tools. One of the last claims to fame for Apollo's C.V.D. rocks is the potential that they will be undetectable from the naturals. Not hardly. Natural diamonds occur in nature, forming paired nitrogen atoms. Synthetics have only single nitrogen atoms. Also, all the samples examined so far fluoresce a very weak yellow-orange under long-wave UV (ultraviolet) light, moderate yellow-orange in short-wave UV, and strong red fluorescence under high-energy UV light.

As of Spring 2012, I am happy to say that Apollo is totally open for business! While I almost didn't believe these guys could pull it off, they have! They are actually growing white, pretty, synthetic diamonds at competitive prices. For now, please keep in mind that the good ones at decent sizes only range from .20ct to .75ct. Don't let others fooled you with a 2ct, synthetic/man-made, white, gem-quality diamond. That's not true. For anyone who is skeptical of blood diamonds and is looking for an honest alternative, these guys are holding the future in their hands. The diamond industry is quite simply not going to be able to keep up with the world's demand for diamonds with off-the-chart growth rates in China and India clamoring for rocks. It's time for the naysayers and skeptics (I was one) to embrace these guys because they have a good product that the world needs.

ICE IN ICE

One thousand miles north of the U.S. border in Lac de Gras, Canada, a remarkable thing has been going on since 1998. They are mining diamonds, and I'm not just talking onesies and twosies but bucketsful! On any given day, Ekati (first ever Canadian diamond mine) will sift ten thousand tons of kimberlite (a rock formation in which diamonds are formed) to obtain a sack of ten thousand carats of diamonds (about four pounds) valued in excess of one million dollars. What's even more amazing is where they find these diamonds. They are buried in ice two thirds of a mile down, chilled to a very uncomfortable 70 degrees below zero. At a cost of six hundred million dollars, BHP Diamond Corporation (Broken Hill Proprietary, an Australian outfit) broke ground with a team of five hundred people who live and work on the frozen tundra, working in shifts (two weeks on and two weeks off) 365 days of the year, including Christmas. To give you some idea how big a diamond find this is, let's put it into perspective. Every year, thirty billion dollars' worth of diamonds are mined worldwide. That's every mine from every country in the whole world to get to that thirty billion. This one little mine is currently producing three million carats a year at a value of a billion dollars. "So what?" you say. Here's what: Only one company is on line right now, but there are 260 companies that have staked claims on a hundred thousand square miles (larger than Texas). They've found 136 kimberlite pipes with five already having enough diamonds to mine. Think about it. If there's only one mine in production (Ekati Diamond Mine), one main kimberlite pipe being used (named Panda, how cute); imagine what will happen when the other mines come on line! Next year, Diavik Diamond Mines, Inc., will be in production, and at their peak, they will be able to produce six million carats a year (twice that of Ekati)! With most of these mines' life expectancy being twenty years, that's over six billion dollars' worth of diamonds to be produced from each single location. Before this decade is out, 12 percent of the world's diamonds will be coming from Canada.

WHAT IT MEANS TO YOU

Nothing! The Canadians as well as all the foreigners they are letting mine don't want to see the price of diamonds fall. It's not in their best interest. They are going to do what's been done for the last hundred years: Allow a certain amount to the market and hoard the rest for future consumption. With the 8 percent consumption increase from India and 12 percent increase from China, the amount of diamonds mined from Canada may not fill the worldwide demand.

Good diamonds still are endangered species.

LUSTING FOR GRAVEL

In Neiman Marcus's 100th Anniversary Edition of *The Christmas Book*, you will find on page 102 the following items: a pencil (sharpened with a used eraser and slightly chewed around the upper wooden barrel toward the point), a sketch (assuming made by the pencil) of something that looks like the profile of a sea monster with algae on its pointed head, a squint for an eye and a mouth that looks like Jimmy Cagney right before he says, "Oh…you dirty rat!" Beneath the picture is a marbleized rock shaped like an upside-down, four-sided pyramid with a cross-sectioned aorta jetting out of the top. The rock is opaque and looks like a petrified mixture of rocky road, vanilla swirl, and peppermint ice cream. The rock floats above a notebook that lays on top of a five-slatted wood countertop. Imprinted in the notebook are approximately 158 words, five numbers (one big one), and a myriad of commas, periods, and spaces. So here's the question: What is the most valuable thing on the page?

Don't spend too long thinking about it because it's a trick question. The answer is the paper because at least the paper is 100 percent recyclable! Now I'm not implying that a pencil, notebook, bookmark, and tabletop aren't valuable. They can be used to solve many problems!

Even the words are priceless because, without them, the seller of this uncut, rough diamond would be unable to convince some lollipop that they should pay a million dollars for a rock that has less utility than the pencil above it! The old saying a fool and his money are soon parted is never truer of the lollipops that are paying top dollar for worthless, uncut diamonds mounted into everything from men's jewelry (cufflinks, necklaces, and rings) to homeopathic crystals mounted into amulets to ward off evil spirits. Anybody who lusts for the gravel that is being pitched as a valuable diamond has more space between his ears than should be allowed by law. If someone tries to sell you a rough diamond, RUN as far and as fast as you can from the sales person!

DIAMONDS ARE NOT FOREVER
By Edward Jay Epstein

HAVE YOU EVER TRIED TO SELL A DIAMOND?
PART 1 OF THE 3 PART SERIES

De Beers' advertising slogan, "A Diamond Is Forever," embodied an essential concept of the diamond invention. It suggested that the value of a diamond never diminishes and that therefore a diamond never need be sold or exchanged. This precept, of course, is self-fulfilling: As long as no one attempts to sell his diamonds, they retain their value (assuming the cartel controls the supply of new diamonds). When, however, an individual is forced to defy this principle by attempting to sell diamonds, the results can prove illuminating. Consider, for example, the case of Rifkin's Russian diamonds.

In the fall of 1978, a thirty-two-year-old Californian computer wizard named Stanley Mark Rifkin discovered an ingenious way to become a multimillionaire overnight. While working as a consultant for the Security Pacific National bank in Los Angeles, he had learned the secret computer code that the bank used to transfer funds to other banks telegraphically at the end of each business day. With this information and his mastery of the bank's computer, he realized that he could transfer tens of millions of dollars to any bank account in America. The problem would be withdrawing the money from the system. In early October, he devised a plan for siphoning this money out of the bank and converting it into Russian diamonds.

The first step was establishing an alias identity. Under the pseudonym "Mike Hanson," Rifkin opened a bank account at the Irving Trust Company in New York, arranged a phony passport and other documentation, and retained a respected diamond broker, Lou Stein, to acquire for him a multimillion dollar consignment of diamonds from Russia. The Russian diamond organization, Russ Almaz, agreed to sell "Hanson" at its fixed wholesale price 115,000 perfectly cut, round, brilliant stones for $8,145,000. For arranging this low price, the broker took a standard 2 percent commission, or $162,000. For the deal to be consummated, Rifkin only had to wire the money to Zurich.

On October 25, Rifkin coolly entered the bank's transfer room under the pretext of inspecting the computer. He picked up a telephone connected to the computer and dialed in the necessary digits. Instantly, the computer withdrew $10,200,000 from a non-existent account and transferred it to the account of "Mike Hanson" at the Irving Trust Company in New York. Rifkin then had the New York bank transfer $8,300,000 to the Zurich account of Russ Almaz.

A few days later, using his phony passport, Rifkin flew to Switzerland, took delivery of the diamonds, which weighed under five pounds, and smuggled them through customs into the United States. He then began contacting dealers in Los Angeles, but none was willing to buy the diamonds.

Meanwhile, the Security Pacific National Bank discovered that more than ten million dollars was missing. It was one of the largest bank robberies in history. The FBI, investigating the loss, received a tip about Rifkin, and arrested him in Carlsbad, California, and found on him the Russian diamonds, as well as the remaining cash.

Initially, bank officials assumed that most of stolen money prudently invested in diamonds would be easily converted back to money. Only a few weeks earlier *Newsweek* had reported in a cover story, "The Diamond Boom," that diamonds were "the ideal asset" and that quality diamonds were soaring in price. While the diamonds that Rifkin had bought were commercial-grade stones used in jewelry, the London-based Economist Intelligence Unit had such diamonds, which had increased by at least 50 percent that year and were still increasing in price. Independent appraisers estimated that the diamonds, which Rifkin had bought at a low price, were worth at least $13 million at the retail level, and so the bank foresaw that it might make a profit of some $5 million with the reported appreciation in value of the diamonds. In anticipation of this windfall, they agreed to pay the 10 percent custom tax on the diamonds which Rifkin had evaded, as well as part of the cost of the FBI investigation. Before this expected profit could be realized, the bank had to await the outcome of the trial, since the diamonds were important evidence.

Finally, in September 1978, the bank announced that it would sell its hoard of diamonds to the highest bidder. Twelve major dealers were invited to the bank's vault to inspect Russian diamonds. They were instructed to submit sealed bids by the end of the business day on September 18. A minimum price of $7.5 million was established to encourage high bids, though independent appraisers assured the bank that the diamonds would fetch far more.

On the day of the auction, bank officials anxiously waited to see how much profit they would garner from the diamonds. However, only a single bid had been submitted, and when it was opened, it was for several million dollars less than the minimum. The bank officials were disappointed at this turn of events. Even though the diamonds had been purchased through a reputable broker at wholesale price, no American dealer would pay anywhere near this price nearly a year later.

The bank offered to sell the Russians back their own diamonds at the original 1978 price. But they refused to buy the diamonds back at any price.

The bankers learned that two Israeli banks were also trying to sell large quantities of diamonds received as collateral from Tel Aviv dealers; and this might make it far more difficult, if not impossible, for the Security Pacific Bank to unload its 115,000 diamonds. So they decided not to wait any longer.

Walter S. Fisher, the vice president of Security Pacific, was charged with the responsibility of selling the 115,000 diamonds. He realized that diamonds were not a standardized, or fungible commodity, as were gold, silver, and platinum. Different appraisals of the same diamonds varied widely, dependent on what the prospective buyer thought he could sell them for. And, though all the bank's diamonds were commercial stones for the mass market, Fisher found that it was extraordinarily difficult to find a buyer. None of the dealers in the United States were willing to buy such a large consignment of diamonds. Fisher found it necessary to deal through De Beers' main broker in London, I. Hennig, and accept the terms dictated by the buyer, if he wanted to sell the diamonds. He then had to deliver the diamonds to an unknown corporation in Liechtenstein, GSG Investments, without receiving any money for them for eighteen months. These were terms that the bank probably would not have accepted in selling any other commodity. With a flourish of understatement, the banker concluded, "Selling diamonds is far more difficult than I had anticipated."

While the Security Pacific National Bank's problem was made worse because it had to dispose of the diamonds quickly, even when diamonds are held over long periods of time, selling them at a profit can prove difficult. For example, in 1970, the British magazine *Money Which* tested diamonds as a decade-long investment. It bought two gem-quality diamonds, weighing approximately one-half carat apiece, from one of London's most reputable diamond dealers for $1,000. For eight years, it kept these diamonds in its vault, inflation ran as high as 25 percent a year. For the diamonds to have kept pace with this inflationary spiral, they would have had to increase in value at least 300 percent. When the magazine attempted to sell the diamonds, the highest bid that it received was $1500 pounds, which led the publication to conclude "As an eight-year investment the diamonds that we bought have proved to be very poor."

In 1976, the Dutch Consumer Association also attempted to test the price appreciation of diamonds. They bought a perfect, over-one carat diamond in Amsterdam, held it for eight months, and then offered it for sale to the twenty leading dealers in Amsterdam. Nineteen refused to purchase it, and the twentieth dealer offered only a fraction of the purchase price.

In 1972, financial speculators in California had a very expensive lesson in the value of diamonds. In January, the West Coast Commodity Exchange began trading diamond contracts. Each contract contained twenty carats of cut and polished diamonds that were certified by diamond appraisers to be in flawless condition. On the first day of trading, speculators, assuming that the value of diamonds would increase with inflation, paid $660 a carat for the diamonds, or $13,200 per contract. Immediately thereafter, diamond dealers began selling contracts on the exchange, and the price plummeted down to the limit allowed by the exchange for the next six days. The following week, the price was down more than 40 percent. The diamond dealers, who had offered the packets for sale at more than $600 a carat, made a vast profit within days on the falling prices. The speculators, who could not afford to keep putting up cash to meet the collapsing prices, lost everything. By the end of the second week, the West Coast Exchange ended trading in diamond futures. The value of diamonds, it turned out, could not be established through an open market.

Even among experts, the valuation of a diamond depends on highly subjective criteria. In 1979, for example, New York Diamond Club president William Goldberg was offered a six carat diamond in my presence by a reputable New York dealer. Both Goldberg and the dealer agreed that the diamond had excellent clarity, with no defects visible under a ten power magnifying glass, a highly desirable blue-white color, and had been expertly cut. The only disagreement was, in fact, over the price of the diamond. The dealer believed it was worth $24,000. Goldberg, after consulting another dealer, believed it was not worth $8,000. The value was in the eye of the beholder, ultimately.

Selling diamonds can also be particularly frustrating for individuals. One wealthy woman living in New York city decided to sell back a diamond ring that she had bought from Tiffany two years earlier for $100,000, and use the proceeds to buy a necklace of matched pearls that she fancied. She had read about the "diamond boom" in news magazines, and hoped that she might make a profit on the diamond. Instead, the sales executive with whom she dealt explained, with a touch of embarrassment, that Tiffany had "a strict policy against repurchasing diamonds." He assured her, however, that the diamond was extremely valuable and suggested another jewelry store. The woman went from one leading jeweler to another, trying to sell her diamond. One store offered her the opportunity to swap it for another jewel, and two other jewelers offered to accept the diamond "on consignment," and pay her a percentage of what they sold it for, but none of the half-dozen jewelers she visited that day offered her cash for her $100,000 diamond. She finally gave up and kept it.

Retail jewelers generally prefer not to buy back diamonds from customers because the offer they would make most likely would be considered ridiculously low. The "keystone," or markup, on a diamond and setting may range from 100 to 200 percent, depending on the policy of the store. If they bought diamonds back from customers, they would have to buy them back at the wholesale price. Most jewelers would prefer not to make a customer an offer that not only might be deemed insulting but would also undercut the widely-held notion that diamonds hold their value. Moreover, since retailers generally receive their diamonds from wholesalers on consignment and need not pay for them until they are sold, they would not readily risk their own cash to buy diamonds from customers. Rather than offer customers a fraction of what they paid for diamonds, retail jewelers usually recommend their clients to other firms.

One frequently recommended is Empire Diamonds, on the 66th floor of the Empire State Building in midtown Manhattan. Empire's reception room, which resembles a doctor's office, is usually crowded with elderly women who sit nervously in plastic chairs waiting for their name to be called. One by one, they are ushered into a small examining room where an appraiser scrutinizes their diamonds and makes a cash offer. "We usually can't pay more than 60 percent of the current wholesale price," Jack Braud, the president of Empire Diamonds, explained. "In most cases, we have to pay less since the setting has to be discarded and we have to leave a margin for error in our evaluation [especially if the diamond is mounted in a setting]." Empire removes the diamonds from their settings, which are sold as scrap, and resells them to wholesalers. Because of the steep markup on diamonds between the wholesale and retail levels, individuals who buy retail and, in effect, sell wholesale often suffer enormous losses on the transaction. For example, Braud estimated that a half-carat diamond ring that might cost $2,000 at a retail jewelry store could only be sold for $600 at Empire.

The appraisers at Empire Diamonds examine thousands of diamonds a month but only rarely turn up a diamond of extraordinary quality. Almost all the diamonds found in Jewelry are slightly flawed, off-color, commercial-grade diamonds. The chief appraiser explained, "When most of these diamonds were purchased, American women were concerned with the size of the diamond, not its intrinsic quality." He pointed out that the flaws were commonly concealed by the setting, and added, "The sort of flawless, investment-grade diamond one reads about is almost never found in jewelry."

Many of the elderly women who bring their Jewelry to Empire Diamonds and other buying services have been the recent victims of burglaries or muggings and fear further attempts. Thieves, however, have an even more difficult time selling diamonds than their victims. When suspicious-looking characters turn up at Empire Diamonds, for instance, they are asked to wait in the reception room, and the police are called in. In 1980, for example, a disheveled youth came into Empire with a bag full of jewelry that he called "family heirlooms." When Brand pointed out that a few pieces were imitations, the young man casually tossed them in the wastepaper basket. Braud buzzed for the police.

When thieves bring diamonds to underworld fences, they usually get a pittance for them. In 1979, for example, New York City police recovered stolen diamonds with an insured value of $50,000 that had been sold to a fence for only $200. According to the assistant district attorney that handled this particular case, the fence was unable to dispose of the diamonds on 47th Street, and was eventually turned in by one of the diamond dealers whom he had contacted.

While those who actually attempt to sell diamonds often experience disappointment at the low price they are offered, the stories circulated in the press by N. W. Ayer continue to suggest that diamonds are resold at enormous profits. Consider the legend created around the so-called "Elizabeth Taylor" diamond. This pear-shaped diamond, which weighed 69.42 carats after it had been cut and polished, was the fifty-sixth largest diamond in the world, and one of the few large cut diamonds in private hands. Except for the fact that it was a diamond, it had little in common with the millions of small stones that are mass-marketed each year in engagement rings and other jewelry. When Harry Winston originally bought the diamond from De Beers, it weighed over 100 carats. Winston had it cut into a fifty-eight-faceted jewel, which he sold in 1967 to Harriet Annenberg Ames, the daughter of publisher Moses Annenberg, for $500,000. Mrs. Ames found it, however, extremely costly to maintain: the insurance premium just for keeping it in her safe was $30,000 a year. After keeping it for two years, she decided to resell it and brought it back to Harry Winston.

Winston advised Mrs. Ames that he could not buy it back for the price for which she had purchased it from him. She then called Ward Landrigan, the head of Parke-Bernet's jewelry department, and explained that because she did not want any publicity, the diamond should be auctioned without her family's name attached to it.

This caveat gave the publicist that Parke-Bernet retained for the auction the idea for a brilliant gambit. The huge diamond, which would appear on the cover of the catalogue, would be called "The No Name Diamond," and the buyer would have the right to rechristen it. In August of 1969, Ward Landrigan brought the diamond to Elizabeth Taylor's chalet in Gstaad, Switzerland, and assured her that it was the finest diamond then available on the market. She expressed interest in it, and shortly thereafter items were planted in gossip columns suggesting that Elizabeth Taylor planned to bid up to a million dollars for the No Name Diamond.

At that point, Robert H. Kenmore, whose conglomerate had just acquired Cartier in New York, saw the possibility of gaining considerable publicity for Cartier by buying the No Name Diamond, renaming it the Cartier Diamond, and reselling it to Elizabeth Taylor. He preferred to pay a million dollars for it, so that the sale would be indelibly impressed on the public's mind as the most expensive diamond ever purchased. He arranged to borrow the million dollars from a bank, and took the $60,000 interest cost on the loan out of his conglomerate's public relations budget.

The auction was held on October 23, 1969, and after sixty seconds of excited bidding, the diamond was sold to Cartier for $1,050,000. Harriet Ames received from Parke-Bernet, after paying their commission and sales tax, $868,600, and Cartier received the diamond. Four days later, Elizabeth Taylor and her husband, Richard Burton, bought the diamond from Cartier for $1,100,000 (which meant that Cartier took a slight loss on the interest charge), and a few days later the diamond was transferred to Elizabeth Taylor's representative on an international airliner flying over the Mediterranean to avoid any further sales tax on the diamond.

Some ten years later, when she was married to John Warner, the United States senator from Virginia, Elizabeth Taylor decided to sell this well-publicized diamond. She announced that the minimum price was four million dollars, and to cover the insurance costs for showing it to prospective buyers, she further asked to be paid $2,000 for each viewing of the diamond. At this price, however, there were no buyers. Finally in 1980 she agreed to sell the diamond for a reported $2 million to a New York diamond dealer named Henry Lambert who, in turn, planned to sell the stone to an Arabian client. The profit Miss Taylor received from the transaction, after paying sales taxes and other charges, was barely enough to cover the eleven years of insurance premiums on it.

Most knowledgeable diamond dealers believe that the value of extraordinarily large diamonds, such as the one bought and sold by Elizabeth Taylor, depends more on cunning publicity than the intrinsic quality of the stone. An extreme example of this is the seventy-carat diamond given to the Emperor Bokassa in 1977 by Albert Jolis, the president of Diamond Distributors, Inc. The Jolis family first negotiated a concession to mine diamonds in 1947 in what was then the French colony of Ubangi. Jolis's father, Jac Jolis, had made the case to the State Department that an American company should have the mining rights for diamonds in French Central Africa, thus ensuring the United States a supply of industrial diamonds. He even hired William Donovan, the wartime head of the OSS, to represent his firm in the negotiations. According to a declassified memorandum from the American embassy in Paris, State Department officials were persuaded that it was important for the United States to gain "direct access to strategic materials such as industrial diamonds." Eventually, with the assistance of Donovan, Jolis's firm gained control over the alluvial deposits of diamonds in Ubangi. In 1966, Bokassa, then a colonel in the provisional gendarmes, seized power in a military coup d'état and proclaimed himself president of what was then the Central African Republic. President Bokassa agreed to continue the Jolis concession in return for the government receiving a share of a profit. A decade later, however, when Bokassa decided to become emperor and rechristened the country the Central African Empire, Jolis was given to understand that he was expected to provide a "very large diamond" for the coronation.

As the coronation date approached, Jolis found himself caught in a difficult situation. His firm could not afford to spend millions of dollars to acquire the sort of supervised diamond that would put the emperor-to-be in a league with the shah of Iran or the British royal family; yet if he presented him with a small diamond, Bokassa might well withdraw his firm's diamond concessions. Finally, Jolis hit upon a possible solution to this dilemma. One of his assistants had found a large chunk of industrial diamond boart, weighing nearly seventy carats, which curiously resembled Africa in shape. This piece of black, poorly crystallized diamond would ordinarily have been crushed into abrasive powder, and as such would have been worth about $2 a carat, or $140. Jolis instead ordered that this large diamond be polished and mounted on a large ring. He then had one of his workmen set a one-quarter carat white diamond at the point in the black stone that would coincide with the location of the capital of the Central African Empire. Finally, Jolis placed the ring in a presentation box with a certificate staring that this diamond, which resembled the continent of Africa, was unique in all the world.

The following week, though understandably nervous about how it would be received by the mercurial Bokassa, Jolis flew to the Central African capital of Bangui and presented the ring. Bokassa took it out of the box, examined it carefully for a moment, and took Jolis by the hand and led him into a room where his entire cabinet was assembled. He paraded around the table, jubilantly displaying to each and every one of his ministers this huge black diamond. He proudly slipped it onto his ring finger. Jolis's mining concession was secure, at least temporarily secure in the Central African Empire.

A few days later, the emperor proudly wore the black diamond during the coronation ceremony. The world press reported that this seventy-carat diamond, which had cost Jolis less than $500, was worth over $500,000. A piece of industrial boart was thus elevated to being one of the most celebrated crown jewels in the world. When the Emperor of Central Africa met Giscard D'Estaing, the president of France, he extended his black diamond to him as proof of his royalty.

The Bokassa empire ended in 1979 when French paratroopers, on orders from Paris, staged a bloodless coup d'état and put the former emperor and his retinue on a jet headed for France. From there, Bokassa went into exile on the Ivory Coast with his prize diamond ring. When Jolis heard that he retained among his crown Jewels the industrial diamond he had presented him two years earlier, he commented, "It's a priceless diamond as long as he doesn't try to sell it."

The value of the Emperor's diamond, like that of most other diamonds, depends heavily on the perception of the buyer. If it is accepted as a unique gem and a crown jewel, it could be auctioned off for a million dollars. If, on the other hand, it is seen as a piece of industrial boart, it will be sold for $140 and used as grinding powder. It is, as Jolis observed, "a two-tier market."

CAVEAT EMPTOR
PART 2 OF THE 3 PART SERIES

In 1977, in Los Angeles, a film producer, who had just closed his account with his stockbroker, received an unexpected call from a stranger with a distinct English accent. The caller, identifying himself as a representative of "De Beers Diamond Investments, Ltd.," began by commending the producer on his acumen in withdrawing from the stock market. "You obviously are aware of the fact that stocks and bonds can't keep pace with inflation," he continued in a soft voice, "but have you considered diamonds as an alternative?"

He explained that diamonds had appreciated "700 percent over the last ten years," and that they were the "most prudent investment available, since the supply is tightly controlled by a private monopoly." Without further ado, the caller offered to sell the film producer a selection of "investment diamonds" for $5,000.

"But how can I buy diamonds over the phone," the producer asked incredulously.

"All the diamonds are sealed in plastic with a certificate guaranteeing their quality," the caller responded. "And of course you have heard of De Beers." The more hesitant the producer became, the more determined the caller became. "We can register these diamonds under your wife's name, which might be helpful for your taxes," the caller went on.

"Think of how surprised she will be when the diamonds arrive…and you are buying them below wholesale."

The caller, it turned out, was one of dozens of salesmen seated around a bank of telephones in Scottsdale, Arizona. Like the rest of the men in this boiler room, as it was called, he was making a pitch to sell diamonds and had been supplied with a list of names of individuals around the country who had recently closed brokerage accounts. For every order he sold, he received a commission of up 20 percent. Since the prices were in reality far above wholesale prices, the company could afford to pay its salesmen, most of them "telephone pros," large commissions. And despite the similarity of its name, De Beers Diamond Investments, Ltd., was in no way connected with De Beers Consolidated Mines. Like a host of other recently formed diamond boiler rooms, with names like Diamond Selection, Ltd., Kimberlite Diamond Resource Company, and Tel-Aviv Diamond Investments, Ltd., this firm was formed to promote "investment diamonds."

When the mail-order diamonds finally arrive at the purchaser's home, they are sealed in plastic with the certificate guaranteeing their quality. The customer is then advised of what amounts to a catch-22 situation: The quality of the diamond is only guaranteed as long as it remains sealed in plastic; if the customer takes it out of the plastic to have it independently appraised, the certificate is no longer valid. When customers broke the seal, many found diamonds of inferior or even worthless quality. Complaints to the authorities proliferated at such a rate in New York that the attorney general was forced to mobilize a "Diamond Task Force" to process the hundreds of allegations of fraud.

"It is incredible," William R. Ralkin, the assistant attorney general said in the New York Times in 1979. "These crooks will get outwardly rational people to buy a sealed bag containing supposed gems…And they have the nerve to tell their victims not to unseal the packet for two to three years, after which they promise to buy back the stones at much higher prices." He added, "It never fails to amaze me how… professional people like lawyers [and] medical practitioners will send checks for thousands of dollars to people they never met or heard of after being contacted by these boiler room operators."

Aside from selling tens of thousands of diamonds a month over the telephone, many of these newly created firms hold "diamond investment seminars" in expensive resort hotels. At such events, they present impressive graphs and data, and typically assisted by a few well-rehearsed shills in the audience, they proceed to sell sealed packets of diamonds to the audience. (Not uncommonly, in dealing with elderly investors, diamond salesmen play on the fear that their relatives might try to seize their cash assets and have them committed to nursing homes. They suggest that the investors can stymie such attempts by putting their money in diamonds and hiding them.

Some of these entrepreneurs were relative newcomers to the diamond business. Rayburne Martin, who went from De Beers Diamond Investments, Ltd., to Tel-Aviv Diamond Investments, Ltd., both domiciled in Scottsdale, Arizona, had a record of embezzlement and security law violations in Arkansas and was a fugitive from justice during most of his tenure in the diamond trade. Harold S. McClintock, also known as Harold Sager, had been convicted of stock fraud in Chicago, and he had been involved in a silver bullion caper in 1974 before he helped organize De Beers Diamond Investments, Ltd. Don Jay Shure, who arranged to set up another De Beers Diamond Investments, Ltd., in Irvine, California, had also formerly been convicted of fraud. Bernhard Dohrmann, the "marketing director" of the International Diamond Corporation, had served time in jail for security fraud in 1976. Donald Nixon, the nephew of President Richard M. Nixon, and Robert L. Vesco, the fugitive financier, were, according to the New York State attorney general, allegedly participating in a high-pressure telephone campaign to sell "over-valued or worthless diamonds" by employing "a battery of silken-voiced radio and television announcers." Among the diamond salesmen were also a wide array of former commodity and stock brokers who specialized in attempting to sell sealed diamonds to pension funds and retirement plans.

Meanwhile, in London, the real De Beers, unable to stifle all the bogus entrepreneurs in Arizona and California using its name, decided to explore the potential market for investment gems. It announced in March of 1978 a highly unusual sort of "diamond fellowship" for selected retail jewelers. Each jeweler who participated would pay a $2,000 fellowship fee. In return, he would receive a set of certificates for investment-grade diamonds, contractual forms for "buyback" guarantees, promotion material, and training in how to sell these unmounted diamonds to an entirely new category of customers. The target was defined by De Beers as "men aged 55 and over with inherited or self-made wealth to spend." Rather than sell fine jewels, as they were accustomed to, these selected retailers would sell loose stones with a certificate for $4,000 to $6,000.

De Beers's modest move into the investment diamond business caused a tremor of concern in the trade. De Beers had strongly opposed retailers selling "investment" diamonds on the grounds that because there was no sentimental attachment to such diamonds, customers would eventually attempt to resell them and thereby cause sharp price fluctuations. Indeed, De Beers executives expressed concern that retailers would not be able to cope with the thousands of distressed investors who tried to resell their loose diamonds back to them. In response to this new "diamond fellowship" scheme, the authoritative trade journal, *Jewelers' Circular Keystone*, observed: "Besides giving De Beers an unusually direct role in retail diamond sales, the program marks a softening of its previous hard-line stand against gem investing." Eric Bruton, the publisher of *Retail Jeweler* in London, added, "De Beers is standing on the edge of a very slippery slope...They say it is unwise to sell diamonds directly as an investment, then [they] go ahead with this diamond investment scheme."

If De Beers had changed its policy toward investment diamonds, it was not because it wanted to encourage the speculative fever that was sweeping America and Europe. Its marketing executives in London realized that speculators could panic at any moment, and by precipitously flooding the market with diamonds they had hoarded, burst the price structure for diamonds. They had, however, "little choice but to get involved," as one De Beers executive explained. Even though the "De Beers Diamond Investments" in Arizona, which had pioneered in selling diamonds over the telephone, had gone bankrupt, more than 200 firms had by then entered the business of selling sealed packets of diamonds to the American public over the phone. And aside from these proliferating boiler rooms, many established diamond dealers rushed into the field to sell diamonds to financial institutions, pension plans, and serious investors. It soon became apparent in the Diamond Exchange in New York that selling unmounted diamonds to investors was far more profitable than selling them to jewelry shops. By early 1980, David Birnbaum, a leading dealer in New York, estimated that in terms of dollar value, nearly one third of all diamond sales in the United States were for investment diamonds. "Only five years earlier, investment diamonds were only an insignificant part of the business," he added.

Even if De Beers did not approve of this new market in diamonds, it could hardly ignore one-third of the American diamond trade. It had to take some action.

Mass-marketed investment diamonds were made possible in the 1970s by the invention of the diamond certificate. Diamonds themselves cannot be valued by any single measure, such as weight, and the factors involved in such an assessment—clarity, color, and cut—cannot be made by an individual investor or financial institution. Moreover, since diamonds are not fungible in the sense that one diamond can be exchanged for another diamond of the same weight, some means had to be found of standardizing the quality of diamonds. Certificates, which guaranteed the color, clarity, and cut of individual diamonds, provided this medium.

The Gemological Institute of America, a privately owned company established to service jewelers, developed a convenient system for certifying the quality of diamonds. For ascertaining the "cut" of the diamond, the Gemological Institute devised in 1967 a "proportion scope." This contraption casts a magnified shadow of the stone in question over a diagram that represents the ideal proportions for a diamond of that size. By comparing the overlap between the image of the diamond and the diagram, the deviation from the ideal can be easily measured and recorded on the certificate. For determining the "clarity" of the diamond, the Gemological Institute developed a "Gemolite" microscope, which has an attachment for rotating a diamond under ten power magnification against a dark background. If no blemishes can be seen in the diamond under this magnification, it is graded "flawless"; if there are blemishes, but they are very difficult to find with this lens, it is graded "VVS," and with imperfections visible at lower magnifications, it is further downgraded. Finally, to establish the exact color of the diamond, the Gemological Institute introduced the "Diamondlite": a boxlike machine with a window in it which allows a diamond to be compared with a set of sample stones that span all the color gradations from pure white to yellow. The purest white on this scale is classified as "D"; the next grade of white is classified as "E." Gradually, by grade "I," the white is tinted with yellow; and by grade "K," the color is considered to be yellow and of much lower value.

By 1978, diamonds were being routinely certified through these methods, not only by the Gemological Institute of America, but also by other Gemological laboratories in Antwerp, Paris, London, and Los Angeles. Since dealers needed certificates for selling investment diamonds, and customers were usually willing to pay a hefty premium for such a document attached to the diamond, the laboratories found it difficult to keep up with the demand. Long lines of diamond dealers usually formed in front of the laboratories, and in many cases, stand-ins were hired to wait in line for impatient dealers.

The certification mechanism, despite all the Rube Goldberg sorts of inventions employed, did not entirely remove the subjective element from diamond evaluation. Not uncommonly, dealers would resubmit the same diamond to the Gemological Institute and receive a different rating for it. It did, however, facilitate the trading of rare diamonds. A diamond certified as D, flawless, was an extreme rarity, and since very few such stones existed, or would ever be extracted from mines, they could be bought and sold on the basis that they were in short supply. The price of these near-perfect diamonds rose from $4,000 a carat in 1967 to $22,000 to $50,000 in 1980. Even though such extravagant prices for D, flawless, diamonds are frequently cited by the press in stories about the appreciation of diamonds, they are atypical of diamond prices. In all the world, there are probably less than one hundred diamonds mined that can be cut into one carat, D, flawless, stones, and only a small proportion of these ever are certified and sold to investors. Moreover, very few diamonds are ever sold for the prices reported in the news stories. "No dealer I know has ever sold a one-carat investment diamond for $50,000," a New York dealer commented.

The high prices quoted for the few available D, flawless, stones do not necessarily hold for diamonds of an even slightly inferior grade. For example, in 1978, when D, flawless, diamonds were quoted at $22,000 a carat, an H grade white diamond, without any visible imperfections, was valued at only $2,750. Once mounted in a ring or piece of jewelry, it would be extremely difficult for the untrained eye to differentiate between a D and H color (especially since the setting reflects through the diamond). But while this subtle difference makes little difference in the sale of jewelry, it creates nearly 90 percent of the value in an investment diamond. For what is measured by this grading system is not beauty, but the comparative rarity of a given class of diamonds.

Most investors have no choice but to rely on the piece of paper that comes attached to the diamond to specify the grade, and hence the value, of their investment. Not all the certificates, however, emanate from the Gemological Institute of America. Many certificates have been issued by less reputable—or even nonexistent—laboratories, and the diamonds might be of a much lower grade than that certified.

Even if the certificate comes from a bona fide laboratory, its evaluation of the diamond may later be disputed by another assessor. Robert Crowningshield, the New York director of the Gemological Institute, observed, "...I've never seen two experts agree on the quality of a particular diamond."

The extent to which the value of diamonds is determined by the eye of the beholder was demonstrated in 1981 by an experiment conducted under the sponsorship of *Goldsmith* magazine. In this test, four leading diamond evaluators were handed 145 diamonds that had previously been graded by the Gemological Institute of America, the European Gemological Laboratories, and the International Gemological Institute. The team of experts was not told how each of the diamonds previously had been graded. After the team had reached its own consensus on the grade of each stone, the results were compared with those of the Gemological institutes. In 92 out of 145 cases, the team of evaluators disagreed with the grades previously given on the certificates. Despite all the scientific paraphernalia surrounding the process of certification, diamond grading remained, according to this test, an extraordinarily subjective business.

To make a profit, investors at some point must find buyers who are willing to pay more for their diamonds than they did. Here, however, investors face the same problem as those attempting to sell their jewelry: there is no unified market on which to sell diamonds.

Although dealers will quote the prices for which they are willing to sell investment-grade diamonds, they seldom give a set price at which they are willing to buy the same grade diamonds. In 1977, for example, *Jewelers' Circular Keystone* polled a large number of retail dealers and found a difference of 100 percent between different offers for the same quality investment grade diamonds. Moreover, even though most investors buy their diamonds at or near retail price, they are forced to sell at wholesale prices. As *Forbes* magazine pointed out in 1977, "Average investors, unfortunately, have little access to the wholesale market. Ask a jeweler to buy back a stone, and he'll often begin by quoting a price 30 percent or more below wholesale." Since the difference between wholesale and retail tends to be at least 100 percent in investment diamonds, any gain from the appreciation of the diamonds will probably be lost in the act of selling them.

Many New York dealers feared that despite the high pressure telephone techniques, the diamond bubble could suddenly burst. "There's going to come a day when all those doctors, lawyers, and other fools who bought diamonds over the phone take them out of their strong boxes, or wherever, and try to sell them," one dealer predicted. The principal ingredient in the Diamond boom is expectations that may not be fulfilled.

CHAPTER TWENTY-TWO:
THE GREAT OVERHANG
PART 3 OF THE 3 PART SERIES

Except for those few stones that have been permanently lost, every diamond that has been found and cut into a gem since the beginning of time still exists today. This historic inventory, which overhangs the market, is literally in the public's hands. Some hundred million women wear diamonds on their person, while millions of others keep them in safe deposit boxes or strong boxes as family heirlooms. It is conservatively estimated that the public holds more than five hundred million carats of gem diamonds in this above-the-ground inventory, which is more than fifty times the number of gem diamonds produced by the diamond cartel in any given year. Since the quantity of diamonds needed for engagement rings and other jewelry each year is satisfied by the production from the world's mines, this prodigious half billion carat overhang of diamonds must be prevented from ever being put on the market. The moment a significant portion of the public began selling diamonds from this inventory, the price of diamonds could not be sustained. For the diamond invention to survive, the public must be psychologically inhibited from ever parting with their diamonds.

In developing a strategy for De Beers in 1953, N. W. Ayer noted: "Diamonds do not wear out and are not consumed. New diamonds add to the existing supply in trade channels and in the possession of the public. In our opinion old diamonds are in 'safe hands' only when widely dispersed and held by individuals as cherished possessions valued far above their market price." The advertising agency's basic assignment was to make women value diamonds as permanent possessions, not for their actually worth on the market. It set out to accomplish this task by attempting through subtly designed advertisements to foster a sentimental attachment to diamonds which would make it difficult for a woman to give them up. Women were induced to think of their diamonds as their "best friends." As far as De Beers and N. W. Ayer were concerned, "safe hands" belonged to those women psychologically conditioned never to sell their diamonds.

This conditioning could not be attained solely by placing advertisements in magazines. The diamond-holding public, which included individuals who inherit diamonds, had to remain convinced that diamonds retained their monetary value. If they saw price fluctuations in the diamond market and attempted to dispose of them to take advantage of these changing prices, the retail market would become chaotic. It was therefore essential that at least the illusion of price stability be maintained.

The extremely delicate positioning of the "overhang" provides one of the main rationalizations for the cartel arrangement. Harry Oppenheimer explained the unique situation of diamonds in the following terms: "A degree of control is necessary for the well-being of the industry, not because production is excessive or demand is falling, but simply because wide fluctuations in price, which have, rightly or wrongly, been accepted as normal in the case of most raw materials, would be destructive of public confidence in the case of a pure luxury such as gem diamonds, of which large stocks are held in the form of jewelry by the general public." During the periods when the production from the mines temporarily exceeds the consumption of diamonds, which is determined mainly by the number of impending marriages in the United States and Japan, the cartel can preserve the vital illusion of price stability by either cutting back the distribution of diamonds at its London sites or by itself buying back diamonds at the wholesale level. The underlying assumption is that as long as the general public never sees the price of diamonds fall, they will not become nervous and begin selling the hundreds of millions of carats worth of diamonds that they hold from prior production. If this overhang ever reached the market, even De Beers and all the Oppenheimer resources could not prevent the price of diamonds from plummeting.

Before the advent of the twentieth century and the mass marketing of diamonds, the "overhang," though it existed, was far less of an imminent danger. Diamonds were then considered to be the almost exclusive possession of the aristocrats and wealthy elite, who were not expected to precipitously sell their jewels—except under the direst circumstances. In times of revolution, however, this stock did threaten to come cascading onto the market. When the Czar of Russia was deposed in 1917, the Bolsheviks announced that they were selling the mass of diamonds that his family had accumulated over the centuries. The fear that this stockpile of diamonds would come onto the market depressed world diamond prices for over a year. Then Solly Joel, the nephew and heir of Barney Barnato, who controlled the diamond syndicate in London, offered the Bolsheviks one quarter million pounds for the entire hoard sight unseen. The Bolsheviks, desperately in need of cash to finance their revolution, accepted the offer, and delivered the diamonds in fourteen cigar boxes to London. Joel then assured the other diamond merchants that he would keep these diamonds off the market for years, and panic subsided.

With the bulk of the diamonds in the hands of the general public, the problem of the overhang became much more difficult to handle. When the demand for diamonds almost completely abated after the crash of 1929, De Beers shut down the supply of diamonds by closing its mines and buying the production of independent mines for its stockpile in London. It could not, however, prevent diamonds from the overhang seeping into the market. Prices for small gems fell to $5 a carat. De Beers, already heavily in debt, continued through the 1930s to borrow money to buy back as many of these diamonds as it could absorb. But despite all these efforts, enough of the overhang came onto the market to make it impossible for jewelers to buy back diamonds. Public confidence in diamonds as a store of value was nearly destroyed, especially in Europe, and it required more than a generation before diamonds were again to reach their 1929 price level.

In the 1960s, the overhang again threatened to pour onto the market when the Soviet Union began to sell its polished diamonds. De Beers and its allies now no longer controlled the diamond supply. De Beers realized that open competition with the Russians would inevitably lead to "price fluctuations," as Harry Oppenheimer gingerly put it. This, in turn, would undoubtedly weaken the public's carefully cultivated confidence in the value of diamonds. Since Oppenheimer assumed that neither party could afford risking the destruction of the diamond invention, he offered the Soviets a straightforward deal: "a single channel" for controlling the world supply of diamonds. In accepting this arrangement, the Russians became partners in the cartel, and co-protectors of the diamond invention. De Beers then devised the "eternity ring," made up of hundreds of tiny Soviet-sized diamonds, which could be sold to an entirely new market of married women. The advertising campaign designed by N. W. Ayer was based on the theme of recaptured love. Again, sentiments were born out of necessity: American wives received a snake-like ring of miniature diamonds because of the needs of a South African corporation to accommodate the Communist Russia.

As the flow of Soviet diamonds continued into London at an ever-increasing rate, De Beers strategists came to the conclusion that this production could not be entirely absorbed by "eternity rings" or other new concepts in jewelry. They began looking for diamond markets for miniature diamonds outside the confines of the United States. Even though they succeeded beyond their wildest expectation in creating an instant diamond "tradition" in Japan, they were unable to create similar traditions in Brazil, Germany, Austria, or Italy. Despite the cost involved in absorbing this hoard of Soviet diamonds each year, De Beers prevented, at least temporarily, the Soviet Union from taking any precipitous actions that might cause the diamond overhang to start sliding down onto the market.

Another threat came in 1977. Sir Philip Oppenheimer and other De Beers executives became concerned about the buildup of Israeli stockpiles of uncut diamonds in Tel Aviv. Most of these diamonds had been pledged as collateral for loans with which the dealers bought still more diamonds. The Israeli banks, who had lent nearly one-third of all of Israel's foreign exchange on the diamonds, began asking the dealers to repay the loans. To do this, however, dealers would have to sell their diamonds, which could cause an abrupt drop in the price. And if the price began dropping, the banks themselves might be forced to liquidate the remaining stockpiles of diamonds, causing the sort of panic in the diamond market that could conceivably unsettle the overhang.

After establishing liaisons with the Israeli banks, De Beers executives worked out what one of its chief brokers termed "a billion-dollar-squeeze play." First, De Beers reduced the number of diamonds provided to the Israeli dealers at the London sights. Then, through a special surcharge, De Beers actually increased the price the dealers had to pay. To get the cash for these diamonds, the latter were forced to reduce their inventories. Meanwhile, De Beers' publicity department churned out a series of press releases about new surcharges and rising prices that distracted attention from the fluctuation in wholesale prices. Before the year ended, according to *Jewelers' Circular Keystone*, about 350 Israeli dealers, unable to repay their loans, were forced into bankruptcy. The wholesale price, cushioned by De Beers' buying the Israeli operations, wavered but did not collapse. By 1979, stockpile had been successfully dispersed.

The most serious threat to the stability of the diamond overhang came in the 1980s from the sale of "investment" diamonds to speculators in the United States. De Beers had methodically nurtured the idea in America that diamonds were not subject to the vagaries of price that affected other consumer luxuries. To maintain this illusion in the public's mind, De Beers made it a sine qua non condition of its marketing strategy that retail prices should never fall. Price competition between major retailers of diamonds was prohibited by the rules of the game prices. *Jewelers' Circular Keystone*, which interviewed dozens of leading retailers in 1979, explained: "If the giant retailers ever declared a predatory price war on 'mom and pop' competitors and each other, they could destroy the image of diamonds as a commodity that always appreciates in value…So a tacit unwritten agreement with De Beers forbids such privileged retailers from engaging in predatory price wars." Under this system, nationwide Jewelry chains, though they get their diamonds either directly from De Beers or a De Beers sight-holder at a lower price, do not attempt to undercut the small jewelry shop (which acquires its diamonds on consignments at much higher prices). What varies is the profit and markup, not the retail price. As long as individuals do not attempt to resell their diamonds and thereby discover the enormous difference in markups, or "keystones," as they are called in the trade, it is possible to retain the appearance of stable and gradually increasing prices.

The situation radically changed when the more unsavory sales organizations began selling millions of carats of "investment" diamonds to men who had no sentimental attachment to the diamonds themselves and acquired them solely for the purpose of reselling them at a higher price. They were not even mounted as jewelry. By 1980, it was estimated that American investors had paid more than a billion dollars for these diamonds. Moreover, many of the companies that had sold the diamonds with the guarantee of a "buy-back" at a fixed price had either gone bankrupt or simply closed their offices and disappeared.

The diamond cartel managed to absorb or get control over these private stockpiles to prevent them from cascading onto the market and unhinging the entire overhang. If they had not, the illusion would shatter. As one dealer explained, "Investment diamonds are bought for $30,000 a carat, not because any women want to wear them on their fingers, but because the investor believes they will be worth $50,000 a carat. He may borrow heavily to finance his investment. When the price begins to decline, everyone will try to sell their diamonds at once. In the end, of course, there will be no buyers for diamonds at $30,000. At this point, there will be a stampede to sell investment diamonds, and the newspapers will begin writing stories about the great diamond crash." When women read about a diamond crash, some might attempt to sell their own, but find few buyers. At that point, people will realize that diamonds are not forever.

Whether this pessimistic scenario ever unfolds remains to be seen. De Beers has billions of dollars of its cash reserves to buy back diamonds. Nevertheless, with new diamond mines in Australia and Canada coming on stream, the time is past when De Beers can manipulate prices merely through the expedient of shutting down mines.

The diamond invention is neither eternal nor self-perpetuating. It survived for the past half century because two critical conditions were satisfied: the production of diamonds from the world's mines was kept in balance with world consumption; and the public refrained from attempting to sell its inventory back onto the market. De Beers satisfied the first of these conditions by owning and controlling the major sources of diamonds and the second of these conditions by fostering the illusion in the public's mind that diamonds are forever. Both achievements may prove to be temporary phenomena. The diamond craze of the twentieth century could end as abruptly as the tulip mania of the eighteenth century. Under these circumstances, the diamond invention will disintegrate and be remembered only as a historical curiosity, as brilliant in its way as the glittering, brittle, little stones it once made so valuable.

State of the Union
(The Future of Diamonds)
As I have written before, the diamond industry is going through a dramatic evolution.

- Diamond production has been declining since 2005; the first time in over twenty-five years.
- On September 10, 2005, De Beers shut down their last three underground mines.

- Of 170 diamond companies globally, less than 18 are actually producing.
- Diamond inventories held by De Beers and other mining companies that totaled over $22 billion U.S. just a few years ago were down to $3–4 billion in 2005. As of 2008, they are gone!
- Since 2005, Rio Tinto's Argyle mine in Western Australia's Kimberly region, the world's largest, has left $30 billion U.S. of demand unfulfilled. Quite simply, one out of every three orders for a diamond is not filled—and it's going to get worse. By 2012, Canada's Ekati mine (run by BHP Billiton) is predicted depleted; Rio's Diavik mine in Canada is next, and the world's largest, the Argyle mine, will be exhausted in the next decade even with a billion-dollar overhaul.

Botswana, which produces approximately one out of every four gem-quality diamonds, can't be expected to carry the load even though they have upped their production by 22% in 2007. With booming economies in China and India, the world demand for diamonds is at a "tipping point." In only the last decade, China has tripled their jewelry purchases. SOLD OUT is going to be a familiar phrase the public is going to have to deal with when they go looking for a non-commercial, gem-quality diamond. Of the average 130 million carats sold each year, only 2.6 million (that's 2%) are noncommercial. Non-commercial is defined as a diamond that is 100% natural, white, eye clean, well-proportioned, and fully bondable. The current "cut rate" (distribution of commercial to noncommercial diamonds) is forty-nine to one. For every good diamond that is sold in the United States, there are forty-nine crummy (commercial) ones. The average resale value of a commercial-grade diamond is 19.7% of the original dollars paid; the average resale value of a noncommercial grade diamond is 85%—worst case, 60%, best case, 100% or better.

To make matters worse, "brick and mortar" stores and online

consolidators are taking advantage of the shortages by offering "cert pretty" diamonds. (These are diamonds that have lab-grading reports by labs that guarantee nothing and appear to be attractive but are actually only commercial grade "seconds.") Also compounding the problem for the public are the bribery scandals at the labs (see page 159 for details), making it increasingly difficult for the consumer to purchase the real thing versus a bluff diamond.

Besides the sentimental attraction to a diamond, there has to be an actual dollar value or the whole industry will implode and the diamond engagement ring may become a thing of the past like $.99-a-gallon gas. Dr. Charles Fipke, world-renowned geologist, predicted in 2008 that diamond prices would double by 2010; they did.

However, diamonds have never been considered an investment instrument after one billion dollars was lost by consumers buying diamonds as a hedge against inflation in 1980. But, it appears, some lessons aren't easily learned. For anyone who has been paying attention, you would have noticed that large, investment-grade (IF, VVS1, VVS2, and D, E, F) diamonds have been skyrocketing in prices! As of May 2011, a 5ct D, IF is selling for over a million dollars. That's about double what it was just a few years ago. However, we don't have to look hard to see other commodities mimicking the same exponential, unrealistic growth. Oil, gold, platinum, rice, wheat, etc…everything is up! Way up! The question is this: Is this the new reality, or have we fallen down the rabbit hole? The prices people are paying for some diamonds is reflecting a market mania. The current diamond climate is creating a craze very similar to the tulip mania in the early 1600s in Amsterdam. Believe it or not, back then at the height of the mania, a tulip went for $76,000 a bulb! Six weeks after smart money got out, the price had fallen to a dollar!

At the same time, the *Wall Street Journal* reports (SmartMoney, May 2011) that America is going through a sell-off. Every day, eight thousand Americans are turning sixty-five, and they want to unload all their stuff.

They've got over $747 billion worth of homes, $407 billion in cars, $251 billion in clothing, $158 billion of electronics, $87 billion worth of jewelry, and $24 billion worth of art. That's a little under $2 trillion worth of stuff.

New stuff is priced through the roof, and old stuff is being given away. See the solution?

SOLUTION

Since diamonds were discovered over two thousand years ago in India, the world has produced over 380 tons of diamonds. If I had to take a guess, I would estimate that there are over one billion carats of diamonds in the hands of consumers. That is over a hundred times the annual consumption gobbled up for weddings, anniversaries, birthdays, and even Super Bowl rings. These diamonds haven't left the planet; they lie dormant in the private sector and represent the largest stockpile of diamonds that could be harvested again.

If the diamond tradition is going to continue to work, the public is going to have to allow diamond companies access to these gems, and the public will have to understand a "used" diamond is better than no diamond at all. While this may be the last generation to own a diamond cut to order, it doesn't have to be the last to possess one. Patek Phillip Watch Company says that nobody truly owns one of their watches, that they just hold on to it for the next generation. If we can adopt the same philosophy with diamonds, we'll be all right.

WANT TO KNOW MORE?

My goal was to cover all you need to know in one medium-sized book, but at best, I've covered the highlights. All the press from industry scandals, rough diamond shortages, giant diamond discoveries, doomsday predictions on availability, not to mention De Beers's class-action $295 million lawsuit, would fill another book. Instead, all up-to-the-minute news that couldn't make the book is on my website at www.diamondcuttersintl.com.

The Alphabet Rules

L-M-N-O-P

Recently, I appeared on a PBS special about diamonds, and the producer asked me if I could come up with four or five easy-to-remember rules for diamond shopping. So I came up with the Alphabet Rules, a quick and simple consumer protection guide that will help even a novice avoid getting ripped off.

L = Loose   Always look at loose, not mounted, diamonds. The setting may hide flaws.

M = Magnify   Always look at your diamond through a jeweler's loupe or a microscope, which will reveal imperfections invisible to the naked eye.

N = Negotiate   Most retailers dramatically increase prices. Never pay the sticker price unless you've shopped around and you know they're already giving you the wholesale price.

O = Opinion   Always insist that the final sale be contingent upon the opinion of an independent appraiser. If the appraiser agrees that you've done well, the sale will be final.

P = Plot   Always have the diamond's flaws plotted on a drawing of the stone. That way you'll be able to identify your diamond by the location of its blemishes and inclusions.

Appendix B

Carat Size Charts

Carat Weight	Shapes				
.50	◯	◇	▢	▢	◯
.75	◯	◇	▢	▢	◯
1.00	◯	◇	▢	▢	◯
1.25	◯	◇	▢	▢	◯
1.50	◯	◇	▢	▢	◯
2.00	◯	◇	▢	▢	◯
2.50	◯	◇	▢	▢	◯
3.00	◯	◇	▢	▢	◯

Carat Weight	Shapes

4.00

5.00

Carat Weight	Round	Carat Weight	Round
1/150	∘	1.25	◯
1/100	∘	1.50	◯
1/70	∘		
1/50	∘	2.00	◯
1/40	○	2.50	◯
1/33	○		
1/25	○	3.00	◯
.03	○		
.05	○	4.00	◯
.07	○		
.10	○	5.00	◯
.15	○		
.20	◯		
.25	◯		
.33	◯		
.40	◯		
.50	◯		
.65	◯		
.75	◯		
.85	◯		
1.00	◯		

Glossary of Terms

SPEAKING THE JEWELER'S LANGUAGE

Annealing   The process of treating a diamond with high temperature and high pressure (HTHP) to remove nitrogen, boon, and other impurities that discolor a diamond. Also known as baking or heating.

Blemish   A flaw on the exterior of a diamond, such as a scratch, abrasion, nick or chip.

Blue-white   Refers to a diamond that glows (fluoresces) blue under ultraviolet light.

Brilliance   White light reflected back from a diamond.

Brilliant   A round diamond with fifty-eight facets.

Carat   A unit of weight equal to two hundred milligrams. In ancient times, one carat was equal to one carob bean or four grains of rice.

Carbon   The raw material of which diamonds are made. Occasionally, a diamond will contain tiny pockets of carbon that can be seen as black spots within the stone.

Cloud   A cluster of small inclusions or internal flaws within a diamond.

Color Matched   The process of taking fancy-colored diamonds and intensifying and equalizing the color through neutron bombardment in order to match neighboring diamonds.

Crown   The top of a diamond. Everything above the girdle.

Culet   The bottom of a diamond, usually very small.

Dispersion   Colored light reflected within a diamond; also called "fire."

Eye-clean   Refers to a diamond that has no inclusions or blemishes visible to the naked eye.

Facet   A polished surface on a diamond. A round, full-cut diamond usually has fifty-eight facets.

Flagship   Standard and box radiants that abide by the 65/65.

Fluorescence   A diamond's reaction to ultraviolent (UV) light, causing the stone to glow in various colors.

Full-cut   A diamond with fifty-eight or more facets.

Fully Bonded   A fully bonded diamond is a natural diamond that is fully warranted by the jeweler and covers breakage, buy-back, and exchange.

Gemologist   A person who has been trained and accredited in diamonds and colored stones.

GIA   Gemological Institute of America.

Girdle   The narrow, unpolished or faceted band around the widest part of the diamond; the girdle separates the crown and the pavilion of the stone.

Head   The prongs that hold a diamond in its setting.

Inclusion   A flaw within a diamond, such as carbon spots or fractures.

Karat   The measure of purity of gold; 24-karat being pure gold. Jewelry is usually made from 18K and 14K gold, which contain other metals for strength.

Laser-drilled   A diamond that has been treated with a laser to remove carbon spots or other inclusions.

Loupe   A small magnifying glass used to view gemstones.

Off-make   A poorly proportioned diamond.

Pavé   A method of setting diamonds very closely together, giving the illusion of one or more larger diamonds.

Pavilion   The bottom of a diamond; everything below the diamond's girdle.

Point   One hundredth of a carat. A diamond weighing one-and-a-half carats weighs 150 points.

Semimount   A setting that is complete except for the main stone, which will be selected separately.

Single-cut   A diamond with only sixteen or seventeen facets.

Sparkle   The liveliness of the light reflecting from a diamond; the sum of the brilliance and the fire (dispersion).

Tiffany   A simple, elegant, 2–3mm ring setting with a head that holds a single diamond.

ROCK SLANG DICTIONARY

In the jewel industry, we throw around a lot of slang terms like, "chubbies," "four grainers," "off-makes," and "glow worms," to name a few. Some of this slang terminology is derived from decades of usage, and other terms are technically correct definitions to describe a diamond like the "65/65 Rule." Here, I've tried to give definitions of the most popular slang terms that jewelers, dealers, and cutters have been using for years. Hopefully, it will make it a little easier for the consumer to understand the secret language we jewelers use on a day-to-day basis.

65/65 Rule   A square or rectangular diamond whose table and total depth percentage does not exceed 65 percent of the diamond's width.

Amplified Light Return (A.L.R.)   The number of visible internal light reflections that a diamond has per every ray (signal) of light that enters it.

As Is   A diamond that comes with no bonding or warranties. Its sale is final, no exceptions after the buyer takes possession from the vendor.

Back Alley   A diamond that has had at least one previous owner and is being purchased on the secondary market. Example: Joe has purchased a back alley diamond. Translation: Joe has purchased a used diamond.

Bananas   A marquise-shaped diamond whose length to width ratio exceeds 2.25 to 1. The diamond appears to have been stretched to look like a banana.

Big Brother   Diamond Trading Company, aka De Beers.

Bling-Bling   A sparkly, valuable diamond or diamond jewelry.

Blue Booked   The dollar value placed on a diamond at time of purchase that the seller agrees to purchase the diamond back at some time in the future.

Bonded Synonymous with warranty. All diamonds are either fully bonded, partially bonded, or not bonded. A new subcategory that has been popularized of late is the fully bonded diamond with an expiration date (i.e., a limited lifetime warranty). The diamond is warranted not for the life of the diamond or person but for the warranty itself. Most of these bogus warranty packages (breakage guarantee, buy-back, exchange) run ninety days. A true fully bonded diamond has no expiration date or restocking fee.

Canaries A canary diamond is yellow in color because of the fact that it is saturated with nitrogen. The four main categories of canaries are light fancy, fancy, intense fancy, and vivid.

Chubbies Diamonds that are poorly proportioned. Typically, diamonds that have oversized girdles or deep pavilions that cause the diamonds to appear smaller than they should when viewed from the top for any given weight.

Cognac A brown diamond dramatized as attractive and valuable with an appealing title.

Commercial Grade Diamonds that are recovered in bulk form and distributed for the masses primarily through online consolidators and chain stores. These goods are typically poor quality. They come with non-guaranteed lab reports that offer little of no warranties and depreciate dramatically after these warranties expire.

Consolidator A clearing house for commercial grade, off-makes, or poor quality diamonds. These seconds are sold both online and in brick-and-mortar locations.

Decorate the Tree How the facets are arranged on a diamond.

Doublet A diamond or gemstone that is made of two pieces. Example: The crown is diamond, but it is epoxied to a pavilion made out of cubic zirconia.

Duping The con of selling a diamond with a lab-grading report that does not match the diamond being sold but rather matches a diamond that was shown loose to make the initial sale and later switched for the understudy.

Efficiency Rating (E.R.) A measure of the refracted light entering a diamond that is returned to your eye.

Estate   A diamond or piece of jewelry that has been previously owned and is up for sale.

Fancies   Has two meanings: (1.) Any shape other than a round diamond or, (2.) any diamond of any particular color of the rainbow but white. These would include blues, pinks, violets, and yellows. The most famous fancy diamond in the world is the Hope Diamond, which is steel blue.

Fisheye   The circular, centrally dark light pattern that appears in the table of a round diamond when it is cut shallow. It derives its nickname because of the fact that the light leakage through the pavilion creates the look from the crown of that of a fish's eye.

Footballs   The opposite of a banana-shaped marquise that closely resembles the shape of a football. A marquise could be described as a football if its length to width ration is less than 1.75 to 1.

Fractional Crystallization A state in which a diamond was not able to fully crystallize because of lack of and/or excessive of heat and/or pressure.

Full-Term Rough   Uncut diamond with a cubic crystal lattice structure and a minimum of eight hundred million years old. This type of rough typically appears in the shape of a cube, octahedron, or dodecahedron.

Fully Warranted   Can be synonymous with fully bonded. A diamond that has a breakage, buy-back, exchange, and market-crash guarantee. When it comes with no expiration dates, it is considered fully bonded. Otherwise it is a limited lifetime warranty.

Glow Worms   A diamond that exhibits fluorescence in the presence of ultraviolet light. Fluorescent diamonds are 20 percent less valuable than nonfluorescent diamonds.

Grade Bumping/Soft Grades   A diamond whose clarity or color grade has been raised by one or more grades by a lab appraiser or salesman to enhance the value of the diamond.

Grainers   In the Orient, diamonds were weighed using grains of rice. (4 grams = 1/5 of a gram which = a 1 ct diamond on a counter balance) Example: a 6 grainer = 1 ½ ct diamond

Grandfather   An old diamond (Old Miners, Old European) or a diamond whose paperwork is outdated. A lab-grading report is considered a grandfather when it is over six months old, and an appraisal is considered a grandfather at two years old.

Guild Store   A guild store is slang for a premium jewelry store. For example, Graff, Van Cleef & Arpels, Harry Winston, or Cartier and other top-tier retailers.

Hot Rocks   Diamonds whose country of origin (South Africa, Sierra Leon, etc.) is linked to wars and oppression fueled with the finds acquired from the sale or barter of diamonds.

Illusion Setting   The placement of a diamond in to a mirrored high-polished plate of metal to give the illusion that the diamond is larger than it appears from a distance.

Laser-drilled   A diamond whose inclusions have been drilled out with a laser.

Melee   Small diamonds, usually used to describe diamonds under a quarter carat in size.

Noncommercial Grade The top 2 percent of diamonds that hold their value and/or appreciate over time. These goods are not found in bulk form and are distributed to guild stores and bonded jewelers. They come with guaranteed certificates (fully bonded appraisals) and unconditional buy-back and exchange policies.

Off-makes   Generally speaking, a poorly proportioned diamond that is either cut too shallow, too deep, or warped. All class III and IV cut diamonds are considered off-makes.

Old European   A round diamond popularly cut in the early 1900s for the public from European cutting houses. These diamonds had the same characteristics as an Old Miners (small table, high crown, open culet) with the exception that they were not squarish round but round in diameter.

Old Miners   A squarish round diamond typically seventy-five or more years old, whose facet arrangement is highlighted by a small table, high crown, and open culet. Old Miners also referred to as heavy makes.

Orphan   A diamond that is being sold at an auction and has no current owner that is wearing it. Orphan can also be used to describe a diamond that does have an owner but the owner no longer wears it. Example: Mary owns a beautiful, two-carat, orphaned diamond. She should rescue it from her safety deposit box.

Padded   See spreads and chubbies. The cutter kept extra weight on the stone that does not optimize the optics of the diamond. The goal is to increase revenue.

P.B.'s   Not peanut butter but "partially bonded." A diamond with some warranties.

Pegasus, Monarch, or Bellataire   Brand names for annealed (heated, baked) diamonds introduced into the market by General Electric and Lazare Kaplan in 1998.

Pickpocketing   A salesman has been said to be "pickpocketing" a customer when he uses the two-month-salary guideline in order to make a bigger sale.

Plot   The mapping of inclusions and blemishes on a paper diagram of the facet arrangement of any given diamond for identification purposes. Similar to a fingerprint.

River Rock   A diamond that is so heavily included (I2 and I3s) that they deserve to be thrown in the river. River rock is synonymous with a bad diamond of little or no value.

Rovals   A poorly proportioned oval diamond that has a length to width ratio under 1.2 to 1, causing the diamond to look not quite round and not quite oval. Hence "roval."

Sandbagger   An appraiser who misgrades an appraisal to sabotage a sale in order to recommend that the client purchase somewhere else.

Single Cuts   Round diamonds that have sixteen or seventeen facets.

Spreads   A diamond that is purposely cut wide to give the impression that the diamond is larger than its corresponding weight when viewed from the top. All spreads are also shallow with less than 38 percent light return.

Warped A diamond whose crown height percentage plus maximum girdle thickness percentage plus pavilion depth percentage doesn't equal the total depth percentage within .5 percent.

Weighted Light Return (W.L.R.) A measure of brightness in a diamond derived by multiplying efficiency rating and amplified light return.

Diamond Guy Q&A

I HAVE PICKED A few of my favorite questions and thought I would share them with you here. If you have any questions of your own, I can be reached at www.diamondcuttersintl.com or through my HelpLine, 1-800-275-4047 or 713-222-2728.

SUBJECT: CLEANING A DIAMOND

What is the proper way to clean a diamond? I use alcohol sometimes, and other times, I use Efferdent denture cleaner. Can either of these damage my diamonds?

ANSWER

I recommend cleaning your ring daily. There is no better home care system than household ammonia and a good ultrasonic toothbrush. Let the ring soak and then use an ultrasonic toothbrush to get to any hard-to-reach crevices. Ultrasonic toothbrushes cost between $30–$200 and are available in most major department stores.

SUBJECT: TIFFANY SETTING

What is a Tiffany setting?

ANSWER

A Tiffany setting is generally a 2–2.5 mm band with a 4-or 6-prong head. No side diamonds.

Subject: Is it really a diamond?

I heard from someone in a chat room of a laboratory that "creates its own diamonds" by "speeding up" the coal-to-diamond process. I heard of someone purchasing a 2.5-carat stone for $500 from this place. The stones are called diamond essence, I believe. Is this too good to be true, or are these legitimate diamonds?

Answer

If it were true, I'd be out of business! The cost for a good quality 2.5ct diamond is around $54,600. This "diamond essence" is a simulant. Translation: not a man-made diamond, just cubic zirconia that kind of looks like a diamond! The correct price for a 2.5 ct "diamond essence" should be $1.00 to $2.50 per carat, not $500. Wow, what a mark up!

Subject: Diamond cuts

What is meant by a miner's cut?

Answer

The miner's cut or old miner's cut was the first predecessor to what is now called the American Ideal cut or the round diamond. Its shape was a cross between a round and a square. It was more like a square with rounded corners, a high crown, and a deep pavilion, with the traditionally chopped-off culet (the culet is the facet on the bottom of the stone). Diamond cutting has come a long way since the old miner's cuts of the early 1900s, and it is a good thing too. Old miner's cuts were nothing more than an athlete fifty pounds overweight. The modern day cuts are more durable, beautiful, and valuable.

SUBJECT: INCLUSIONS

My diamond has a small but visible (with the naked eye) inclusion toward the base. You can see it only from looking up through the bottom. How does this affect the value?

ANSWER

There are two ways to describe any diamond: commercial or noncommercial. Commercial represents the average, low-quality diamonds that are generally sold. They are diamonds with one or more of the following faults: not eye-clean, tinted yellow, poorly proportioned, treated, or fluorescent. Noncommercial grades are eye-clean, white, well-proportioned, nontreated, and nonfluorescent. The diamond you're describing, due to the fact that the inclusion can be seen without magnification, would in most cases classify the diamond in the commercial category. Unfortunately, this is a bad thing. With approximately 97.5 percent of all diamonds sold being commercial, you're probably holding onto a diamond that is not extremely rare. And with that lack of uniqueness comes the following problems:

1. It will appreciate in value little or not at all.
2. It probably has no trade-in value.
3. Its cash-liquidation value is approximately ten cents on the dollar.

A noncommercial-grade, natural diamond with SI1, I color, Class II, no fluorescence, at a minimum will:

1. Appreciate in value by an average of 6 percent per year
2. Have trade-in capabilities
3. Have a cash-liquidation value (or dump value) of sixty to eighty cents on the dollar

If it's possible to trade in or get a new diamond, I would recommend it.

Subject: Natural/Treated Diamonds

In your responses, you occasionally refer to a diamond as being "natural" as opposed to being "treated." I am not familiar with what that means. My assumption is of some type of bleaching process to aid the color of a diamond. Could you please explain the meanings of those terms and what the effect of "treating" a diamond has on its quality and value.

Answer

Approximately one out of every three diamonds is treated after the faceting process. By treated I'm referring to laser-drilled, fracture-filled, heat-treated, coated, and irradiated. Treated diamonds have very poor to no secondary market value and in many cases are not structurally sound. A noncommercial-grade diamond that is natural could expect to appreciate 6 percent to 8 percent per year. Treated diamonds do not appreciate.

Subject: Natural/Treated Diamonds

How can one ensure that a diamond one is looking at has not been treated?

Answer

With the exception of baked diamonds (e.g., Pegasus), the only way to be sure that you are getting a natural diamond is to get it in writing at the point of purchase. Then have it verified by an independent appraiser. The only way to ensure against a baked diamond is with a bonding document.

Subject: Basic Question

1.   How much does it cost to get a GIA lab-grading report?

2. How long does it take?

3. What is the best way to ship and insure a diamond in the mail?

4. Will they also point out any sort of treatment, if any, that's been done to the stone?

ANSWER

1. The price of a GIA lab-grading report is based on the size of the diamond. The average cost for a GIA lab-grading report is around $177.

2. They say four to five business days, but it is more like two weeks.

3. Registered mail is your best choice.

4. If the diamond is treated, GIA should catch it.

SUBJECT: DIAMOND COLOR GRADES

I read somewhere about diamonds being referred to as white but still having further divisions: Blue White, Fine White, White, Commercial White, Top Silver Cape, and Silver Cape. It said that any of these diamonds could all be referred to as "white" by a jeweler. Is this true? What is the difference in these diamonds?

ANSWER

The terms you've listed are called "old-school terminology." No one who is trying to be straight with you should use these terms. Only some places in Europe still use them. Blue White refers to D, E, F colors. Fine White refers to G, H. White refers to I, J. Commercial white and lower are slightly tinted yellow diamonds. Blue White can also refer to a fluorescent diamond.

SUBJECT: HARRY WINSTON

I wandered into Harry Winston in New York the other day and was surprised to find that they don't sell loose stones—only the finished product! I took a look at their little booklet that describes everything, and

I can't believe people are buying these expensive rings already set! Is it because of the name and that they are historically known for quality?

I've been really learning a lot about diamonds and have been doing a lot of research—I should be able to get a fine diamond and setting just as good as the Harry Winston on my own, right? Also, I never asked my jeweler about the polish—should I? What should I be looking for? Is there a way to check it against what the jeweler's telling me? Is this going to hugely devalue the ring if it's not right?

ANSWER

When buying a diamond, everyone generally has two main concerns: getting the right diamond and getting it at the right price. While satisfying any one of these isn't difficult, getting both takes a lot of time, patience, and work. The high-end stores like Graff, Van Cleef & Arpels, Cartier, Winston, etc., cater to one type of client—a person who wants quality but does not have the time to shop around to get it. Harry Winston's customers feel that their time is extremely valuable. They feel that the price difference between buying at Harry Winston's quickly and spending hours to find the same thing at a lower price are equal because they can take the time they would have spent shopping and use it to make money.

Harry Winston is practically beyond reproach. They represent quality with a capital "Q." But is it possible to get the same quality for as much as a half to a third of the price? Absolutely! It just takes work!

In regards to polish, I can't recall ever seeing a well-proportioned diamond with bad polish. Don't worry about it.

SUBJECT: PLACE OF PURCHASE

I want to purchase an upgrade diamond for my wife. I'm on a budget. However, I still want to buy the biggest, clearest diamond for my buck. Can you recommend a vendor that doesn't mark up extremely high?

Answer

Look for a wholesaler. Their average markup is 10 percent to 15 percent above their cost. They should be cheaper than retail outlets. Call the International Diamond HelpLine at 800-275-4047 or 713-222-2728 to locate a wholesale near you.

Subject: Lab-grading report, appraisal, or both?

I have a trusted diamond dealer whom other members of my family have bought from before. He told me that he can get a diamond with an appraisal, but it won't have a lab-grading report. Is it OK to not have a lab-grading report? What is it REALLY for? Is it necessary?

Answer

A lab-grading report is nothing more than an opinion. When you consider that for every one thousand diamonds that are sold in the United States, less than twenty-five would classify as good or noncommercial, do you think your jeweler is getting you one of those elusive gems? If so, I guess, don't worry about it. But even if you don't get a lab-grading report, you need to get an independent appraisal. Lab-grading reports are definitely required with investment-grade diamonds or fancy, colored diamonds.

Subject: Price Of Diamonds with Lab-Grading Reports

If a diamond comes with a lab-grading report, should it be more expensive than a diamond that is of the same quality and grading but does not come with a lab-grading report?

ANSWER

Diamonds with a lab-grading report should not cost more than diamonds without one. If the jeweler is working very tightly on the price of the stone, there is an argument (small) that the diamond would cost approximately $177 more because that is the average cost of the typical lab-grading report.

SUBJECT: BASIC QUESTIONS

1. How can you tell for sure that a diamond has been laser-drilled? In a diamond we recently purchased can be seen a straight line that I've been told is a laser drill mark. Two jewelers told me this, and I saw it myself. Then, just to complicate things, another jeweler told me he didn't think that's what it was but that it was a natural inclusion. How can I be sure? I've heard everything from looking for "orange light" to putting it under high heat. Can one be sure?
2. Is it required by law that it be disclosed if a diamond has been "laser-drilled?"
3. Why would a diamond lose its sparkle over the years?
4. Will I get the same general appraisal from several qualified appraisers? In other words, is one appraisal enough?

ANSWER

1. Your best shot is to go to one of the labs.
2. Yes, it is now required by law that it be disclosed if a diamond has been laser-drilled.
3. Improper cleaning or a poorly cut diamond that becomes abraded will cause a diamond to lose its sparkle.
4. One independent appraisal is enough.

Subject: Is the price set?

Are prices on rings from those chain jewelry stores at the mall always set? Is there any room to bargain or bring the price down? I wasn't sure if shopping for engagement rings was anything like buying a new car.

Answer

The average jewelry store in the United States charges twice what they should. No one pays sticker price. Generally, the price listed in the average store can be cut in half. Go negotiate!

Subject: Lab-grading report

Does a lab-grading report ever become dated?

Answer

Yes. A lab-grading report must be recent (within six months), and the diamond must not have been worn since it was graded.

Subject: Jeweler Questionnaire

While shopping for a diamond, one jeweler told me that they use their own scale that has been in existence since the 1940s, which they say is longer than GIA's scale. They said they would provide a chart that shows how their grading scale correlates with GIA's scale. You said to disqualify any jeweler who does not use GIA-grading scale; would this be okay, or should I still disqualify the store? They were the most friendly and helpful of all that I contacted. Also, a store told me that they specialize in "Lazare diamonds," and they mailed me some info on them. The information says that they have higher standards for these diamonds, and they have a logo and an individual identification number specially inscribed on its circumference. It says that the inscription is visible under a 10X microscope and does not affect the clarity grade of the diamond. Is that true? Are these diamonds really better than any others? Can any jewelry store get them, or are they rare?

ANSWER

To question #1, disqualify the store or make all sales contingent on a lab-grading report or independent appraisal. That way you will be able to see if you are getting what you really want.

Some Lazare Kaplan diamonds can be equivalent to Class I or Class II diamonds. They are very well cut. As long as the price is in line, Lazare Kaplan stones can be a good choice. Only stores that have an account with Lazare Kaplan can get their diamonds.

SUBJECT: FOUR ELEMENTS

During an interview on MSNBC, you referred to the four elements to any purchase. Can you go over those again?

ANSWER

In any purchase, not just diamonds, there are four factors that must be taken into consideration before purchase:

P–Price Q–Quality

S–Service W–Warranties

So, mind your Ps and Qs, but don't forget your SWs. Let's start with price first. Everyone in this world, including jewelers, has a right to make a living and a profit. But a living and price gouging are not the same thing, which is why you have to be educated and know what a fair price is. Otherwise, you'll leave yourself open to the wolves. In quality, it is true that beauty lies in the eyes of the beholder. But with 99 percent of the public unable to tell the difference between a cubic zirconia and a diamond, appraisals, lab-grading reports, and independent evaluations can sometimes be the only things that can keep you from making a big mistake beyond knowing what to ask for. Thirdly, service. Most people don't realize that even diamonds need to have checkups every now and then, as do their settings. An annual polishing, cleaning, and tightening of your jewelry is a must. Top-notch jewelers will provide the annual checkups free of charge. Last but not least are warranties. It is my honest opinion that bonded diamonds are going to be prerequisites to any serious diamond buyer from now on. The prior president of GIA, William Boyajian, said in an interview that baked diamonds are the biggest threat to hit the diamond industry in the twenty-three years he's been with GIA. As long as laboratories can no longer guarantee a diamond is 100 percent natural and untreated, a diamond without at least a buy-back policy and breakage guarantee isn't worth the setting it's in.

SUBJECT: ROUND

What do you think of the following: round, one-carat, 6.44–6.49 × 3.89 mm, depth: 60.2 percent, table: 55 percent, girdle: medium to slightly thick, culet: none, polish: VG, symmetry: G, clarity: VS1, color: D, fluorescence: none. It also has in the comments: "Additional pinpoints, internal graining, and surface graining are not shown." What does this mean?

ANSWER

At this point, the diamond looks "cert pretty," meaning that with all the data present the diamond looks good. But please remember that, just like beauty can be only skin deep, so too can a diamond be only "report pretty." You need to find out the crown angle, pavilion angle, crown height, and pavilion depth to make a total evaluation. As far as the extra comments, pinpoints are just inclusions the size of the head of a pin that the grader was too lazy to plot. Graining, whether it be internal or surface, is just like graining you might see in a piece of wood. It is nothing to worry about.

Subject: Total depth does not equal crown + pavilion + girdle

I have done quite of bit of diamond shopping, and I have found that when I add up the pavilion depth plus crown height plus girdle (produced from a megascope report), the total is about 1–2 percent off of the total depth listed on the lab-grading report for diamonds from what seem to be reputable jewelers. For example, a (EGL lab-graded) G, VS1, 1.02-carat, total depth: 59.8, crown height: 14.5, pavilion: 42.6, girdle: 1.1. When I add the last three numbers, the total is 58.2, a 1.6 percent difference from what is listed on the total depth. When I brought this up, the dealer seemed just as perplexed as I because those were the printed numbers from his megascope report too. Is there any reason the total depth would not be exactly equal to the sum of those three measurements?

Answer

Boy, you are a sharp cookie! You are absolutely correct that they must add up! So why in God's name are they off on so many stones? There are three possible reasons: (1) The sarin or megascope machines have been calibrated to choose just the perfect crown or pavilion angle instead of a large multiple average. Then, taking the tangent of the angles, the machine calculates the crown height or pavilion depth. Now, if the crown angle and the pavilion angle that were chosen were warped angles, the rest of the data will be wrong! (2) Some graders "guesstimate" instead of actually measuring correctly. (3) Some sarin and megascope reports are scanned into a computer, altered, and reprinted. The most the totals should ever be off is one-half of 1 percent.

Subject: Bonded dealers on the Internet

Are their any fully bonded diamond dealers on the Internet?

Answer

Yes. FullyBondedDiamonds.com (our sister company) is up and running. They are the first online retailer to follow to the exact letter all the guidelines outlined in *How to Buy a Diamond*. Come on, which would you rather have? A cheesy, thirty-day return policy or the security of a lifetime return? What does it say about a company that it will not buy back their own merchandise after thirty days?

I'll tell you what it says. They don't believe in their product. Go ahead and get a fully bonded diamond. Give them a call at 800-825-2616 and tell them The Diamond Guy sent you!

Appendix E

Getting into Shape

◆————————————————————————————◆

A PALM READER SUPPOSEDLY can tell you your future, and numerologists say they can do the same thing by adding and subtracting the numbers of the day, month, and year you were born. Astrologers go so far as to say they can tell you who you are, where your future lies, and what you're going to have for lunch by what phase the moon was in when you were born!

According to all these mystics, who we are and why we do what we do is all predetermined by fate. All we have to do is know how to read the signs to tell us what path our lives will follow and what our final destination will be. "Yeah, right!" you're probably saying. "I am the captain of my own ship and the creator of my own destiny." Well, maybe so, but how can you explain the fact that every time you check your daily astrology guide, it seems to be pretty accurate? Lucky guess? Maybe. So vague it could apply to anyone? Maybe. Or maybe it's just as simple as thought creating reality. If you are told something and you believe it, I guess it doesn't make a difference whether it's true or not. If it's true for you, even if it's just a perception, it's your reality, your truth.

Now, probably at this point (if you're still reading), you're thinking, "What the heck does this have to do with diamonds and 'Getting into Shape?'" which I know you have figured out doesn't mean doing push-ups or jumping jacks. What we are delving into here is why women like and/or choose one shape of diamond over another. Believe it or not, what shape a woman chooses for an engagement ring tells a lot about the woman doing the wearing. After almost two decades of watching women choose different shapes and sizes, I found that certain personality types tend to gravitate toward one particular shape or another. I've also found that certain shapes tend to have a higher divorce rate than other shapes! Oh, I've got your interest now, have I? Yes, I've actually been able to graph which shapes tend to have the highest divorce rates, which ones result in the best marriages, and which ones are more likely to fool around! Am I crazy? Probably. But if you're interested in one guy's observations, here it goes. Astrologers, numerologists, palm readers, and tarot card readers step aside. (Drum roll please.) I'd like to introduce for the audience's enjoyment the wonderful world of Dia-shape-ology!

Fill out the following questionnaire and answer honestly to determine what your diamond says about you.

1.   Do you have a diamond? (Circle one)

Yes   No

(If no, please stop taking this test.)

2.   What shape diamond do you have? _____

3.   What size diamond do you have? (Circle one)

   A.   Microscopic

   B.   Nice Size

   C.   A Boulder

   D.   I can't lift my hand from the weight.

4.   How long have you had your diamond? (Circle one)

   A.   Less than 2 years

   B.   2–5 years

   C.   5–7 years

   D.   I can't remember it's been so long.

5.   Are you still with the person who gave you the diamond? (Circle one)

Yes   No

(If you bought it yourself, the answer will always be yes.)

6.   How often do you clean your diamond? (Circle one)

   A.   Once a day

   B.   Once a week

   C.   When it gets dirty

   D.   I'm supposed to clean my diamond?

7.   Pick the statement that best describes your relationship with your diamond. (Circle one)

   A.   I will keep my diamond 'til the day I die. We are inseparable.

   B.   I will keep my diamond 'til the day I die unless something better comes along.

Check the following answer guide to see how you've done and determine what your diamond means to you and what it says to the world about the person you are.

Question #1: Obviously, for the purpose of this exercise, having a diamond is a prerequisite. Not to say that if you are not the owner of a diamond, you are any less loved and appreciated. It just seems that way.

Question #2: Here's the meat and potatoes; the meaning of the top shapes:

Round—Congratulations! Round is the most popular, faithful, traditional, and religious. Most round-wearers chose a round for its clean lines and symmetry. The idea that a circle has no beginning and no end adds to the romance of a round. Round-wearers tend to be old-fashioned and honest with values and beliefs they would fight for. The only downside to some who choose a round is their lack of spontaneity and leadership abilities. Round-wearers tend to be more team players than team leaders. If a round-wearer is married, her main goal in keeping a long, loving relationship is to not be afraid of change.

Oval—Look, you would have gotten a round if everyone in your family, including your aunt Gertrude, didn't have one. You have all the same values of a round, but there is something inside you that cries out to be different and not go with the crowd. Oval-wearers make great wives! On one side, they are predictable, stable, and dependable, but every now and then, they have wild hair and let loose! If not for the poor brilliancy of an oval, I believe a lot more women would be in this camp.

Pear—Where round-wearers tend to go with the crowd, pear-wearers want to create the crowd. Pear-wearers want to be different, pure and simple. If also being better comes along with the package, so be it. Pear-wearers tend to be more demanding and higher maintenance. Everything has to be just right, or "don't do it at all" is their battle call. Pear-wearers are the third most likely to get a divorce. (Top two coming up.) Due to, in many cases, forgetting that happiness isn't always asking, "What's in it for me?" The happily married pear-wearer never forgets that there is no I in team and applies the same standards of excellence to herself as to her partner.

Emerald Cut—Here's a tough nut to crack. Emerald-cut-wearers are old-fashioned like round-wearers, but being in the crowd or following the crowd are not the drumbeats they follow. In fact, the interesting thing about emerald-cut-wearers is their lack of ambition to do anything to impress others. Not that other people's opinions don't count, it's just that they don't see themselves through the eyes of others. Emerald-cut-wearers are leaders. They are attracted to an emerald cut for its quiet elegance, its regal temperament, and bold strokes. The emerald-cut-wearer doesn't need pop to sell her diamond—that's what she's there for.

Princess & Radiants—Princess- and radiant-wearers are electric.

They are fun, exciting, cutting edge, and not afraid to take chances. They live life to the fullest. Because princess and radiant are the most sparkly shapes, wearers of these rocks don't mind bringing attention to themselves. They love the spotlight. Whitney Houston, for example, is a proud wearer of a radiant. The only time princess and radiant wearers split up with their mates is if the guy can't keep up.

Heart Shape—The heart shape, aka "Black Widow" and "Three Strikes," holds the title of the least sparkly, second-highest divorce rate, and most-cheated-upon diamond in the group. (Hence the alias "Three Strikes.") A lot of analysis has gone into why this diamond and its wearer have so much trouble, but I think it can best be explained by what type of woman and couple gravitate toward the heart—pure romantics. And when I say pure romantics, I'm not just saying soul mates. I'm talking maple-syrup, knight-in-shining-armor, Romeo-and-Juliet kind of romantic. Heart-shape people tend to live in fantasyland. Their motto is love conquers all, love has no restrictions, love has no boundaries. Then they get married and quickly find out that even though love in its own little world is perfect, life isn't. Life isn't fair or just or evenhanded. Life equals change. The heart-shape-wearer tends to have a problem with this. If love is perfect, there is no need for change and certainly no need for reality. So, when they come to the conclusion that their mate isn't perfect (he never was, nobody is) and discover pure love doesn't seem to pay the bills, they flee—into the arms of another, into another job, into another life—constantly searching for the equation of pure love equals perfect life, which doesn't exist.

Marquise—The marquise, in all its grandeur and magnificence (one of the largest looking shapes), is the crown jewel for divorce—even more so than the heart. Heck, at least the heart had good intentions. Marquise-wearers tend to be very concerned with first impressions, second impressions, all impressions. They are very goal-oriented and certainly believe that size matters. Marquise-wearers believe in division and being "better than." There is the wrong side of the tracks, and it's never the side they are on. A lot of socialites and wannabe socialites choose marquise because, when cut correctly, they look bigger than they really are. And that's where the problem is. Marquise-wearers, not all but quite a few, spend the better part of their lives trying to be something or someone they are not. Success never lies in not being and loving who you are. For a marquise-wearer to survive, she must realize that regardless of how nice a package is, it always fades away—inner beauty doesn't.

Question #3: What actual carat size you have is irrelevant to how you perceive it. To some people, the one-carat diamond they have is puny. For others, it's the rock of Gibraltar. But that's the key here: not what you have but how you perceive it. Is the glass half full or half empty? It appears that the happiest marriages tend to be those in which the engagement diamond is viewed as magnificent and substantial. The minute a woman finds fault in the rock, it's not long before she finds fault in the giver. Want to appreciate your diamond? Just think of the one out of three women who got married and didn't get one.

Question #4: If you had to write a list of all the things you want, how long a list would it be? Long? Short? How about a list of all the things you need? Long? Short? The three steps for creation are thought, word, and action. To get anything done, you have to think it, verbalize it, then take action. When you announce to the world that there are things you need, want, or expect, you cannot be whole 'til you get them. And if your brain perceives that it is without or not whole, it won't be happy. The key to any long-term happiness is not getting everything you want but wanting everything you have. The longer you've had your diamond and the longer you appreciate it, the better your life and marriage will be. The diamond is a symbol of where you were and where you are going. To always embrace your past as you do your present will empower you to learn from your experiences and not repeat those events that no longer define who you are today.

Question #5: Well, I think this one is pretty self-explanatory. If the diamond is a symbol of two that have joined to become one, and one of you is not on the scene any more, chances are your rock means very little to you today.

Question #6: "To have and to hold" doesn't necessarily equal "to love and to cherish." I've lined up a hundred couples and asked them the condition of their marriage and relationship, and I found a direct correlation between clean rings and great marriages and filthy rings and relationships that are no longer connected or were drifting apart. Just a coincidence? Could be. Or maybe it's that any good marriage takes work, care, and effort. Marriage isn't easy. When a problem arises, a lot of people just let it go, thinking it will fix itself. It won't. A clean ring will always get dirty unless you don't allow it. A good marriage will do the same unless you work at it and keep the dust off.

Question #7: Fifty-four percent of women who receive an engagement ring say they would never get rid of their original engagement ring. They would keep it until they die. Forty-six percent, however, say that even though they have fond memories of their original engagement ring, they wouldn't keep the first car they ever had or first home they ever had! If something better comes along, they will snatch it! That being said, here's how the divorce bug attacks each group. Seventy-five percent in group one—"The I'll keep it forever" folks—tend to stay married, while 80 percent in group two are splitsville.

Appendix F

Wedding Traditions

◆————————————————————◆

BY JULIE SEITZ

IS THERE TRULY ANY actual reasoning that is involved in a woman's frantic search for something old, something new, something borrowed, and something blue? Have you ever seen a bride "freak out" because her guy accidentally caught a peak at her a few hours before the wedding? Not a pretty sight. But is there any factual basis to why this is a bad thing? I was curious, so I did some research. I was surprised by how important and, yes, necessary, many of these customs were at one time. Of course, some were silly then and are still silly today, but learning their origin will make you understand them in a more sensible way. But who are we kidding? The bride(zilla) is always right, and is under no obligation to be sensible.

Did you know that several of our wedding traditions are based on the concept of the bride being too ugly for the groom? I'm serious! Seeing the bride before the ceremony is considered bad luck because there was a time when marriages were completely arranged by the families. To keep the groom from backing out, he wasn't permitted to see the bride until the ceremony just in case he considered her unattractive. The custom of wearing a veil came about for same reason. But in this case, the groom wasn't allowed to see the bride's potentially ugly mug until he actually lifted the veil to kiss her. Cruel? Maybe. But necessary at the time.

Watching a groom remove his bride's garter at the reception is always fun. She's usually quite embarrassed, he's usually way too comfortable with the whole thing. Everyone gets a big kick out of it. What's the purpose? In certain parts of Europe in the fourteenth century, it was considered to be good luck to come away from a wedding with a piece of the bride's clothing. Inebriated guests would destroy the poor bride's dress trying to get a scrap. So, over time, it evolved to the tossing of the garter, providing safety for the bride, but making the dispersion of luck more of a lottery. This same idea of protecting the bride is also why the bride has always stood to the groom's left. This was so the groom could have his right hand free to draw his sword against sudden attack. I guess this could still be considered a convenient concept. How else is the poor guy supposed to retrieve his cell phone from his right pocket on the first ring?

You've all heard, I'm sure, the term "to tie the knot." I always thought it referred to tying your lives together. It actually goes back to Roman times, when the women's girdles had many strings on them that were tied securely. Of course, the groom had the "duty" of untying the knots on the wedding night.

Stag parties have had the same meaning since they started. Stag parties, or bachelor parties as they are often called, are a farewell to bachelorhood and celebration of camaraderie between the groom and his friends. Although the reason has changed over the years, there has always been a shroud of mystery and secrecy when it comes to the bachelor party. It's a sort of unspoken rule that details of the party usually aren't revealed to women. I've heard rumors and hints, but after fourteen years of marriage, I'm still not 100 percent sure what happened at my husband's bachelor party. I only know that he lost his shoe and never did find it. Interesting. I think I feel an in-depth article on bachelor parties coming on.

Of course the bride has her own festivities to attend in the weeks leading up to her wedding. The first bridal shower is said to have come about from a Dutch folktale in which well-meaning townspeople gave household items to a poor, newly married couple. The father of the bride disapproved of the union, so he had not provided a dowry. Anything goes today. Many bridal showers even become "bachelorette parties."

Have you ever wondered where the word "honeymoon" came from? I have. I've even asked around. Not surprisingly, few people know the origin of the word or original meaning. Teutonic newlyweds drank wine made of honey and yeast from one full moon until the next full moon after they were married. I guess I should refer to my post-nuptial vacation as my "margaritamoon."

Speaking of drinking, I found out in my research that the word "toast," as in toasting the happy couple, actually comes from toasted bread. An old French custom is the source of this tradition. A piece of toasted bread was placed at the bottom of a glass filled with wine. After passing the glass around at the wedding, the bride would finish the wine and eat the wine-soaked bread at the bottom, thus receiving all of the good wishes of the guests.

Now to the tradition that most brides take very seriously. I know I did. Did I understand what the meaning of "something old, something new, something borrowed, something blue" was? No. But now I do. Something old signifies continuity. I had my great-grandmother's wedding band to wear on my little finger. Something new signifies optimism. This is the easy one. The dress is new, the rings are new, the shoes are new, you get the picture. Something borrowed signifies future happiness. A friend of mine borrowed her uncle's Ferrari to drive to the church. Hey, whatever works for you. Something blue signifies modesty, fidelity, and love. It's funny to me that most brides I've known have gone with the blue garter. The garter is removed in front of hundreds of people! Fidelity and love? Maybe. Modesty? I'm not sure.

There are enough stories about the origin of the customary white wedding dress to fill an entire page. But I couldn't find a single story that had anything to do with wearing white only if you were "pure." It was mainly just a fashion trend credited to Ann of Brittany in 1499 and again by Queen Victoria in 1840. I did come across a great poem about the topic, however.

> Married in White, you have chosen right
> Married in Grey, you will go far away,
> Married in Black, you will wish yourself back,
> Married in Red, you will wish yourself dead,
> Married in Green, ashamed to be seen,
> Married in Blue, you will always be true,
> Married in Pearl, you will live in a whirl,
> Married in Yellow, ashamed of your fellow,
> Married in Brown, you will live in the town,
> Married in Pink, you spirit will sink.

> *–Author Unknown*

When a girl wore a green dress, the implication was that she was of questionable morals and her dress was green from "rolling in the fields."

There are many traditions, customs, and superstitions that are not covered here. There are, simply, too many to mention. Depending on race, culture, religion, and geographic location, there are literally thousands of different particulars that brides must organize and prepare for her wedding. Some are silly, meaningless things that are done "just because it's always been done." Others have been passed down from generation to generation and, for whatever reason, have true meaning for the bride and her marriage. Do we have any conclusive answers to whether following wedding tradition will lead to a happy marriage? No. I do know, however, that I have never met a divorced person who told me that the reason for the split was that rice wasn't thrown at the reception, or he didn't carry her over the threshold, or cans weren't tied to the bumper of their car. Not that I'm trivializing the value of these actions. In fact, it may be many little things combined that will make or break your wedding day. But remembering the "little things" AFTER that one day is what will make or break a marriage in my opinion. Rice may or may not have been thrown at the reception, but taking the time to throw your arm around each other for no reason… now that's important. He may or may not have carried her over the threshold, but has he ever carried the groceries in from the car without being asked? I don't feel that I missed anything by not having cans tied to the bumper of my car on my wedding day. Seeing my husband teach my son to tie his shoes for the first time, however, I wouldn't have missed for the world.

Wedding Traditions: A Quick Reference Guide	
Bachelor Party	A party given for the groom to say good-bye to his bachelorhood and celebrate the camaraderie between him and his friends.
Bad Luck for Groom to See Bride Before Ceremony	This came about as a means to keep a groom from backing out of an arranged marriage to an unattractive woman.
Bouquet Toss, Garter Toss	In the fourteenth century, it was thought to bring luck to have a piece of the bride's clothing. To prevent the bride from harm, brides began throwing their garters. That later evolved into the groom throwing the garter and the bride throwing her bouquet.

Wedding Traditions: A Quick Reference Guide	
Breaking the Wine Glass	The Jewish tradition of the groom stomping on a wine glass at the conclusion of the ceremony signifies the fragility of the relationship and also the irrevocable act of breaking something. "Mazel Tov!"
Bridal Party	This tradition has many different origins depending on culture. The groom would use the help of his "bridesmen" to capture or escort his bride from her village. They were also responsible for getting the bride to the wedding and to the groom's home after the ceremony. The women who assisted the bride were called her "brideswomen."
Bridal Shower	Dating back to the 1800s, a bride receives gifts from her friends to prepare her for marriage.
Bride Standing on Groom's Left	This goes back to ancient times, when the groom would need to keep his right hand free to draw his sword against sudden attack.
Carrying the Bride Over the Threshold	It is considered very bad luck for the new bride to trip and fall upon entering her new home for the first time. To eliminate the risk, the groom traditionally carries her through the door.

Wedding Traditions: A Quick Reference Guide	
Engagement Ring	Pope Nicholas I decreed the engagement ring a required symbol of intent to marry. The diamond became popular because of its long-lasting and enduring qualities.
Flowers	The practice of matching the groom's boutonniere to the bride's bouquet goes back to medieval times when knights would match the colors of their lady in tournaments.
Honeymoon	Teutonic newlyweds would drink wine made of honey and yeast from one full moon to the next immediately following their wedding.
Kissing	The kiss between the bride and groom dates back to the earliest days of civilization. A kiss has almost always been used as a legal seal for contracts and agreements, thus the obvious use of the kiss for the end of a wedding ceremony.
Money Dance	The money dance that many people see at wedding receptions has its roots in dozens of cultures around the world. Basically, guests pay the groom money for the privilege of dancing with his bride. The money is then used for the honeymoon.
Ring Finger	Greek belief was that the third finger was connected directly to the heart by a vein they called "the vein of love."

Wedding Traditions: A Quick Reference Guide	
Something Old, Something New, Something Borrowed, Something Blue	Old signifies continuity. New signifies optimism. Borrowed reflects future happiness, and blue is a sign of modesty, fidelity, and love.
Throwing Rice	This is a symbol of fertility and also a wish for the couple to always have a full pantry. Note: Birdseed is often used as an alternative that is nature-friendly.
Tie the Knot	This dates back to Roman times when the bride would wear a girdle tied in little knots.
Toasting the Bride and Groom	Originates from the sixteenth century. A small piece of toasted bread was placed in the bottom of a glass of wine. Guests would pass the glass until it reached the bride, who would drink the last drink, eat the bread, and receive the good wishes of the guests.
Tying Cans or Shoes to the Car	In England during the Tudor period, shoes were thrown at the carriage as a sign of luck. Eventually, it became more common to just tie the shoes to the vehicle. Today, it's usually tin cans that are used.
Veils	Veils were originally worn to keep the groom from seeing his bride until he lifted the veil to kiss her in case she was unattractive. In Roman times, veils were also thought to ward off evil spirits.

Wedding Traditions: A Quick Reference Guide	
Vows	Vows are spoken promises between the groom and his bride in front of witnesses. Today, many religions and cultures allow and encourage the bride and groom to write their own vows.
Wedding	The Anglo-Saxon word "wedd" refers to the promise of a man to marry a certain woman, but it also refers to the money or land, or social status to be paid to the woman's family for her hand.
Wedding Bells	Like many wedding customs, bells are rung to protect the couple from misfortune.
Wedding Cake	In the first century, cake was thrown at the bride for fertility. It is considered very good luck to all who eat wedding cake.
Wedding Ring	Ancient belief was that the ring was protection against evil spirits. Early Rome is the source of our modern symbolism of love and commitment.
White Wedding Dress	A fashion trend credited to Ann of Brittany in 1499 and again to Queen Victoria in 1840.

Appendix G

One Guy's Opinion

My job is to talk about diamonds. How to get a good one, how not to get ripped off, how to get the most for your money. But I'm seeing a society where the "truth" belongs to the one who can tell the best story, not the one based on the facts.

For example, every year five thousand people are indicted, convicted, and sentenced for a whole list of horrific crimes from petty theft to rape, assault, and even murder. What is even more horrific is that all these crimes hold three special things in common; the men and women who are convicted and were primarily incarcerated on eyewitness testimony spend an average of ten years in prison, and all of these criminals are eventually set free because they are later proven to be innocent. How must it feel to spend a decade of your life telling the whole world you didn't do it, to lose your family, friends, and livelihood all based on what someone else believes they see. As it turns out, magicians knew it a long time ago. The hand is quicker than the eye. The eye can be fooled! It happens every day. In our streets and in automobile showrooms with tires, we're told are safe enough to drive our families around on. Now I'm not here to talk about how our justice system is broken or about slick car salesman who try to sell us the virtues of undercoating and who roll back odometers to give us the perception of more value. For me, it's still about diamonds.

"Seeing is believing," you might say. But does believing constitute the truth? Does it constitute a fact? Well, try this on for size. For the last few years, the diamond industry has been fighting the Federal Trade Commission (FTC) so they will not have to disclose laser-drilled diamonds. The industry felt it was an insult. For starters, to require disclosure of a treatment that alters the value or durability by changing the FTC guidelines would be paramount to announcing to the world that jewelers are dishonest. Jewelers can't be trusted to tell the truth. For God's sake, the industry can police itself. But every year, over five thousand complaints are registered at the Better Business Bureau, the FTC, and Jewelers Vigilante Committees. People were and are buying diamonds every day based on who has the best story to tell and a constant reminder, "See for yourself. Isn't it a beautiful diamond?" Even in the casinos with no clocks and free liquor, you know what your odds are. But in a jewelry store with its hundred canned spotlights, lab-grading documents, and very good stories, we lay our money down. Is it worth it? It must be. It's an A.G.S. 000. Is it worth it? It must be. It's GIA graded. Is it worth it? It must be. It's 100 percent natural. Is it worth it? It must be. Just look how pretty it is. And that is where they get you. That is where they set the hook. Then to reel you in, the jeweler says, "How can you put a price on something that lasts forever?" The love card. So you forget about the months or years it took you to save your money or the loan you have to take out or even the Visa you're going to max out at a 22 percent interest rate, because how can you put a price on love? The illusion is complete. Like the frog that turns into the handsome prince. The rock becomes the magical diamond. Seeing is believing, or maybe better said, believing is seeing. That's where any good salesman will get you. Recently, the FTC changed their guidelines and made it mandatory to disclose laser-drilled diamonds or, for that matter, any form of treatment that would give you the impression that something is better or more valuable than what it is. Let me ask you this: If five thousand men and women are convicted for crimes they didn't commit and if there are over five thousand complaints each year about nondisclosure in treatments, how many people are still in jail that are innocent, and how many worthless diamonds are on the fingers of our loved ones?

Here's one more thing to chew on. It has just been announced (to the jewelry industry, not the public of course) that a company by the name of 3-Beams Technology (a separate division of Norsam) has created a process called focused ion beam technology (FIB for short). Apparently taking ideas from Los Alamos National Laboratory, FIB instruments can focus a beam of ions down to a diameter of seven nanometers (that's .000007 millimeters or .00000028 inches). Using this technology, they can drill a diamond to remove carbon, leaving a drill hole one thousandth the size of the current technology. According to 3-Beams's CEO, Jayant Neogi, with a special modification a gas can be injected into the void, which will solidify, making the drill hole practically invisible.

FTC makes a law that treatments must be disclosed. Then the industry we were supposed to trust announces a new way not to get caught.

What's the moral of this story? Seeing is not believing. Take everything with a grain of salt, and please cut the deck before you're dealt a hand.

Index

M

Magnification, 12, 127, 307

Market

    cartel arrangement, 297

    control of, 191, 297, 298,
        301, 302

    demand, 272–273, 274

    of married women, 299

    overhang, 295–302

    price stability, illusion of,
        297, 300

    supply, 298

Market-crash protection policy,
    118

Marketing, 10, 128, 171–172,
    198, 296, 299

Markets, new, 299

Marriage. *See also* Proposal

    determining time for,
        222–223

    and diamond consumption,
        297

    Newlyweds' Prayer, 240

Martin, Rayburne, 289

McClintock, Harold S., 289

Measurements. *See also*
  Proportion

    determining, 42

Medad, 266

Megascope, 42, 45

Melees, 96–97

Men

    advice about, 227–234

    advice for, 219–222, 224–
        226, 238–239

Mines, 272–273, 302–303

Moissanite, 164

Money-back guarantee, 130

Money Which, 279

Moses, Tom, 54, 56, 146, 263,
    264

Multiple stone viewing, 132

N

N. W. Ayer, 296, 299

Necessities, 238–239, 299

Negotiation, 307, 329

Newlyweds' Prayer, 240

Newspapers, 249–250

New York Diamond Club, 280

New York Diamond District,
    123–125

Nixon, Robert L., 289

No Name Diamond, 283–284

O

Off-makes, 37, 38

Onassis, Aristotle, 250

Onassis, Jacqueline Kennedy,
    250

O'Neil, Thomas F. III, 262

Opinion, 307

About the Author

FRED CUELLAR, THE FOUNDER and president of Diamond Cutters International, is one of the world's top diamond experts. Diamond Cutters International (DCI) is one of America's few diamond houses open to the public by appointment only. He is an importer and creative designer of jewelry. His clients include First Lady and President George W. Bush, the Saudi Royal Family, hundreds of professional athletes and various celebrities, including Oprah. Mr. Cuellar is accredited in diamonds and colored stones by the Gemological Institute of America and is ranked as one of the top diamond experts in America by *National Jeweler*. He is also the author of *How to Buy a Diamond*, the number-one selling book on diamonds in the world.

CAREER HIGHLIGHTS

- Ranked as the number-one diamond expert by Google.
- Consulted by *The Guardian* regarding the world's largest diamond discovery.
- Diamond expert to the *Wall Street Journal, Chicago Tribune, USA Today, Kiplinger's, Modern Bride, Maxim, Men's Health, Women's Health, ESPN, Money, InStyle, Glamour, Woman's Day* magazines, and Sony Pictures.
- Author of the number-one selling book on diamonds in the country, *How to Buy a Diamond*, as well as critically acclaimed books *Diamonds for Profit* and national bestseller *World's Greatest Proposals*.

- *How to Buy a Diamond* and its National Diamond HelpLine is endorsed by the National Bureau of Fraud Prevention in Washington, DC.
- *How to Buy a Diamond* is featured by The Smithsonian Institute.
- Most acknowledged jeweler in the *Guinness Book of World Records 2000: Millennium Edition.*
- Official diamond expert to AOL's theknot.com and the Wedding Network.
- Official diamond expert to the Wedding Pages (America's #1 Wedding Source) and columnist for twenty-nine of their magazines.
- Has been featured, discussed, and/or guest expert on the *Tyra Banks Show, Montel Williams Show, The Today Show, The Tonight Show with Jay Leno, CBS Morning News, Donahue, Fox News, CNN, ESPN,* as well as over five hundred other news and talk shows.
- 2007 Entrepreneur of the Year finalist.
- Runner up "Power Player of the Week" for *Fox News Sunday with Chris Matthews.*
- Diamond advisor to MSNBC.
- Diamond advisor to Standard & Poor's.
- Diamond advisor to *60 Minutes.*
- Diamond advisor to *Saturday Night Live.*
- Diamond expert to NBC Universal.
- Diamond expert to the Fine Living Channel.
- Diamond expert to bankrate.com.
- Diamond expert to slate.com.
- Spokesperson for Korbel Champagne, 2003.
- Has been featured and discussed in *GQ, People, Self, FHM, Cosmopolitan, Men's Health, Us Weekly, Newsweek, Washington*

Post, *Chicago Tribune*, *L.A. Times*, *Dallas Morning News*, as well as over one hundred other magazines and newspapers.

- Inventor of the Interlocking Diamond Bezel, Interlocking Diamond Logo, Interlocking Logo Trophy, Gem Sculptured Logo, Tight Knit Pave, and Bullet Train Frame.
- Created the 2006 and 2007 MLS Championship rings for the Houston Dynamo.
- Designed the 2001 Super Bowl Championship rings for the Baltimore Ravens.
- Created the 2001 NHL Stanley Cup Championship rings for the Colorado Avalanche.
- Created the 2000 NHL Stanley Cup Championship rings for the New Jersey Devils.
- Created the 1999 New York Yankees Twenty-Fifth Championship Players World Series rings.
- Created the 1999 NHL Stanley Cup Championship rings for the Dallas Stars.
- Created the 1998 and 1997 NHL Stanley Cup Championship rings for the Detroit Redwings.
- Created the 1998 Super Bowl Championship replacement rings for the Denver Broncos.
- Created the 1997 Super Bowl Championship rings for the Denver Broncos.
- Created the 1995 Super Bowl Championship rings for the Dallas Cowboys.
- Created the World's Greatest Athlete Ring for Olympic Gold Medalist Dan O'Brien.
- Created the Stanley Cup Championship rings for the New Jersey Devils in 1995 and the Colorado Avalanche in 1996.
- Created the "Million Dollar Puck" for the Houston Aeros made of platinum, diamonds, and emeralds.

- Created the International Hockey League Championship rings for the back-to-back champion, Utah Grizzlies, and was the first American chosen to create the Canadian Football League Championship rings for the 1995 champion Baltimore Stallions.
- Created Cal Ripkin's commemorative ring for breaking Lou Gehrig's record of consecutive major league baseball games (2,131).
- Created the first ever baseball bracelet for the Houston Astros, made of mini ruby and diamond baseballs.
- Created the two-million-dollar "Super Pizza" consisting of over six hundred carats of diamonds and colored stones in five pounds of gold for Little Caesars Pizza.
- Creator of the $200,000 "Gem Prowler" in conjunction with Chrysler Plymouth.
- Created the "world's most expensive toy," The Rubik's Cube Masterpiece—a full size, fully working Rubik's cube covered with 185 carats of precious gems.
- Created the "Harley of Gold," a gold and diamond scale replica of a Harley-Davidson motorcycle.
- Created Playboy's Millennium Playmate Pendant.

Other Books by the Author

THE WORLD'S GREATEST PROPOSALS

In an Internet contest, Fred Cuellar (aka "The Diamond Guy") offered a beautiful, sparkling diamond in return for the most hilarious, creative, or inspirational proposal story. As a result, he received thousands of wonderful engagement stories and has collected the best here in *The World's Greatest Proposals*. A perfect shower gift, this beautiful little book will bring tears of joy, love, and laughter to everyone who knows what it means to find the love of their life.

The price is $14.99.

DIAMONDS FOR PROFIT

Diamonds for Profit will benefit any reader who wants to sell (or buy and sell) diamonds or colored stone jewelry—from the one-time seller to the entrepreneur. With *Diamonds for Profit* as your guide, you can make money buying and selling diamonds! It will show you how to determine the immediate cash-liquidity value of your jewelry so you don't get talked into buying them for less. Also learn how to treasure-hunt for diamonds and jewelry in the classified ads, going-out-of-business sales, and national and local estate auctions in your spare time—and make money at it!

The price is $23.95.

FREDISMS

Fredisms are the culmination of a personal life experience that you will be intrigued to discover as you read the Fredism on each page of this uniquely formatted book. Mr. Cuellar touches upon subjects of interest to us all, such as attitudes, health, humor, relationships, God, philosophy, and many others, in a way which will endear the book to a wide variety of readers. It will make a great gift for almost anyone and is easy to read. In fact, you will probably find yourself repeating your most favored Fredism to family and friends before long!

The price is $14.50.

These books are available in stores or through your favorite online bookseller, or you may order copies through the mail by calling (800) 275-4047 or 713-222-2728.